Wr
President
calls

Trevor Birney
and
Julian O'Neill

GUILDHALL PRESS

ry

When the President calls

has been produced in Association with

I think everybody remembers when President Bill Clinton came to Northern Ireland, but a few of you may know how significant this day was for
CableTel. It was a very important occasion for us as an American company
taking our first steps in the Province, particularly when the then US Secretary for Commerce, the late Ron Brown, announced a £600m investment
on the morning the President arrived. More importantly it was a unique
moment in history for the people of Northern Ireland.

CableTel is delighted to support *When the President calls*, written by two
very talented local journalists and surprisingly the only commemorative
book on the visit. It provides an extraordinary insight to this momentous
occasion, when the visit of an American President lifted our spirits and
showed Northern Ireland at its best on the world stage.

Owen Lamont, Managing Director, CableTel Northern Ireland

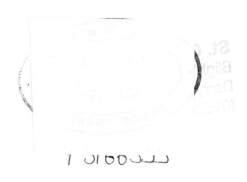

First published in November 1997 by
Guildhall Press, 41 Great James Street,
L'Derry, Northern Ireland BT48 7DF
Tel: (01504) 364413 Fax: (01504) 372949
E-mail: gpress@compuserve.com

ISBN 0 946451 44 3

Guildhall Press receives support from the Training & Employment Agency
under the Action for Community Employment scheme.

Printed by Coleraine Printing Company

Special thanks to Manus Martin (T&EA), and Derry City Council's Recreation
and Leisure Department for generous Community Services Grant Aid, and to the
Derry District Partnership and NICDA for invaluable aid towards the development
of Guildhall Press. Guildhall Press would also like to thank Colm & Anne Murray-
Cavanagh and the other members of the Management Committee for their dedica-
tion over the past 18 years.

For our parents

Acknowledgements

B ill Clinton's visit to Northern Ireland in November 1995 was an exhilarating news event to cover. It was history and a good story to tell. It was as it remains, a pinnacle in the peace process, one that deserves to be recounted with the benefit of insight and hindsight. In doing so we seek to offer no judgement on Clinton as President. We are too far removed for that.

This book owes a debt to a great many people, not least to those in the American Government who from the outset rewarded our enthusiasm with a tremendous degree of co-operation. Few can be given the recognition they warrant here as their assistance was granted only under guarantee they would remain anonymous sources. However, one of those who can be thanked by name, and very deservedly so, is Kathleen Stephens. She gave generously of her time and we would not have been granted high-level access at the White House but for her. We would also like to express our appreciation to Blair Hall, whose help proved equally invaluable.

Regrettably, representatives of the British Government displayed an initial reluctance to match this American goodwill. That it was brought to something nearing parity was due to one source, who must remain anonymous, and we would like to thank him again.

Approximately two hundred interviews were conducted in Belfast, Derry, Dublin, London, New York and Washington. It says something about people's affinity with the subject that of all those involved in the Clinton trip, be it centrally or on the periphery, only two people were unable to help, one did so for security reasons, the other was Van Morrison.

Our appreciation goes to everyone who gave of their time. There are too many to list them all, but we would like to put on record our special thanks, in no order of merit, to the following: Jim Lyons; Mike McCurry; Jamie Lindsay; Pat Dougan; Gary McMichael;

Admiral William Crowe; Bill Flynn; Niall O'Dowd; Bruce Morrison; Sir Patrick Mayhew; Sir John Kerr; Albert Reynolds; Dick Spring; Jackie Redpath; Sammy Douglas; John Hume; Peter Sheridan; John Keanie; John Kerr; David Trimble; Jeffrey Donaldson; Peter Robinson; Ian Paisley Jr; Chris Dodd; Peter King; Dermot Gallagher; Gerry Adams; Richard McAuley; Jim Walsh; Tom Manton; Richard Neal; Tony Lake; Ed Emerson; Lord Alderdice; David Ervine; Doug Heady; Billy Hutchinson; Bill Stewart; Brian Hanna; and Gerry Burns.

We are grateful to our publishers Guildhall Press for their part in salvaging the project when difficulties arose late in the day at our initial publishing house, Brandon Books, and who pulled out all the stops to meet our target publication date. We also express our deep gratitude to CableTel, who shared in the rescue operation by generously sponsoring our endeavours.

Our respected fellow journalist Eamonn Mallie was always a source of inestimable guidance and encouragement, particularly through difficult times. We acknowledge him for sharing his wisdom. Also thanks to Deric Henderson, David Davin-Power and Denzil McDaniel who cast an eye over extracts and offered advice and support. Mention too must go to John Harrison and his team of photographers, Marie Therese Hurson, Norman Evans and Arron McCracken; Crispin Rodwell and the White House for kindly allowing us to reproduce their photographs. Thanks also to the BBC, Sky News and GMTV for providing us with footage of the Clinton trip and to Yvonne Murphy and her staff at the Linenhall Library in Belfast.

Others helped in their own way: our employers Downtown Radio; Sheila Briggs, whose transcription of interviews saved us so much valuable time; Douglas Marshall who copy-edited the manuscript; Peter Malone who came up with the title; and Dylan O'Neill at Sam Hutchinson and Co. who assisted with technical support.

Finally some editorial notes. The introduction is drawn from responses President Clinton made to a series of questions from the authors. The titles and ranks of the personalities in this books are given as they were at the time of the President's visit.

Julian O'Neill and Trevor Birney
October 1997

Contents

Introduction

Our day in Northern Ireland was indeed one of the most remarkable of our lives and a highlight of my Presidency. Today, almost two years later, I am still deeply moved by the warmth of the reception we were given and the palpable desire of the people we saw to come together in peace and reconciliation.

Though my expectations were high, my visit exceeded them in every respect. Even the weather co-operated. It was a great privilege to be the first sitting US President to visit Northern Ireland. I was there to show the desire of the United States to help and to support the peace process, not to impose a vision or a solution of our own. I'll never forget the faces of the people, young and old, of both traditions, who reached out to Hillary and me as we travelled through Belfast. I was very proud to represent the American people and to be able to share our ideals and experiences with the people in Northern Ireland.

I was already committed to supporting the peace process, but my visit gave that commitment a more personal dimension. I saw it as an outpouring of friendship for my country as well as an expression of hope and determination to move beyond the mistrust and bitterness of Northern Ireland's past, and I felt an even heavier duty to do what I can to help. Having the chance to meet people in their communities, to hear their hopes, shake their hands and see their enthusiasm for peace first-hand certainly strengthened my conviction that there is widespread support for a lasting settlement of the conflict. Since my visit, in spite of the setbacks in the peace process, I remain convinced that the prize is within reach and that America's support can help bring it about.

I said then, and I have said it many times since, that those who use violence must not be allowed to dictate the agenda for the rest of us. The courageous people who work for reconciliation and a lasting settlement are the ones who are shaping the future. The people of both communities who extended us such a warm welcome were expressing their commitment to a future built on dialogue and trust, not on violence and hatred. Their commitment to that goal is lasting, as is mine.

I welcome the restoration of the ceasefire. I have always believed that inclusive talks, on the basis of an unequivocal ceasefire, offer the best prospect for achieving a lasting settlement. The United States has loaned one of its great statesmen, Senator George Mitchell, to the talks process. I hope the parties and the British and Irish Governments will move forward with substantive negotiations.

I deeply hope that the parties and Governments will have reached a negotiated settlement during my Presidency. America's role has been helpful in supporting the peacemakers. I am confident we will continue to play that role. But, as with any situation in which people have been divided by a long-standing conflict, the process of building trust and ties between Northern Ireland's two communities is one of the most difficult. There are many parallels with the American experience. I certainly hope I would be able to play a part in the historic process of long-term reconciliation even after I leave office.

William J. Clinton
42nd President of the United States of America
October 1997

I

Glad we're finally making it

*Yes, it had all been painstakingly planned but what
happened virtually from the moment of his arrival is
the spirit began, and that is not something you can
write into a scenario.*

**Kathleen Stephens,
United States Consul General, Belfast**

William J. Clinton's Irish adventure was the pinnacle of his
first term in the White House. That it was a triumph which
briefly flirted with catastrophe made it all the more breathtaking.
Just hours before boldly stepping directly into the maelstrom of
Northern Ireland politics, the leader of the world's one surviving
superpower faced the unimaginable prospect of being locked out of
the venue for a keynote speech which he envisioned providing a
fresh impetus in the pursuit of lasting peace. And it was all because
of Gerry Adams, the leader of Sinn Féin, the IRA's political off-
shoot. "Everything about this visit came right down to how we
handled the radioactive question of when, how and where we dealt
with Gerry Adams," said one of the key American trip planners. As
Clinton sat up reading a book of Adams' short stories at the US
Ambassador's London residence, his courtiers burned the midnight
oil as they endeavoured to solve a crisis which had the potential to
destroy a visit that had taken months in painstaking planning. But

15

solve it they did by morning. A night owl, the President slept little on returning from a black-tie banquet of seafood salad and venison hosted by British Prime Minister John Major for sixty-five guests at 10 Downing Street.

The 42nd President's impending visit to Northern Ireland was an incredible endorsement of two monumental years of unflagging effort which had silenced the weapons in one the world's most enduring conflicts, which had cost in excess of 3,000 lives since 1969. It began with the Downing Street Declaration in December 1993. The complex, 12-point agreement between the British and Irish Governments was trumpeted as a charter for peace and reconciliation. Clinton said the declaration reflected a "yearning for peace that is shared by all traditions in Ireland and creates an historic opportunity to end the tragic cycle of bloodshed." Within ten months the Irish Republican Army (IRA) and Loyalist paramilitaries had both declared ceasefires and in February 1995 the two Governments built on the Declaration with a blueprint for the future known as the Framework Document. Clinton again was quick off the mark to endorse it: "The publication of this document marks another significant step forward in the peace process."

Though out of its infancy, the peace process had grown to a troublesome age as the clock ticked down on Clinton's historic journey. It had been driven into the sand over the issue of IRA weapons. Unionists and the British were clinging to an unrealistic insistence that there could be no negotiations of substance on a political settlement involving Sinn Féin until its military ally decommissioned at least some of its vast arsenal. But the President's imminent arrival stirred both Governments into action. Just eleven hours ahead of his landing in London the peace process was dramatically resuscitated by a kiss of life known as the twin-track agreement, a deal which, although on the table for some time, Major conceded had had a difficult dénouement. In it the British and Irish established an international commission to provide an independent assessment of how the controversial arms issue could be dealt with. It was to be headed by the former United States Senate Majority Leader, George Mitchell, who since his political retirement in January 1995 had been Special Advisor to the President and [US] Secretary of State for Economic Initiatives in Ireland. London and Dublin had lined him up for the job long beforehand but prior to accepting Mitchell, concerned it could somehow impinge upon his Washington economic brief, cleared it with Clinton first. He was under no illusions as to the difficulty of the task. It was a minefield where there had been "candidly substantial disagreement." The affable man from Maine was later to assume a more significant role as chairman of multi-party talks on Northern Ireland's future. In parallel with the arms commission there would be preparatory talks with the region's political groupings with the aim of securing all-party negotiations by the end of February 1996. Unionists said the twin-track fudged the arms issue and wasted no time in ganging up to chide Major for seeming to rush into it to please Clinton. Major, while accepting the President's coming had "concentrated the mind," denied Washington had a more substantial role in the agreement.

The White House media pool was left with a different impression by Presidential Press Secretary Mike McCurry on the flight from the US to London and Clinton himself gave Tony Lake, one of his closest advisors, a bottle of champagne to toast the deal. The drink had been procured from a reporter by McCurry who later said Lake deserved immense credit for the visit's achievement. "He's the one who believed we could pull it off. He's the one that had to do the very delicate negotiations with the British to convince them the trip had merit, that Clinton could go to the North and do it," said McCurry. A joyous Lake heard news of the twin-track breakthrough in a telephone call from the Irish Ambassador to Washington, Dermot Gallagher, who had been in contact with him or his assistant Nancy Soderberg sometimes as often as six times a day to report on the progress of negotiations. A US diplomatic source said: "I think the timing of the announcement speaks for itself. As we started to get closer [to the visit] we kept telling the Governments the President will find it difficult to come if we don't have this road-block cleared. We had many conversations and offered our views and it happened, but it was never 'let's hit John Major over the head with a hammer until he gives in.'" The Northern Ireland Secretary Sir Patrick Mayhew, who had extolled the virtues of twin-track during a trip to Australia that September, admitted: "The Americans knew very well that attempts to crack heads are not productive. I think the imminent arrival of the President secured an earlier signing of that agreement and a meeting of minds perhaps a little earlier than would have been the case." The announcement got the visit off to a perfect start. Said Soderberg: "We were delighted. It set the mood for the whole trip." In London the President urged wavering Republicans to accept the twin-track. Americans said privately afterwards that the fact Adams "had not dumped on it" in the crucial period following its launch was a factor in securing a Belfast rendezvous between Clinton and the Sinn Féin President.

The US President spent the one-hour hop between London Heathrow and Belfast Aldergrove shut off in a suite of private offices at the front of Air Force One for a final review of material for the visit. One of Clinton's aides, Andrew Friendly, went through the itinerary with the President a last time. "We ran through the specifics of the schedule again, gave him a quick overview of what he was going to be doing, and how all the events fitted together so he had it in his mind how important it was to remain on time and to stay focused," said Friendly. Mitchell and Lake, the head of the National Security Council (NSC), which advises Presidents on foreign policy, were further back in a conference room along with White House staff. Two members of Clinton's cabinet were also making the trip to Northern Ireland – Commerce Secretary Ron Brown, who already held the distinction of being the first US cabinet member to visit Northern Ireland when he attended an investment conference in Belfast at the end of 1994, and Richard Riley, Education Secretary. Mitchell reported the mood was hopeful and expectant, but he had a degree of doubt about the welcome that awaited Clinton. "I felt he would get a good reception but I was not certain of it. Clearly there was some risk in the trip but he felt it was well worth it. I had been many times and had come to know and admire the people and I was glad that the President was coming and I felt it would be good for the people of Northern Ireland and good for the peace process."

He was positive Clinton was eagerly anticipating the visit following a 20-minute discussion they had had on the trans-Atlantic flight two days earlier. Serious doubts had been raised as to whether the President could travel because of a domestic budget crisis, but with some relief he told Mitchell: "I'm glad we're finally making it." Most of their conversation revolved around Mitchell's appointment as chairman of the arms commission. The ex-Senator recalled: "I don't think I knew enough about it then to be able to give him much of a briefing except to tell him I would obviously do the very best I could and was pleased to be able to make some contribution.

He expressed his gratitude for what I had done." A lighter moment on the journey was provided by Jim Lyons, one of the President's closest friends and US observer to the International Fund for Ireland (IFI). "I asked the steward for some Irish whiskey and he blanched. I said, 'What? We're going to Ireland and you've no Irish whiskey?' So I reached down into my bag and pulled out a half gallon of Bushmills and said, '*Now* you've got Irish whiskey.' A little bit later word came down from the front cabin: 'Who's got that whiskey?'"

A weak sunshine struggled to peep through the clouds at a blustery Aldergrove, 17 miles north-west of Belfast, on the morning of Clinton's arrival. It was a hive of activity. Planes in and out were to have operated around the President's scheduled arrival. Air Force One, which flies above the ceiling of commercial aircraft at 45,000 feet and within its own exclusion zone, was delayed and subsequently came down in a slot between ordinary flights, a fluke which delighted airfield managers who had been anticipating disruption. Members of the American advance team had been at the airport day in, day out for months beforehand, checking and double checking every detail. They even measured the runway, even though it was used to accommodating other Boeing 747s. Huge Galaxy transporter planes from the US Air Force had come and gone, unloading a dazzling array of hardware as airport workers scratched their heads in bewilderment. Hangars 145 and 146 were bristling with helicopters, communications technology, unmarked medical vehicles with blacked out windows, and armour-plated trucks. One was called the 'road runner'. "It's a car that has direct satellite communications so if they have to press the button it can be done," said one of the American team. Meetings involving the airport's executives, Presidential security staff and White House forward planners had at times been hot and heavy. Airport Operations Director James Mairs said: "If the Americans had their way the place would have been closed down a week beforehand. It was like a pantomime at times. Our view was this was way, way over the top. At the end of the day we had a business to run." So much so that, despite history being in the making, Air Force One had to pay landing fees.

The airport was infested by an army of security personnel drawn from the United States, the Royal Ulster Constabulary (RUC) and Aldergrove's own police force. The airport viewing gallery was screened off and rooms at a nearby hotel which overlooked the area cleared because of their potential use by snipers. In a break with routine, fire engines had been strategically placed along the almost 3,000 metres of landing strip, which that morning had undergone one final bomb sweep. Air Force One's flight across the Irish Sea was tracked by local air traffic controllers with Americans at their shoulders. Its progress was relayed to dignitaries who for upwards of two hours had been assembling in Lounge 20, mixing with shivering Secret Service agents who drifted in from the cold for tea and scones. One of the VIPs, Ulster Unionist MP for South Antrim Clifford Forsythe, felt he and everyone else was under watch. "There seemed to be dozens of American gentlemen with trench coats and short hair who all had the same expression which treated everyone with suspicion. The main difference I noticed between this and Royal visits was that the security, physically on the ground, was intense." Others in the room off the runway apron included Mayhew, his deputy Michael Ancram, the Queen's representative in County Antrim, Lord O'Neill, and the RUC Chief Constable, Sir Hugh Annesley. Three thousand of his officers were on duty for Operation Venice, the most for any one task in the force's then 73-year history. In their midst was a largely anonymous Wisconsin law professor by the name of Brady Williamson who had earned a reputation for his adroit handling of challenging overseas trips by the President. He'd been appointed by the Office of Presidential Advance to control the Belfast leg of his master's carefully choreographed territorial tightrope walk between the two communities in Northern Ireland. A colleague said: "He's the best advance person I've ever seen. He's smooth, steady, listens to professionals but also makes his own judgements."

Throughout the planning stages, but particularly at the outset, the White House staff had found themselves at loggerheads with the British. "They cited security concerns, they cited logistical concerns, they cited the weather. You name it, there was an excuse why this wasn't possible. I got my eyes opened. Their resistance was stunning," said one high-level American official. Within the British Government the Americans detected differing degrees of enthusiasm for the President's trip between the Northern Ireland Office (NIO) and the Foreign Office. Said the same official: "The Northern Ireland folks were much more receptive than the British were to the fact that he would be there at all. When you have an American President shine that big a light on a problem they haven't been able to resolve it is very uncomfortable." A member of the US team charged with thrashing out an itinerary with London recalled the initial meeting with between 30 and 40 personnel that September in the splendour of the Foreign Office in Whitehall. "They try to wow you by taking you into these incredibly beautiful rooms – just to remind you we used to be a colony. Unfortunately it has the reverse psychological effect. It makes you understand that you are now the world's only superpower. They had a certain agenda, we had a certain agenda and there were only certain things we were going to share."

Conversely, a great deal of the British side's frustration stemmed from the fact that Clinton was going to Northern Ireland at the invitation of Her Majesty's Government. "Establishing he was our guest put us in pole position," contended one source charged with liaising with the Americans. "There were often vigorous debates." One of the President's primary objectives was to meet the people at grassroots level, at which the British balked to start with. They pressed for set-piece, formal events at Queen's University, Belfast, and a speech, perhaps at Belfast City Hall. Moving on to the second city, mainly-Nationalist Londonderry, or an excursion to Fermanagh, reputed home of the President's ancestors, would not have figured in their plans, nor would a stopover. "The President was very excited about overnighting in Belfast," said a US Government source, "but if the British had their way we would have flown in, we would have flown out." An Irish-American among the Presidential party, Bruce Morrison, believed the behind-the-scenes wrangling reflected differences in how British and US politics were conducted. "Bill Clinton's hands-on, reaching out to the person in the street, trying to be broadly inclusive, is the American way of going at a problem. I think the British were not altogether comfortable with that but I think after seeing what he did I think they might have learned a lesson."

Mayhew, who had outlined his objectives for the trip in letters to Major and the Foreign Secretary Douglas Hurd, had adopted a keen personal interest in the day's fine detail and, though not unusually for him, had driven and walked the route days previously to the point where he felt comfortable with it in his own mind. He and

21

Ancram in particular were more relaxed as a result of the twin-track deal which, like the bitterly cold weather, figured in much of the small talk in the VIP room at Aldergrove. "I took the view that the President wanted to do his best to help secure a political settlement, wanted to assure the community across the divide of America's good will," recalled Mayhew. "I didn't think the President would come here wanting to boost Nationalist ambitions." Some circles were buzzing with speculation about the noticeable time gaps in the early part of the President's publicised engagements. Absent from it, but widely referred to about the room, was a walkabout on the Loyalist Shankill Road which would include the President calling at a shop.

At 9.04am Air Force One landed on the puddled surface of runway 0725 at Belfast International Airport at Aldergrove, sending spray rolling up around its four roaring engines. The date was 30 November 1995, and Clinton had become the first sitting US President to visit Northern Ireland, home of so many of their forefathers. As the Presidential Boeing began its six-minute crawl to the international pier, the welcome party prepared to set out to meet it. Forsythe reached to put on his nap coat but bowed to protocol when told the robust Mayhew, a former soldier in the Royal Dragoon Guards, was to brave the cold without one.

Clinton's was the second of two VIP plane-loads that arrived within 12 hours. The night before his touch down, a cross-party Congressional group and Presidential guests had flown in aboard what had been John F. Kennedy's Air Force One. It had brought Kennedy to the Republic of Ireland in 1963 and months later borne the assassinated President's casket on the sombre trip from Dallas during which Lyndon B. Johnson was sworn in as his successor. Republican Congressman Jim Walsh of New York, Congressional delegation leader, spent the flight from Andrews Air Force base outside Washington DC to Northern Ireland in Kennedy's old suite. It heightened his sense of occasion. "My father's father, my mother's father and mother were all from Ireland. I'd never been and going to Ireland for the first time and at the same time being involved in this tremendously optimistic visit by an American President, my head was just spinning." Publisher Niall O'Dowd, a native of Tipperary who emigrated to the US at the age of 25, was the only Irishman who shared the journey. He found himself beside the Mayor of Pittsburgh, Tom Murphy, and the Mayor of Los Angeles, Richard

Riordan. "There were people who were clearly useful to the President in re-election and the Mayor of Pittsburgh would have been an interesting example. He didn't know that much about Ireland. By the end of the visit he had transformed into this guy who just couldn't get enough of what he saw." For O'Dowd the whole experience was to eclipse his role in brokering the IRA ceasefire. "There was an extraordinary mood on board of celebration. It was a great way to go home. It sure beats Aer Lingus."

At 9.19am President Clinton, hand in hand with the First Lady, and both wrapped in thick overcoats, emerged from the front door of the blue-and-white jet emblazoned with his seal of office. Said the dry-humoured Forsythe: "I was wondering what was keeping them because it seemed to take a long time before they came out. I suspect they looked out and decided they needed their coats and there we were standing foundering and he and his wife came down lovely and warm." In fact, before leaving Air Force One, Clinton had turned to Lyons, a regular visitor to the country, and asked: "Any last minute advice?" The Denver lawyer replied that Clinton would have to listen more attentively than usual to make out what people were saying, and that the climate was bad. Mid-way down the steps the President flashed a smile that, before the day's end, was to become almost a fixed expression. Directly behind him were Mitchell and the US Ambassador to London, Admiral William Crowe, who would later write that the trip was "one of the most politically challenging and logistically daunting Presidential missions ever undertaken." Unnoticed by most observers was a plain clothes superintendent in the RUC's Close Protection Unit, Henry Ervine, who, having travelled from London on Air Force One, was effectively a Secret Service agent for the day and at Clinton's shoulder for all public appearances throughout the duration of his stay in Northern Ireland. "Henry was there for his local knowledge, his expertise. It was demonstrative of the co-operation we had with them," said an RUC colleague. "It was a very significant vote of confidence in the RUC and in an obvious way showed this was very much an integrated operation."

At the bottom of the steps, the President snapped a return salute at the capped O'Neill who was in regimental dress complete with sword. The Queen's man, who shook Clinton's hand in welcome, was struck by his appearance and stature. "He had an almost film star style about him. I remember noticing his height – and his breadth, which surprised me because of his reputation as a jogger." The official greeting was fleeting but the following day, on a slightly less formal departure, the two would strike up a conversation about a mutual love of jazz music. It turned out they had visited the same club in New Orleans. Mayhew provided the introductions for the rest of the dignitaries, though US Consul to Belfast Kathleen Stephens, fourth in a line of nine, did not need one. Clinton remembered her from her time as Director for European Affairs at the NSC from 1994 to 1995. She had drafted his response to the Downing Street Declaration, briefed him on numerous occasions and had accompanied him on a state visit to Canada only that February. Sent to Belfast in August, this was the zenith of her career to date. She was joining an elite few US staff serving around the globe who got the chance to play host to their leader. As the wind swirled about, the President and Mrs Clinton kept moving down the line which included the head of the Northern Ireland Civil Service, Sir David Fell, and Aldergrove's Managing Director Jim Dornan. "They didn't appear to be in any hurry but they didn't waste any time," said Forsythe, who drew succour from the fact that the first local politician the President had met in Northern Ireland was a Unionist. Dornan presented a visitor's book which both Clintons duly signed. After waving to airport workers and the world's media, most some distance away behind crash barriers that were in hot demand but short supply for those charged with security arrangements across the province, the President ducked into his bullet-and-bomb-proof car, to be joined in the back by his wife and Stephens.

Obscured by the smoked-glass windows President Clinton slumped back into the comfort of his limousine seat and sighed. While his long day was only beginning, he was already running late. Clinton had a reputation for poor time-keeping, especially during the first years of his Presidency, because of his schedulers' failure to take into account the genuine personal interest he took in the lives of those he came into contact with. "One thing Bill Clinton is is late," said one of the Presidential advance party. "He's not late because he's sloppy or he has no discipline. It's because he wants to hear, to meet, to communicate." As the political circumstances changed it had taken little or no coaxing to get him to come. He wanted to taste a peace he had fostered. And for many people in Northern Ireland his visit would in turn provide the first tangible evidence that they had been experiencing 13 months of peace. Never before had Protestant and Catholic united in a day of such euphoric celebration.

Stephens, somewhat nervous, sat erect in one of two jump seats facing the President and First Lady in the seclusion of the car's rear cabin. Up front, bodyguards squeezed in alongside the driver. The cavalcade, numbering over forty vehicles, had yet to sweep off from the runway apron but already Stephens noticed how weary Clinton appeared. She herself had had little more than two hours rest, having had one of the starring roles in the tiny cast of officials who had toiled into the small hours on the mechanics of the troublesome Falls Road handshake between Clinton and Adams, the last piece of the itinerary jigsaw to be slotted into place. Indeed Stephens was so uneasy about how the encounter would play that it made the drive less enjoyable and more apprehensive than it should have been. "By the time morning had come the time for second guessing about what was going to be done or what might happen was gone," she later recalled. "We all knew what the plan was and it was just a matter of executing it."

On an enthusiastic note, she congratulated the President on his performance in London, where he had pumped hands during a Westminster walkabout, had two hours of discussions with John Major which touched upon Northern Ireland, addressed both Houses of Parliament on the 'special relationship' between America and Britain and had tea with Queen Elizabeth. Responding to Stephens he said the day had been great but exhausting. Now he needed to focus his mind on what had really brought him across the Atlantic, to a country about the size of Connecticut, which was in the throes of a blooming but delicate peace and whose divided peoples numbered about a sixth of the population of New York City. He took out the keynote address he was due to deliver in an hour's time at an engineering factory near the 'peaceline' in west Belfast. By then it had been meticulously crafted by many pens, including Stephens', but as usual he wanted to rework aspects of it. (A Clinton speechwriter once joked that his function was to provide a sheet of blank paper.) The President asked Stephens to direct most of her conversation at his wife, while he would eavesdrop as he went over the text.

Beside him was a briefcase bursting with books, including *The Street*, the Adams story collection which the author had signed and

25

presented to him the previous St Patrick's Day at the White House and which had kept him up to five o'clock that morning. Clinton would later stun the Sinn Féin leader by telling him he was moved by the tale of a brother and sister tragically driven apart over politics. Another of the books he carried, *The Ulster Covenant*, the story of the 1912 Home Rule crisis, was a gift from David Trimble, head of the Ulster Unionist Party (UUP). Trimble had chatted to Clinton at Major's dinner and departed more impressed than after their first encounter in Washington four weeks earlier. "He was slightly ill at ease at the White House, looking to [National Security Advisor] Tony Lake for reassurance. In the discussions I had just before he came to Northern Ireland he was quite different, totally up to speed. It was a different person. He blitzes subjects. They get him fully up to speed."

Two motorcycle outriders led the Presidential convoy bound for Belfast. Williamson blazed the way in the lead car, a liveried RUC vehicle. His link to the driver's cabin of the Presidential limousine was one of several channels of communication rigged up to the car. One each for internal RUC and Secret Service traffic, the other between the two organisations.

Travelling with Williamson were Assistant Chief Constable Bill Stewart, who was responsible for crowd and route security, and Rick Alto, lead advance man with the Secret Service, the President's personal protection staff. Alto's gaze was always one of suspicion. RUC officers nicknamed him "Shifty". A path had been cleared for the motorcade. The M2, one of the country's busiest highways, had been closed to traffic for hours in order to ease the President's safe and speedy passage. He had barely left the airport when the first well-wishers cheered him through a roundabout. He lifted his head from his speech and waved back. "They were enjoying the people," said Stephens of the President and First Lady. "At one point we went through a motorway overpass and there were people leaning over and waving and they remarked upon that. They were really pleased that this was a great, friendly beginning to their day." The early part of the drive from Aldergrove is picturesque and quintessentially Irish. The Clintons marvelled at the rolling hills, a patchwork blanket of green and brown hues whose seams were snaking hedgerows. Cattle and sheep were grazing here and there and the President enthusiastically pointed out a farmhouse to his wife and enquired if she had ever been to Ireland before. Stephens' memory went back to the first time she had taken the same journey, accompanied by her eight-year-old son James. She told Mrs Clinton how he had innocently remarked that there were no bad views in Northern Ireland. The First Lady, apparently so struck by his observation, passed it off as her own when later asked by the press about her initial impressions of the country.

In Templepatrick, a large, affluent village near the start of the route, knots of people had been drawn to the one main road by the novel spectacle of a pre-dawn security operation that had effectively quarantined its two thousand inhabitants. Routes in and out were blocked. Estate agent Ray Chapa, a Texan who married a Northern Ireland woman and moved to her homeland in 1986, tried in vain to take his nine-year-old daughter to school by way of their usual car journey but had no choice other than to join the swelling ranks of spectators. The thrill of glimpsing an American President, though not for the first time, started to build within him. The uncommitted Democrat had seen Richard Nixon walk the beaches of San Clemente, California, as he surfed between the President's guard boats in his youth. "Even in the States it's hard to get close to this guy but we were maybe ten feet from the road as the President drove by – you could actually see him waving with a big smile. People were clapping and screaming, 'President, President.' I thought it was amazing. It made me aware of how important this person is, but also how important Northern Ireland is for him to come over here." In the lead car, Agent Alto spied two RUC officers waving at the passing cavalcade from the footpath and snapped to Stewart that he would have to remind his men to stick to their task of watching the crowd, not Clinton.

In between the scenery and the spectators the President was poring over his speech, bouncing ideas off his wife. "He already knew the speech and felt comfortable with it, and his initial reactions had gone back to the speechwriters and been taken into account," said Stephens. "From my experience at the NSC this was his *modus operandi*. He works on his speech right up until the last minute, putting his own imprint on it." Clinton quizzed the Consul about Mackie International, the factory selected as the venue for his keynote address, which the President traditionally liked to deliver as early as possible. She informed him it manufactured textile machinery and this became the inspiration for one of a number of script changes during the car journey: "The textile machines you make permit people to weave disparate threads into remarkable fabrics. That is now what you must do here with the people of Northern Ireland," wrote the President after working on the metaphor with the help of his wife. Another amendment, a quotation by a Governor from his home state of Arkansas in the aftermath of the American Civil War, was pulled from his briefcase. Clinton, a voracious reader, had come across this post-conflict plea for forgiveness and reconciliation a few days earlier and felt it pertinent to the Northern Ireland situation.

As the limousine sped towards Belfast Stephens at times felt uneasy, fretting she was encroaching on what she perceived as private moments for America's first couple. But she had little time to dwell on the thought as the two became increasingly inquisitive. Mrs Clinton showed an interest in women's issues and the role of the churches in Northern Ireland. When she asked why Protestants and Catholics didn't get along, perhaps the most fundamental question for any curious visitor, Stephens, a masters graduate from an Ivy League college, was left groping for an adequate answer like many before her. In another exchange, this time with the President, Stephens gave a rough percentage of the religious breakdown in the region only for her boss to go one better by being more exact. The 20-minute ride to the city with the scenery, the crowds, the speech and the conversation served as something of a Presidential wake-up call. By its end vigour had supplanted fatigue. Observed Stephens: "What happened over the course of that drive from Aldergrove to the first stop was a visible energising, truly. By the time he got out the man was really up. Yes, it had all been painstakingly planned but what happened virtually from the moment of his arrival is the spirit began and that is not something you can write into a scenario. That is what made the drive really fun."

What was to follow became a powerful manifestation of how deeply Washington's engagement in Northern Ireland had become in the short space of time since 1993. "The mere fact of his presence as a way of conveying his personal interest would indicate the priority he accorded to the issue and conveyed the sense that the United States wanted very much to be helpful to the process as best we could," stated Mitchell. Past Presidents had largely paid cursory lip-service in support of London and Dublin's efforts to solve the age-old Irish question but the Clinton Administration broke new territory in becoming directly involved. Previously a disjointed Irish-American lobby had scored some noteworthy successes on Capitol Hill but now with a changed vanguard it was able to exert an influence in the Oval Office which went beyond its wildest dreams. "It's unprecedented that the Irish issue had found such a home in the White House," said a leading Administration official. Ireland and Britain welcomed this timely interest from the world's most powerful nation, but to a differing extent. For many reasons, Clinton's elevation from State Governor to President meant the much-vaunted 'special relationship' between America and Britain, while remaining important, was never going to be as centre stage as it had been in the earlier course of the twentieth century. After setbacks at home and abroad, Northern Ireland, like the Middle East, afforded the Clinton Administration an opportunity to enhance its prestige as global peace broker. It became locked into the quest for a lasting political settlement and, in George Mitchell, put its representative at the very heart of negotiations. Clinton, the man from Hope, had grasped the Irish nettle and not been stung – at least not until the IRA ceasefire collapsed in spectacular fashion in February 1996. His visit though prevented it disintegrating sooner. Mitchel McLaughlin, a leading Sinn Féin strategist, said: "The peace process was virtually over. I suspect the IRA was at the point of calling off its cessation and the President's visit bought another three months. It was a minor miracle we got that additional time but it wasn't used very productively." Aspects of Clinton's policy raised eyebrows in Washington as well as London. There was friction between the White House and the State Department, which was no longer in the driving seat on thinking on Northern Ireland and from within which there were serious reservations about going to the province ahead of a final political settlement. As New York Democratic Congressman Tom Manton, another member of the House of Representatives who accompanied the President, put it: "We had the wedding reception before the marriage." Clinton's embassies in London and Dublin, under the imposing personalities of William Crowe and Jean Kennedy Smith respectively, were also at odds, reflecting the attitudes to the peace process of the countries they served in. "With her it was always a zero sum game – if somebody won, somebody lost. It was never as though we were part of the same team," said a London Embassy source.

The White House's unprecedented involvement also led Northern Ireland's political parties into a re-evaluation of the worth of their relationships with Washington. Doors which down the years had been ajar for Social Democratic and Labour Party (SDLP) leader John Hume suddenly began swinging open for other politicians. Hume would claim with some justification that he acted as an obliging doorman ushering them in. Access to the highest level of the US Government was staggering. Sinn Féin and the UUP both set up offices in Washington. Nationalists, long proponents of an international dimension to the quest for an answer to the Northern Ireland problem, were keen to ensure America was in to the finish. Unionists, traditionally insular and distrustful of America, started to travel Stateside with greater regularity and higher profile. Increasingly the missions became positive rather than negative, more about articulating their own case rather than bidding to throw a spanner in the works of the well-oiled Irish Republican propaganda machine. "We were totally wrong to ignore the importance of America," argued UUP deputy leader John Taylor. "Most Unionists dismissed America as a lost cause and we've missed out for two decades." Even the Democratic Unionist Party (DUP), the most privately and publicly hostile of all towards US involvement, sensed the tide was turning. "I think the Unionist case is far, far better known now in the States than it ever has been," leader Ian Paisley said. Clinton's magical 24 hours in Northern Ireland, together with the intense preparation put into it, could claim much of the credit.

II

Fascinated from the day it began

*The President saw, and all of us saw, an opportunity
to try and be helpful in putting an end to, or at least
make progress on, an issue all of us had grown up
knowing about. Everybody was aware of the
Troubles and it seemed the right thing to do.*

Tony Lake, National Security Advisor

Bill Clinton was 46 years old when he achieved the highest
political office in the United States, billing himself along the
campaign trial as the man from Hope, the sleepy southern Arkansas
town where he was born William Jefferson Blythe III on 19 August
1946. The future President was named after his father, who was
killed in a car smash three months before he was born. His mother,
Virginia Cassidy, who had possible ancestral links with County
Fermanagh, moved to New Orleans to study nursing, leaving the
child with her parents, Eldridge and Edith Cassidy, owners of a
small grocery store. Returning newly qualified when her son was
four years old, she wed a car salesman, Roger Clinton, one of four
marriages in her colourful life. He was an abusive drunk who
sometimes fired shots from his revolver into the interior walls of
the family's home. They moved forty miles north to a resort and
gambling town called Hot Springs when Billy Blythe, as he was
then known, was seven. It wasn't until he started school that year
that he adopted his stepfather's name.

Clinton, though raised a southern Baptist, was initially educated by nuns at a Catholic school. In the classroom over coming years he began to display the academic excellence which would win him scholarships. Outside it he started playing the saxophone. It became his favourite pastime and each summer he went to band camp in the mountains. One of the most formative – and now most celebrated – events of his youth came on a visit to Washington in 1963 as a Boys' Nation delegate at a special leadership conference. Invited to the White House, the teenage Clinton seized his chance to shake President Kennedy's hand in the Rose Garden. Kennedy praised the visitors for passing a motion the previous evening attacking racism – civil rights was the biggest domestic issue of the day. Clinton, a young civil rights idealist, had helped carry the resolution. As good fortune would have it, their encounter was captured on black-and-white film which proved useful in future political campaigns. (The footage is also replayed as part of an exhibit at the JFK Library near Boston before President Clinton appears on screen to pay homage.) Clinton, like millions of other Americans, was captivated by Kennedy. From then on, as the Clinton fable goes, he repudiated any notion of a career as a Baptist minister and chose instead the path of politics.

Clinton attended Georgetown, a Jesuit-run university in Washington acclaimed for producing diplomats, and earned a Bachelor of Science degree in International Affairs. There he met Irish-Americans from the eastern seaboard and developed a passing interest in Catholicism. His first girlfriend came from a well-to-do Irish Catholic family in New Jersey. Fellow students later told biographers of Clinton's support for the civil rights struggle by African-Americans. It was said he was so deeply moved by Martin Luther King's 'I Have a Dream' speech that he memorised it. During college his political education developed as an intern in the office of a Senator from Arkansas he admired, J. William Fulbright. After Georgetown, Clinton went to Oxford in 1968 on a prized Rhodes Scholarship. While there he made a weekend trip to Dublin with a friend. North of the border, the Troubles were breaking out. Deeply interested in the civil rights cause at home, it was natural Clinton would follow the story of Catholic agitation for equality in Northern Ireland through the British media, particularly as it derived inspiration from the American movement and adopted some of its strategies. Even the protest songs were the same. Television vividly recorded heads being cracked by the reserve police force, the B-Specials, and by Protestant mobs. To Bill Clinton, watching from Oxford, the pictures could easily have come from Birmingham, Alabama, but for the skin colour of those whose skulls bled.

The extent to which those images burned in the mind of Clinton only became apparent three decades later. "I was there when the Troubles began, you know," he told the *Irish Times'* Washington correspondent Conor O'Clery. "I was living in Oxford. It occupied the attention of the country, obviously. We went through the whole thing at home. I could see it coming, that religious differences were likely to lead to the same kind of problems that racial differences had in my childhood. You know, I've been fascinated by it for 25 years, from the day the Troubles began." When he reminisced about his Oxford days with others, he spoke of his interest in the career of Bernadette Devlin, the fiery civil rights activist who in 1969, at the age of 21, became the youngest woman ever elected to Westminster. Another figure he watched and read about was Ian Paisley, then a politician-in-training as a firebrand Protestant preacher. It was Paisley's sparkle as an orator that caught his attention. Clinton disclosed this when the two met for the first time on the President's visit to Northern Ireland.

After Oxford Clinton, the boy who grew up on the wrong side of the tracks, went to Yale to study law. He kept his hand in politics by campaigning for a Senate candidate in Connecticut. It was at the Ivy League college that he meet his future bride, Hillary Rodham. He graduated in 1973 and went back to his roots. He was a good old boy from the American south, a 'Bubba' as they are known. But a Bubba with brains. Commentators would later testify that therein lay the essence of Bill Clinton, a man who could balance his easy, populist charm and his intellectual prowess. Clinton taught law at the University of Arkansas and began preparing for political office but his first shot, in 1974, ended in failure – defeat in a Congressional contest at the hands of the Republican incumbent. Hillary Rodham joined him on the stump and she too started teaching at the state university. The pair married in 1975. A year later Clinton was elected Arkansas Attorney General and in 1978 built on that success by becoming state Governor. He was 32 and the youngest state Governor in America. Although he lost in 1980, he was re-elected in 1982 and every time thereafter until he decided to run for the Oval office. Clinton was dubbed the 'Comeback Kid' in 1982 and again in 1992, when he shook off setbacks to first win the Democratic Party's nomination and then the ultimate prize itself.

The Irish issue had no place in Arkansas state politics. It was, after all, the south, not New York, Chicago or Boston where there was a sizeable and sometimes electorally significant concentration of those of Irish descent. It therefore wasn't until his national campaign that Clinton was confronted with the Irish question. Even then foreign policy was not top of his agenda; one of the slogans he was electioneering on was 'The Economy, Stupid.' Ireland surfaced in national American politics in April 1992 during Clinton's tussle for the nomination during the primaries, when candidates from within each party run-off against each other. He was going into a tough primary in New York, having narrowly lost in Connecticut to his one remaining rival, Jerry Brown, a former Governor of California. Clinton's campaign had been dogged by a spate of controversies and was in crisis. There were claims he'd dodged the draft during the Vietnam War, allegations of an affair with Gennifer Flowers and, famously, an admission he'd experimented with marijuana, but not inhaled. Desperate to win New York – where one in four Democratic voters was undecided – Clinton agreed to attend a forum on Irish issues. The forum, began in 1984 and the brainchild of an assemblyman from the Bronx by the name of John Dearie, was an opportunity to quiz the Democratic hopefuls on a question they held dear. "John Dearie deserves enormous credit for helping focus Presidential candidates on the Irish issue," said one observer of the New York political scene.

An urbane Wall Street lawyer and Democratic Party strategist, John Connorton, played a part in cajoling the candidates along. A former naval officer in Vietnam, his grandparents came from Roscommon, Mayo, Kerry and Cork. Connorton was well aware of the trepidation with which presidential candidates and their teams approached this probing of issues Irish. Al Gore, whose unsuccessful campaign for the nomination he ran in New York in 1988, had gone to a similar event but only after considerable debate right up until an hour beforehand. "Dearie called me in a panic on a Saturday morning," Connorton recalled. "He said, 'I think I've got Clinton committed to the forum but I'm afraid I'm going to lose him if Brown doesn't come.'" Connorton said he'd help. He tracked down Brown at a rally and secured the pledge of attendance, keeping the event alive.

Clinton was weary when he appeared before the Irish-Americans in a small function room at the Sheraton Hotel in Manhattan on the night of 5 April, two days before the crunch primary. There were about one hundred people at the event, at which Clinton and Brown were appearing separately as agreed. The questions were posed by a panel which included Mayor Raymond Flynn of Boston, later Clinton's Ambassador to the Vatican, some newspapermen and Martin Galvin, the public face of Irish Northern Aid (NORAID) which fundraised for the Irish Republican cause in America, and editor of its paper the *Irish People.* He'd gained notoriety for defying a British Government order which banned him from Northern Ireland until 1990, popping up on several occasions at Sinn Féin rallies and the funerals of IRA men. His presence at the forum had been a potential spanner in the works and sparked interest in some quarters. Said Connorton: "I remember Conor O'Clery turned round to me and said, 'Martin Galvin on the platform is big news.' I said, 'If you say it's big news it'll be big news in Ireland but I can tell you it's not going to be big news in the United States.' No-one from the mainstream US press was interested." (As Clinton left, O'Clery broached the subject of Galvin's presence. "Come on, give me a break. I'm doing my best," the candidate told the reporter.)

The first question at the forum came from Flynn who asked if Clinton would consider sending a peace envoy to Northern Ireland and encourage United Nations involvement. "I would," replied Clinton. "I think sometimes we are too reluctant to engage ourselves in a positive way because of our long-standing relationship with Great Britain and also because it seemed such a thorny problem." As well as encouraging sides to reach a peace settlement, he said his envoy would focus on the work of Amnesty International concerning breaches of human rights by the security forces and others. He drew loud applause. The envoy idea had been pushed for years by Dearie, who got the New York State legislature to adopt a resolution backing it in 1983. The same year Daniel Patrick Moynihan, one of the so-called 'Four Horsemen' of Irish-American politics, introduced a resolution in the Senate, backed by Ted Kennedy and Chris Dodd, urging President Ronald Reagan to appoint an envoy. The defeated Democratic candidates for the

Presidency in 1984 and 1988, Walter Mondale and Michael Dukakis respectively, had also backed the proposal. The British, however, detested the prospect of such overt meddling. "We do not need a peace envoy, thank you very much," was the brusque response of Sir Patrick Mayhew.

Clinton was asked by Galvin if, as President, he would reverse US policy and order that a visa be granted to Gerry Adams, allowing the Sinn Féin leader into the country to express his views. Clinton replied he would. "I think it would be totally harmless to our national security interests and would widen the political debate in this country." Adams' visa requests had been denied down the years because of the then west Belfast MP's association with the IRA and his refusal to renounce the organisation's violence. At the forum, Clinton also endorsed a set of fair employment guidelines for American companies operating in Northern Ireland, the MacBride Principles. Since their launch in 1984, countless states and cities across America had adopted the guidelines, named after their late architect, the former Irish Foreign Minister and Nobel peace laureate Sean MacBride, which sought to ensure firms didn't discriminate against Catholics. (They were based on the Sullivan Principles which had been applied in South Africa as part of the disinvestment campaign against apartheid.) While Sinn Féin backed them, SDLP leader John Hume felt they could discourage potential investors. Ted Kennedy also shunned them, but candidate Clinton disagreed. "I see it as a way of encouraging investment because it's a way of stabilising the political and economic climate and the workforce," he said.

Nodding approvingly in a front row seat was a Redemptorist priest, Fr Sean McManus, head of the Irish National Caucus, a Washington-based umbrella group for numerous Irish-American organisations. Its attention had focused on promoting the Principles, with success, since the mid-eighties. "The way he addressed the issue was very heartening," recalled the Fermanagh-born McManus, whose brother Frank was the former Nationalist MP for Fermanagh-South Tyrone. "I was quite impressed with Clinton. I thought to myself, the media has got this guy wrong. On television he comes across a little bit soft but I was struck by his intensity and steel. He spoke excellently. He had been very well briefed. I felt that this time, this time, we might just be able to push the Irish issue." Also present at the forum was Congressman Tom Manton, a first generation Irish-American Democrat for the New York district of Queens. "We'd already endorsed him in Queens where I'm Democratic County Chairman," he said. "He was already my candidate as a Democrat, not necessarily as an Irishman, but with the forum he kind of locked it up both ways. He wanted to win the election so it was reasonable for him to make the commitments. If you don't want to make these promises you don't come. Dukakis was fairly good on the issue. He didn't have to be prepared too much, but then he was from Massachusetts. Clinton came across as knowing the issues, but how much he'd had to be briefed I'm not sure."

Clinton won the New York primary, boosted his campaign and went on to secure his party's nomination. To what extent his pledges secured votes in the New York Primary was debatable however. Brown gave much the same undertakings at the forum and suggested the next President could perhaps go to Northern Ireland himself. It wasn't until the Democratic Party Convention in August that Clinton looked capable of beating sitting President George Bush.

His attempt to oust Bush at the November poll was run from Little Rock, capital of unfashionable Arkansas. Ordinarily it's off the map for most visitors from Ireland but in 1992, as Clinton sought to become the first Democrat to win the White House since fellow southerner Jimmy Carter in 1976, it attracted, of all people, a senior aide to DUP leader Ian Paisley.

Nigel Dodds, a former Lord Mayor of Belfast, was in town for five days to see the campaign in action as part of a month-long study programme run by the US Government. In an office deep within a Clinton headquarters staffed by some of those who went on to become leading lights in the subsequent Administration, Dodds and his fellow foreign observers were briefed on the candidate's policies. Paisley's man buttonholed the election worker on what Clinton's views were on Ireland. "I'd a pretty good idea but I just wanted to hear what he'd say," recollected the mischief-making Dodds. "He said, 'Oh, we've taken care of that, Bruce Morrison's looking after it', and I immediately said, 'But he's coming from one particular angle.' Bemusement and bewilderment crossed his face but as far as they were concerned Morrison was it, so they were coming at it from the Irish-American, Nationalist-Republican point of view. I came back from that trip fervently hoping Clinton wouldn't get elected on that basis."

Morrison, a Yale Law School classmate of the future President's and a former Congressman for Connecticut, was co-chairman of 'Irish-Americans for Clinton', a group which campaigned for Clinton and in return sought to influence the candidate's pronouncements on the Irish situation. He'd penned the legislation for Congress which gave 48,000 visas to a new wave of Irish immigrants at the turn of the decade. Together with a group of others – publisher Niall O'Dowd, insurance magnate Bill Flynn and Charles "Chuck" Feeney, billionaire owner of a chain of duty free shops – he would become an emissary of peace in Northern Ireland in the wake of Clinton's election to the White House, playing a role in securing the IRA ceasefire in August 1994. Despite his popularity over the 'Morrison visas', he was a rather unlikely figurehead for an Irish-American group. He wasn't Catholic and by his own admission was more German than Irish. The source of his interest in the issue was human rights.

'Irish-Americans for Clinton' was established after Chris Hyland, a Clinton campaign worker, got in touch with O'Dowd at the *Irish Voice*, a New York-based weekly tabloid. In each other they'd found what they'd been looking for. Hyland, in charge of ethnic outreach, had to ensure Irish-American backing for the campaign was properly harnessed; O'Dowd was searching for a Democratic candidate to get hooked on the cause. "Hyland was very important," recalled O'Dowd, who had contacts with most if not all the players in the Irish-American community. "He just picked up the *Irish Voice* and called me out of the blue. He said, 'Would you chair a group?' I said, 'No, Bruce Morrison would be the guy to do that.' And that's how it started. We represented Irish-American grassroots opinion. People like Bruce Morrison are absolute saints in Irish-America. You try and fill a room of Irish-Americans with John Hume and it's hard, very hard. You could fill a room overnight if Bruce Morrison was going to speak." Morrison, who'd accepted the position with Mayor Flynn as co-chairman, believed the candidate's commitment was partly based on *realpolitic*. "It wasn't like he was pondering the issue for 20 years. He does not claim, never has claimed, that there was a straight line from Oxford to 1992. What he had was an image in his mind of Northern Ireland and of civil rights, and a negative and repressive response. Then there was Arkansas, and nobody talked much about Northern Ireland in Arkansas. Then he came to the New York primary and there were those of us who brought the issue back to the fore. When it became a current-day political reality and a political imperative he got involved."

Two weeks before his election to the White House, Clinton put in writing to Morrison what was effectively a manifesto on Northern Ireland. It was in fact penned by Nancy Soderberg, former aide to Senator Kennedy, who had joined the campaign foreign policy team. As number three at the NSC in the Clinton Administration, she became a hate figure for Unionists and some British Government officials, who misguidedly perceived her as being pro-Nationalist. Said a senior diplomat at the British Embassy in Washington: "This embassy didn't have the problems with Nancy Soderberg that legend has it. She wasn't deceptive. She was always intellectually honest." That view was echoed at the Irish Embassy. "I don't think Soderberg leant towards us more than the British," said an insider. "I think it is a perception related to the fact she'd worked in Kennedy's office, but she was professional and objective." Soderberg herself would become irritated by her treatment in the British media. "The portrayal of me was always inaccurate. All the press stories focused on me because I worked in Ted Kennedy's office. I thought the whole reaction was first of all very naive about how the decision process works in the White House and secondly just over-reacting and hysterical. The way they portrayed it was that I single-handedly talked the President round on the Irish issue. You can't do that. One person, particularly at my level, number three person at the NSC, can't single-handedly talk the President into something." In Clinton's letter to Morrison. Soderberg wrote: "Senator Gore [Vice Presidential running mate] and I share the goal of all Irish-Americans for peace in Northern Ireland. We believe that the United States must reflect this concern more effectively in its foreign policy. A Clinton Administration will take a more active role in working to achieve a just and lasting settlement of the conflict. I believe the appointment of a special US envoy to Northern Ireland could be a catalyst in the effort to secure a lasting settlement." The letter went on to express Clinton's belief that the British could do more to tackle job discrimination against Catholics. And there was more. "We also believe that the British Government should establish more effective safeguards against the wanton use of lethal force and against further collusion between the security forces and

Protestant paramilitary groups." There was no mention in the letter of a visa for Adams, but no matter. The blood was starting to curdle in London at the unthinkable prospect of direct Presidential intervention in Northern Ireland against the wishes of Washington's closest ally. (The furthest any White House occupant had gone was when Carter blocked the sale of over three thousand weapons to the RUC.) Major's Tories were backing Bush, many openly so. Officials even opened Clinton's passport files from his Oxford days in a search for anything damaging. Election pledges though were one thing, honouring them another. And so it was in 1993, Clinton's first year in the Oval Office.

Ironically it was the Irish, not the British, who were decisive in killing off the peace envoy idea. Taoiseach Albert Reynolds had it placed on the back burner on St Patrick's Day at the White House. He briefed the President on the spadework he and Major were doing on what nine months later was to become the Downing Street Declaration and on the clandestine contacts with Sinn Féin designed to end IRA violence. Hume, the most influential figure from Northern Ireland with Washington's political elite, had also been against the idea of a peace envoy. He argued instead for an economic emissary. Following a shamrock presentation in the Roosevelt Room, Clinton said the United States couldn't make peace in Northern Ireland and, while a final decision on an envoy hadn't been made, the most important thing was the resumption of stalled peace talks. Said a high-level source at the Irish Embassy in Washington: "Albert Reynolds was very doubtful about the idea. He'd serious negotiations underway at the time with John Major and he didn't want any extraneous factor that might be unhelpful in any way. If an envoy had gone over there there would've been a lot of resentment, so it was put on the shelf. It was very pragmatic."

The St Patrick's Day occasion was also used to announce the appointment of Jean Kennedy Smith as Ambassador to Ireland. JFK's youngest sister had no diplomatic experience but her brother, Senator Edward Kennedy, had lobbied hard for her appointment, which reinforced the notion among cynics that Clinton was in awe of or beholden to the first family of American politics. (The morning of his inauguration Clinton had knelt at the graveside of President Kennedy.) The appointment of Kennedy Smith, then 65, caused alarm among Unionists, not only because of her family's Nationalist leanings. In a break with previous Ambassadors to Dublin, her brief was to be pro-active in the search for a settlement in Northern Ireland. In Ireland, where fond memories of JFK and his triumphant 1963 visit hadn't been much diminished by the tarnishing of his reputation, Kennedy Smith's arrival was seen as complementing Clinton's regard for the issue. "We have an American Ambassador driven by her zeal to make a contribution to solve the Irish problem at a time when you have a President in the White House who has a far more abiding interest obviously than Bush or Reagan," said Irish Foreign Minister Dick Spring. "She has been a very important person in this whole business."

In May it became public that Clinton had reneged on another campaign commitment, the granting of a visa for Adams. The US State Department said the request, in order to undertake a book promotion tour, had been denied under rules which excluded those with terrorist associations. It had been blocked on the advice of, among others, Attorney General Janet Reno and US Secretary of State Warren Christopher. Clinton claimed that he had only promised to review the evidence if Adams sought entry to the United States. A sticking point was also made of the fact that Adams had lost his House of Commons seat since the New York forum pledge. "I asked that his case be reviewed by the State Department and others and everybody that reviewed it recommended that the visa not be granted and pointed out that he was no longer a member of parliament," said the President. Soderberg explained: "It just wasn't appropriate to have the President take a hit for giving somebody associated with the IRA a visa. It was a bad anti-terrorist message."

The ban on Adams entering the US raised its head five months later during the re-election campaign of New York Mayor David Dinkins. Keen to capitalise on the Irish vote, he wrote to Clinton asking that the Adams visa denial be reconsidered given that the dialogue now taking place in Northern Ireland between the Sinn Féin leader and Hume was showing encouraging signs. Dinkins' timing however couldn't have been worse. The spotlight was back on Northern Ireland because an IRA bomb had killed ten people on Belfast's Shankill Road. The letter was dismissed out of hand and a response sent. The White House's reply, cleared by Soderberg, used the abbreviation PIRA (Provisional IRA being the favoured term of reference of the British Government and the Anglophile State

Department) and angered Irish-Americans already made impatient by Clinton's breaking of campaign promises. Recalled Fr Sean McManus: "For months we'd hammered away at him for not keeping his campaign pledges. We did extensive mailings to supporters and included postcards for them to forward to the White House to keep the pressure on. It was absolutely important the pressure was kept on."

Despite the visa and envoy setbacks, the White House was interested in the Northern Ireland situation. After the Dinkins letter, members of the Ad Hoc Committee on Irish Affairs had an audience with leading Clinton foreign policy aide Tony Lake. Among its number were Congressmen Ben Gilman, Peter King, Richard Neal and Tom Manton. Lake, who was accompanied by Soderberg, was keen to emphasise the Administration was still taking the issue seriously – a fact underlined by the meeting itself. Never before had the group got to address such a high-ranking Administration figure. Neal, a Congressman from Massachusetts, recalled afterwards: "I give Tony Lake a lot of credit. I remember vividly him leaving the meeting saying, 'The only promise I will make to you is that I will elevate Ireland to the same status as the Middle East.' We left almost astounded that somebody so close to the President would say something like that." The meeting made an impression on Lake too. In an interview with the authors, he admitted: "That meeting early on in the Administration had an impact on me. It helped me put the issue on my agenda and it got more and more interesting as we went along. The President saw and all of us saw an opportunity to try and be helpful in putting an end to, or at least make progress on, an issue all of us had grown up knowing about. Everybody was aware of the Troubles and it seemed the right thing to do." Morrison was keeping faith with Clinton regardless of the meeting. "There was a whole year it took him to get on track, to get out from under the same old, same old. Did I question his commitment? No I didn't, because I had a lot of good conversations with people at the White House, including the President, which suggested he was focused on it. But it was a contest about how we would present an opportunity for him to act that would be compelling and that was all of the work on Bill Flynn's forum."

Flynn, head of the Mutual of America insurance group, was behind a conference on Northern Ireland on 1 February 1994 in New

York – the vehicle by which Adams eventually got into the United States. Adams and other politicians from the country's political parties were invited, though the UUP and DUP refused to send anyone. The conference was organised by an independent but influential think-tank, the National Committee on American Foreign Policy, of which Flynn was chairman. Highly respected in corporate America, Flynn had a powerful emotional draw towards the Irish issue. He was an Irish Catholic whose father, from County Down, and whose mother, born in County Mayo, were "driven out by poverty and lack of opportunity." He supported the unification of Ireland, but by peaceful means. His company, which had a Nobel laureate on its board, sponsored a series of 'Beyond Hatred' conferences, including one in Derry in 1992.

The first real glimmers of a new dawn were becoming visible in Northern Ireland at the time Adams applied for a visa at the US Embassy in Dublin in January 1994. The political landscape was brightening. The Downing Street Declaration had been signed and there was speculation about an IRA ceasefire. Reynolds and Hume believed Adams could shepherd the Republican movement down the road of non-violence and believed America had a significant part to play. Alliances were formed to get Adams in. Key to its success were the Kennedys. Jean Kennedy Smith and Ted Kennedy were convinced of the visa's merits by Hume and Reynolds. Said Senator Kennedy: "During the campaign the President clearly indicated his interest in involving his Administration in the Northern Ireland issue. But it was the situation on the ground – the Hume-Adams initiative, the Joint Declaration of December 1993 and the indications many of us received that the IRA wanted to end violence – that caused the President to make the issue the priority he did."

When the Ambassador's recommendation that the visa be granted arrived in Washington, her brother sent a letter to Clinton supporting her stance. It was also signed by fellow Democratic Senators Chris Dodd, Daniel Patrick Moynihan and John Kerry. Later, 36 more members of the House of Representatives put their names to it, including the Senate Majority Leader, George Mitchell. Powerful politicians were now on the Adams visa bandwagon – men crucial to the President's legislative agenda in Congress. Kennedy and Moynihan were chairmen of major Senate committees whose co-operation was essential to the passage of Clinton's health care and welfare reform programmes. Also the National Committee on American Foreign Policy placed a full-page advertisement in the *New York Times* backing the visa, signed by the heads of more than 80 corporations and one hundred other leading Irish-Americans. Dodd, who was also chairman of the Democratic National Committee, believed the Adams visa issue was developing into a defining moment – either there would be direct Presidential involvement in a peace process or Clinton would back away and offer verbal encouragement. "I think there was a sense that the moment was right to try something different – the right moment to be bold – and the President is a great instinctive politician," said the Senator. "One thing this President isn't given enough credit for is the fact he has a great feel for the moment. Most of the paid advice he got from his own staff and others was, 'Don't get near this thing.' In the scale of things in the world Northern Ireland doesn't register. China, Russia, new independent states, India, Pakistan, Latin America, Middle East. The list is almost endless before you get to this one. Why did he get involved? I think it was perplexing to him, it was irrational to him and he was ready to give of himself to try and think of some answers."

The British Embassy in Washington sensed the tide was turning. The fact that secret contacts between London and Sinn Féin going back years had been exposed in the British media three months earlier didn't benefit the argument that Adams was a pariah to be shunned by all right-thinking democracies. Still, while allies were hard to come by on Capitol Hill – Speaker of the House of Representatives Tom Foley being a notable exception – big names in the Administration remained against an Adams visa. Secretary of State Christopher and Attorney General Reno were joined in opposition by the head of the FBI Louis Freech and the Ambassador to London Raymond Seitz, a career diplomat rather than a political appointee. Vice President Al Gore, though, came down in favour of the visa. The White House considered another option. "We thought about just resuming contact with Sinn Féin, finding other ways to reach out without giving the visa," said a leading White House official. "But ultimately it came down to the visa and nothing short of a visa was enough for Adams." Downing Street and the British Embassy were making their objections known to Lake at the National Security Council. "We weren't going to roll over and say, 'Oh well, it's your decision, Mr President'," said a source at the Embassy. "For us Adams was the mouthpiece of an organisation still in the middle of a campaign of terror. Our Ambassador, Robin Renwick, strongly represented that. But there was the political pressure, Congressional pressure, people like Kennedy. People like that made the key difference to Clinton."

In the end the White House viewed the visa as what Soderberg later termed a "win-win decision." There would be kudos for the Administration if the lifting of the ban on Adams helped bring about an IRA ceasefire. If he didn't deliver it would expose him as a fraud, someone not interested in peace who could then be isolated from Irish-America. Clinton's advisors, whom he met in the Oval Office on 29 January, three days before the New York conference Adams wanted to attend, also believed Anglo-American relations were solid enough to weather the looming diplomatic storm. The President had agreed to grant the visa before news of a bizarre episode reached him. Hoax bombs were planted in British stores in San Diego by the unheard of 'South California IRA'. Trouble was promised if Adams didn't get his visa. The Sinn Féin leader's subsequent condemnation of the incident, elicited by the White House through O'Dowd, sealed the visa for him, his first in nine attempts spanning two decades. Adams would be allowed into the US for 48 hours to attend the one-day peace conference on Northern Ireland and his movements restricted to a 25-mile radius of New York. "It was a gut thing," Clinton advisor George Stephanopoulos was later reported as saying of the decision. The President himself told journalists it was a "judgement call." Lake said: "The Adams visa made us concentrate on the issue. A decision to grant it or not to grant it would have an impact on the situation in Northern Ireland and we wanted to make sure we got it right. Once we had made the decision to grant it we were involved." A senior White House colleague agreed, adding: "Once we took the step to give him a visa we were committed. Had we not given him a visa we probably could have stayed on the sidelines."

There were predictable howls of disapproval from the British and Unionists. Said David Trimble: "One never regarded the American Administration as merely a creature of the pan-Nationalist front but it made us concerned about the fundamental alignment of the US Government. Over the years British influence had far outweighed any influence that could be demonstrated by Irish-America. The visa was significant in indicating Irish-America could actually exert enough influence in the White House to overrule something the British Government put a major effort into fighting." Sir Patrick Mayhew, who went to Washington to help heal the rift that April, later admitted the British might have suffered a backlash to their robust opposition. "I think we might have slightly overdone it when we expressed these things strongly. It develops a kind of equal, or more than equal lobby in the other direction. We felt very strongly that it was not a good idea." The outrage at the decision wasn't lost on the Clinton Administration. Said Presidential Press Secretary Mike McCurry: "We see eye-to-eye with Britain on many issues – they are our closest ally – but this was a disruptive element, a source of tension and some conflict. You could sense that it was something really personal that was rubbed there. Their sense of disappointment was profound and yet our intentions were only the best because we really did believe we could make a difference and ultimately we did make a difference in accelerating the process."

Adams arrived in New York on 31 January, checking into the $350-a-night Waldorf Astoria Hotel under the name Shlomo Brezhnev as a security precaution. He was looked upon as a curio by the American news media, in part due to the extraordinary lengths the British had gone to to demonise him during the visa war. CNN's Larry King tried to use the bogey-man factor to the advantage of his chat show. "Tonight the New York visit of a man so controversial his very voice is barred from British television," said King in dramatic tone as the opening credits rolled. (At the time Adams' voice was banned from the airwaves in Britain under law, as the organisation he belonged to supported violence.) Hume and Alliance Party leader Dr John Alderdice were also attending the peace conference, but they never got a look in. Alderdice left before Adams spoke. The Sinn Féin President called on the Clinton White House to be actively involved in the search for a settlement in Northern Ireland. "The US Government can play a significant and positive role in encouraging the peace process by helping to create a climate which moves the situation on," said Adams.

In March, IRA mortar shells were fired at Heathrow Airport in London. That none exploded was irrelevant to politicians in Washington who'd wagered their credibility on Adams. Moynihan sent Kennedy a note which said: "Have we been had?" Joined by others on Capitol Hill they issued a statement condemning the attack and urged Sinn Féin and the IRA to accept the Downing Street Declaration. Speaker Foley launched another of his blistering broadsides against the IRA, saying the mortar incident was "the worst kind of terrorist threat – the threat to innocent civilians was contemptible." At the White House, Lake and Soderberg kept their cool. On St Patrick's Day Clinton defended the Adams visa decision. "We all have to take some chances for peace. I think when Gerry Adams came here he saw that the Irish in America want peace. They want him to be part of the peace process."

A three-day IRA ceasefire at Easter precipitated "a complete cessation of military operations" announced by the organisation on 31 August. There was relief and joy at the White House, banishing lingering doubts about the prospects of a ceasefire which had surfaced following a Sinn Féin conference in Letterkenny in June. Soderberg had phoned O'Dowd, a conduit to Sinn Féin, and asked: "Where's the ceasefire you promised me?" In a statement welcoming the declaration, Clinton said: "We join the Governments of Ireland and the United Kingdom in the hope and expectation that today's step will help bring a lasting and just peace to Northern Ireland. The United States continues to stand ready to assist in advancing the process of peace in Northern Ireland."

A second visa decision by the President had been crucial in bringing about the ceasefire. The week before it was declared Albert Reynolds was informed by an intermediary that the IRA wanted to send an emissary, Joe Cahill, to the US to sell the peace strategy to supporters. The Irish premier was taken aback. He realised he'd have his work cut out to get Cahill into America, but it might well be that the ceasefire depended on it.

Born in Belfast in 1920, Cahill was a living legend, a man who commanded the respect of generation after generation of Irish Republicans. He'd been sentenced to death in 1942 for killing a policeman in his native city, but had been reprieved. When the IRA split in 1969, Cahill was among those who led the Provisional IRA and soon afterwards was involved in the forming of NORAID. On suspicion of arms procurement he was twice deported from America, which he had been banned from entering since 1971. Cahill however had proven he didn't need visas. He'd earned the nickname the 'Emerald Pimpernel' for his half dozen or so illicit trips over the years. In 1973 he was arrested aboard a ship laden with Libyan arms and explosives off the Waterford coast and sentenced to three years in jail. Released early due to ill-health, he had redirected his efforts to working for Sinn Féin.

Reynolds got in touch with Kennedy Smith who was holidaying in France and the Ambassador began badgering Soderberg, first in Spain where she was on leave, and then in Los Angeles where she'd gone for a nephew's christening. Clinton, on holiday in Martha's Vineyard, Massachusetts, was informed and spoke with Reynolds, who got an indication of the wording of the IRA ceasefire statement for the President before Cahill's visa was finally approved. Cahill left Dublin for New York at noon on 30 August, having arrived at the Irish capital's US Embassy at 9.00am with his suitcase but no guarantee of a visa. "The night before it was very doubtful I was going," recalled Cahill. "I'd unpacked but got a call telling me to go to the Embassy next morning. I was told my visa hadn't been granted but the fact I was told to go to the Embassy made me hopeful." He'd applied for a 21-day visa, but was given one for five. "I was on the verge of saying, 'I'm not going', to tell you the truth," the Republican veteran disclosed. "Then I was told, 'Get your foot in the door and see what happens.' The extension came through when I was out there, as the ceasefire was called. The way I was received was fantastic. We needed the support of die-hard Republicans, who naturally feared the Brits were duping us, but I'd taken out a message of hope that something would come out of it though it would take some time." Cahill's big regret was that he was away from Ireland for the celebrations which greeted the announcement in Republican quarters.

Post-ceasefire, the United States began deepening its engagement and was anxious to make overtures to Unionists. In September, Vice President Gore invited Ulster Unionist representatives to Washington. Party leader James Molyneaux had other commitments so couldn't travel. Instead MPs David Trimble, Ken Maginnis and William Ross went, accompanied by Jeffrey Donaldson, a party official with the American brief. The four were received at the White House by Gore who told them: "I've been doing some research and my grandmother was a Denny who came from Ulster. So I guess that makes me one of you lot." SDLP leader John Hume hadn't been forgotten either. He was at the White House the same week, meeting both Clinton and Gore, proof he was the one still carrying most clout. In a statement the White House said the President "underscored his deep admiration for the role Mr Hume has played in promoting peace and reconciliation in Northern Ireland."

Adams, back in September too, was the top draw. With IRA guns silenced, there was no dilemma this time over a visa. The British fought to ensure the Administration kept him at arms length and pressed it to tease out of Adams a declaration the ceasefire was permanent. Although Adams didn't get to the White House, he did receive a phone call from Gore who informed him Sinn Féin was no longer a banned organisation. On Capitol Hill, they fell over themselves to meet the Sinn Féin leader. The irony wasn't lost on New York Congressman Peter King, an Adams supporter through the wilderness years. "Congressmen were lined up to get their picture taken like kids waiting to see Santa Claus," recalled King, who first met Adams at the home of dead IRA hunger striker Kieran Doherty in 1981. "They were saying the dopiest things, trying to say something to endear themselves." King felt vindicated. "Gerry always says he was the guy that brought me in from the cold. Democratic people told me Tom Foley told them not to be associated with me, be around me, because I was a friend of Gerry Adams. Then when Gerry gets to Capitol Hill everybody's calling me up." Senate Minority Leader Bob Dole greeted Adams in his office. King pointed out the window to the White House and said to Adams the next time he came Dole – the Republican Presidential candidate in 1996 – might be living there. "And I'll bring you in the front door, not the back door," quipped Dole. Adams acquired celebrity status on the trip, being feted at a party in Hollywood by the likes of director Oliver Stone and actors Angelica Houston, Sean Penn and Gabriel Byrne. In New York, Mayor Rudi Giuliani presented him with a proclamation marking his peace effort. The British tried to slow the Adams publicity juggernaut by flying out former Northern Ireland Office minister Michael Mates to put its side of the story, and Ken Maginnis became the first Unionist to debate with Adams on television when they appeared on CNN's *Larry King Live* show.

Loyalist terrorist groups, under the auspices of the Combined Loyalist Military Command, called their ceasefires on 13 October. Clinton said the step, when taken with the IRA truce, presented "the best hope for peace in a generation" and encouraged negotiations

49

for a lasting political settlement. Six Loyalists arrived in the United States within two weeks on a visit co-ordinated with the White House and backed by Bill Flynn's National Committee on American Foreign Policy. In publicity terms, they got the crumbs from Adams' table, but were well received by the Irish-Americans they encountered. In New York they shook hands with the Irish President Mary Robinson.

The Sinn Féin leader's stride towards political respectability took a symbolic step forward in December 1994 when he got into the White House, although an encounter with the President was a few months and an Anglo-American diplomatic row away yet. He turned up at 1600 Pennsylvania Avenue without identification and was kept waiting until Kathy Stephens, then working in Tony Lake's office, went to the guard post to affirm who he was. As well as his meeting with Lake, Adams had given equal priority to securing a lifting of the ban on Sinn Féin raising funds in America. But the Administration had resisted and Adams had to bide his time – until his next trip in March 1995 – before the party could tap into the riches of Irish-America. Senators Kennedy and Dodd, Congressmen Gilman, King, Neal and Manton and Ambassador Kennedy Smith all backed the move.

In the lead up to St Patrick's Day, Mayhew went to Washington to argue against permission to fundraise and attempt to block the prospect of Adams being received at a White House party by Clinton. Said an official at the British Embassy: "OK, the money raised in the US might be used for perfectly legitimate reasons and we had no evidence to suggest that it wasn't going to be. But it would release other cash for illegitimate purposes and a case can be made as to that it is what happened." Mayhew made a big play of the need for the IRA to make a gesture on disarmament before Sinn Féin could be treated like other political parties in Northern Ireland and gain entry to peace talks. With Sinn Féin being permitted to fundraise in Britain, his argument against it was undermined somewhat. Admiral William Crowe, soon to replace Seitz as Ambassador in London, said: "I always felt it was a little odd for a country to criticise us for allowing somebody to fundraise when they allowed him to fundraise in Great Britain. That's the reason I thought we could defend our decision. Their answer is, 'Well, he didn't raise a lot of money in Great Britain.' That's not an answer. I mean if you don't like these people doing these things then you shouldn't let them do it yourself."

With Lake and Soderberg wary of allowing Sinn Féin to fundraise, because of the difficulty of knowing how the cash would be used, it was down to Clinton. Dodd brought up the issue with the President on the seventeenth green during a round of golf. Clinton informed him: "All the advice I'm getting is not to, but I think I might." The comment triggered a final push. A pledge from Adams that decommissioning would be addressed in subsequent peace talks, secured again after Soderberg spoke with O'Dowd, was enough to do it. With the Administration in such outreach mode to Sinn Féin, it would have been incongruous to decline Adams an invitation to the White House on St Patrick's Day. (London was so incensed by the double whammy that Clinton was unable to reach Prime Minister Major by telephone for five days.) Clinton and Adams didn't in fact have their first encounter at the White House but a day earlier at a St Patrick's luncheon on 16 March on Capitol Hill, hosted by the new Speaker of the House of Representatives, Newt Gingrich. It was brief and off-camera.

Clinton and Adams wouldn't be captured together in public until the President's visit to Northern Ireland eight months later. And even then, though the ice had been broken, Adams handshakes were never straightforward.

III

Nailing the balance

*The President was concerned that we ensure all
sides were touched, that we were not seen to be
favouring one side or the other, that we were there to
promote the peace process as a whole. That was the
overriding aim of the whole trip.*

Andrew Friendly, aide to the President

Albert Reynolds was the Ireland visit's salesman-in-chief outside
the White House. On President Clinton's first St Patrick's Day
in 1993, the wheeling-dealing Reynolds enquired when the President
would be returning to Dublin. Clinton seemed somewhat surprised
Reynolds knew he'd weekended in the city during his college days.
"So you've been looking up the records too," joked the President.
Reynolds was in touch in December and extended an invitation.

The following 17 March at the White House Ambassador Jean
Kennedy Smith whispered to Reynolds that Clinton was going to
Europe. "Ask him to drop in," she suggested. But Reynolds had set
his sights higher than a whistle-stop. "I said, 'Jean, I want to see
him longer in Ireland than just a couple of hours on his way over
because the system will convince him that that's enough.'" He advanced the argument to Clinton, saying a two or three-hour stop-off
wouldn't do Ireland, or the President, justice. Reynolds said they
were in agreement. "He wasn't for this couple of hours thing. He

wanted longer than that. I said to him, 'You can bring your mother as well,' and he said, 'No, there's too much racing in Ireland for her.' His mother is a real racing woman." (Clinton made reference to his mother's passion for horse-racing in an address in Dublin. She had passed away by then.)

Reynolds was undeterred by the fact violence was still raging in Northern Ireland, although he was only too well aware that efforts at securing an IRA ceasefire were underway. Leaving sentiment aside, the White House couldn't sanction a trip, certainly to Belfast, ahead of a truce and given Clinton's pronouncements and interest in the Northern Ireland situation he would have exposed himself to criticism in steering clear. "When he rang me after the IRA ceasefire I said a visit would be an opportunity for the Irish people – north and south – to say thank you," Reynolds said. "I knew he was certainly committed to do it. It was only a question of making the arrangements and that was up to other people." The President's desire was detected by his staff. Susan Brophy, Clinton aide and trip planner, recalled: "The President had always expressed an interest in doing a trip to Ireland and soon after the ceasefire he was always talking about going. The ceasefire made the prospects more interesting, certainly to go to the north. He may've only gone to the south otherwise." (Reynolds was bitterly disappointed he'd been forced from office by the time Clinton came, enabling his replacement John Bruton to bask in the glory.)

In May 1995 the White House hosted an investment conference on Northern Ireland in a bid to encourage American companies to underpin the peace with dollars. By then the White House was working with London and Dublin on a trip schedule which had become a nightmare. In public, Washington couldn't yet commit to a visit in 1995, or indeed the prospect of Clinton going to Belfast. Privately, however, that was never in doubt. "What really turned the Clinton team on was the idea of going to Northern Ireland," observed one American source. "It was almost like they would suffer through the visit to London because they knew they couldn't just go to Belfast. Most of the energy and most of the intensity of the trip and the planning had to do with the Northern Ireland angle." It had been envisaged that the dates would be agreed in time for the President to dramatically announce his visit during a conference finale speech on the White House lawn.

An enterprising Northern Ireland journalist in Washington for the event put the President on the spot after his address. Broadcaster Eamonn Mallie managed to slip into a line-up as the President worked the crowd and with microphone at the ready was introduced to the unsuspecting Clinton by Gerry Burns, Chief Executive of Fermanagh District Council. Mallie bounced in with a question on when the President would call. "I hope to be there in the fall," responded Clinton. Burns, like the reporter, had a duty to perform. He'd brought with him scrolls purporting to trace the President's ancestors, the Cassidys, back to Fermanagh in the eighteenth century. "He expressed great interest," remembered Burns. "It gave me an opportunity to at least say back home that I had delivered these things in person to the President."

Behind the scenes, the Americans accused the British of giving problems on dates for a Presidential visit, be it Major's diary or the Queen's. The whole concept of Clinton venturing into Northern Ireland was something Downing Street wanted to give the utmost consideration to. The timing had to be helpful in terms of the peace process and it didn't want Sinn Féin or the IRA to be able to exploit it. The Irish, who had no such scheduling predicaments, grumbled that London's awkwardness was indicative of what they interpreted as being reservations about the visit. Irish Foreign Minister Dick Spring later ventured: "The British do not like or want Northern Ireland up in lights for lots of reasons. It is one of their unsolved, unresolved historical problems and they probably wouldn't have wanted Bill Clinton in Northern Ireland if it had been a straight choice." But the British Ambassador to Washington, Sir John Kerr, quashed the theory they were lukewarm on the trip, recalling a conversation he had had with Prime Minister Major when he was the UK's Permanent Representative to the European Union. "I first talked to Major about it at some European meeting in June – I was still over in Brussels. Major was keen on the idea."

The NIO had a say on timing, but like the Foreign Office it was purely in an advisory capacity to Downing Street which, through Private Secretary Rod Lyne, was negotiating with Lake at the White House on dates, together with the trip's objectives. Edward Oakden, Assistant Private Secretary whose brief covered foreign policy and Northern Ireland, also spoke at length and with frequency to Lake and Soderberg. A British source described the Lyne-Lake working relationship as "good and easy." However, a US official admitted that while that might have been the case on issues like Bosnia, their rapport on Northern Ireland wasn't an especially good one. It had been poisoned by distrust flowing from the granting of the first Adams visa. The episode had also undermined Lake's standing among some staff within the US's London Embassy to such an extent that when he asked Clinton to withdraw his nomination to head the Central Intelligence Agency in the midst of bruising Senate confirmation hearings in spring 1997 one source said: "There were no tears shed in Downing Street or this Embassy when the nomination went down the tubes."

At the White House, Director of Communications Mark Gearan was expending considerable energy in attempting to pin down dates, mulling over various options that could have seen Clinton do it on the way to or from this or that, but all the while not wanting to let the politically opportune moment slip. Gearan, whose grandparents were Irish immigrants, said: "The stars were aligned, so to get it locked into the schedule was most important. It's hard to read the tea leaves of what you get up from the State Department and what people's own views are versus the British Government's views. Sometimes things are what they are and schedules don't work. Sometimes schedules are used for a reason. At the end of the day it all did work out, but it did take a determined push that it was going to happen." Days in August, September, October were all floated, but finding dates agreeable to the three leaders proved frustratingly elusive for more than a month.

A communiqué from the White House finally came, on 6 July, in a statement from the Office of the Press Secretary. "The President is pleased to accept the invitations of the British and Irish Governments to visit the United Kingdom and Ireland, November 29-December 2. In the UK the schedule will include meetings in London with Prime Minister Major and a visit to Northern Ireland; and in Ireland a meeting with Prime Minister Bruton. The goals of the trip include strengthening the transatlantic partnership in which the United Kingdom plays such a special role, nurturing our close ties of friendship and culture with Ireland, and underscoring the President's support for the joint efforts of the Irish and British Governments and the people of Northern Ireland to achieve a lasting and peaceful settlement."

For the British Government, great emphasis had been placed on ensuring Clinton went to London, then Belfast, before setting foot in the Republic. The possibility that British 'partnership' could be subverted by Irish 'friendship' was almost inconceivable to them, but in view of the open warfare with the Administration over the Adams visas they weren't going to leave anything to chance. "The British Government was clear the order of the visit should be London, Belfast, Dublin, rather than the other way around. It might have been the American idea too, but for us that was quite an important point," said Kerr. Mayhew backed him: "It was very important the President, as the head of state of our most powerful and closest ally, should come to London first." Logistics were on their side. London, as the UK's capital, had, for reasons of protocol, to precede Belfast so visiting Dublin first would have meant the Presidential party and its large support staff having to cross the Irish Sea twice in a period of a few days. The case was strongly put by the British Embassy in Washington from the outset and was reinforced by Kerr on his arrival as successor to Sir Robin Renwick in September.

Kerr, an engaging 55-year-old Oxford-educated Scot, quickly decided to go on the offensive, endearing himself to Unionists in the process. "He's the first Ambassador not afraid to dish the Irish," said one prominent Ulster Unionist MP. By then he'd won over Northern Ireland's three members of the European Parliament after helping secure multi-millions from Brussels coffers for a special Peace and Reconciliation Fund following the double ceasefire. Other politicians were delighted his appointment reversed a trend of London diplomats disadvantaged by cutting too much of a colonial dash in America. Kerr, who established a tradition of St Patrick's Day luncheons at his residence, had formerly headed up the vast Embassy's political section and had dealt with tricky Irish-related issues such as the MacBride fair employment campaign, high-profile IRA extradition cases and NORAID fundraising.

His insight into the intricacies of the peace process while out of the loop in Brussels came courtesy of none other than John Major, whom he believed cared passionately for it. "He used to tell me quite a lot about things. I would brief him on some European Community problem and quite frequently his eyes would glaze over and he would say, 'Jolly interesting, John,' then tell me about Northern

Ireland." As Ambassador, Kerr ensured letters from the public which questioned British policy in Northern Ireland received answers. On hot issues these could number three hundred per day. He was also wont to ring up to register protest at what he judged unreasonably harsh newspaper editorials. However, he realised his Embassy couldn't do battle alone and one of his first acts was to call the UUP leader David Trimble and urge him to travel to Washington for talks with the Clinton Administration at the first available opportunity. Kerr told him he would do all in his power to ensure Trimble enjoyed face time with the President. "It's a great mistake to stay back the other side of the Atlantic and complain about the debate in America. The parties need to do their own thing. They'd got to join the debate," argued Kerr. When he presented his diplomatic credentials to Clinton and the conversation inevitably turned to Northern Ireland, Kerr suggested the President might help soothe Unionist anger at the treatment of Adams and lingering unease about his Administration's agenda by meeting its leaders.

Like his predecessors however, Kerr found himself playing catch-up with the Irish Embassy based further down Washington's Massachusetts Avenue. With Britain's considerable interests in the US being much more diverse – it was for example the nation's biggest foreign investor – the Irish had been free to concentrate resources on cultivating Washington's movers and shakers over the Northern Ireland issue for years, long before it was a topic of discussion in the Oval Office. Their links with politicians on Capitol Hill impressed Kerr. An Irish Prime Minister, like no other world leader, knew he had the President's ear on a predetermined date each year, 17 March, St Patrick's Day. Under Clinton the day had been elevated in social importance. To the traditional handing over of a bowl of shamrock and a meeting between the President and Taoiseach was added a soirée at the White House. The Speaker of the House of Representatives also hosted a lunch for them.

Irish Ambassador Dermot Gallagher set out to conquer Clinton the minute the polling booths closed in November 1992 and counting started. "While other Ambassadors watched the results on their television sets our man was on his way to Little Rock," crowed Reynolds, who dubbed Gallagher Ireland's greatest Ambassador. Gallagher, Leitrim born and Ambassador since 1991, travelled to the Arkansas state capital the night it toasted victory and tracked down the President-elect at a party. Hovering around Secret Service agents positioned on a staircase, he waited, then collared his man. "We had a good conversation," recalled Gallagher. "This is when we first learned he had spent a weekend in Dublin while at Oxford. He told me he had a glorious weekend. He intended to see part of the country but he didn't get beyond Dublin he enjoyed it so much." As fate would have it Clinton wouldn't get beyond the Irish capital on his forthcoming trip either, despite the best laid plans. (In the end Clinton's Ireland trip had a day shaved off at the end. What was to have been day two of his visit to the Republic, with a round of golf planned at Ballybunion in Kerry, got axed as he'd to fly to Germany and see-off US troops bound for Bosnia.)

The Office of Presidential Advance at the White House has a staff of just eight, surprising given that it pre-plans the movements of the world's most powerful man at home and abroad. The Vice President has his own even smaller version. The office's foot soldiers are drawn from the ranks of volunteers who have enough flexibility in their nine-to-five jobs to take two weeks' holiday to go and work for the President. Many are young – sometimes party activists who cut their teeth zigzagging the US on election campaign events. "Volatile 24-year-olds who can come and break all the crockery," was how an American with experience of numerous Presidential trips described them. The prestige makes up for the pay, $30-a-day on top of accommodation and travel. A director heads the office. For the visit to the UK and Ireland it was 44-year-old Paige Reefe. By the end of his two-year tenure he'd have been to 26 countries but none he felt was fraught with anything like the political dangers and the potential for catastrophe as the Northern Ireland trip. At his disposal were specialists, like Brady Williamson, and personnel at US Embassies and Consulates.

Williamson was involved in Democratic Party politics in his home state and had been an assistant to former Senator and defeated 1984 Presidential aspirant Walter Mondale. His father's side of the family had relatives from County Antrim but he had never been to Ireland. A job in the Administration didn't appeal to him, though he enjoyed attachments to Presidential Advance on trips to Japan and Russia that had earned him a tremendous respect among his peers. "He is sophisticated about overseas things and he's very good at delegating and keeping people in tune," said a colleague. Williamson seized the opportunity to do the trip, firstly as it was virgin soil for a President and secondly because of the political and logistical challenges. Doing Paris or London, for example, was too ordinary. There were templates that could lifted from previous visits and there was a certain drill to be followed regardless – seeing the Queen and dropping by the Elysée Palace. "It would be a waste of Brady's talents to send him out to do an easy one," said one of those who worked with him in Belfast.

The Belfast leg of Clinton's visit was to re-unite Williamson with a career diplomat, Blair Hall, who in the summer of 1995 was a political counsellor at the London Embassy and who would become "one of the top three brains on Northern Ireland," according to a Grosvenor Square associate. Hall's education in the sectarian geography of Belfast began in late summer on a first guided tour of the likes of the Falls and Shankill Roads, riding with an official from the Belfast Consulate in its armour-plated car. His and Williamson's mutual admiration and friendship grew out of the President's first foreign excursion, a G7 summit in Tokyo in July 1993, where Hall was then posted. "When you find really good State Department people who understand the magnitude of a Presidential visit you grab them. No matter where in the world they are, if you get anywhere close to them again you grab them back. Blair was one of those kind of people," said a trip organiser. Hall, key with Stephens in finessing the President's itinerary, also acted as the main on-the-ground liaison with the NIO through David Watkins at the Central Secretariat. The two got on well.

The United States and British Governments had both shared and diverging objectives on what the trip to Northern Ireland should achieve. London wanted the visit to further anchor down the peace process; to give Clinton a more balanced view of the region; and to promote Northern Ireland in investment terms, thus building on the Washington trade conference. Washington had two distinct agendas. The first was to demonstrate that Clinton was genuinely interested in promoting peace in Northern Ireland and that in doing so he wasn't partisan. Given what had gone before, it would therefore be imperative that he reached out to a suspicious Protestant majority. Presidential aide and trip briefer Andrew Friendly said: "The President was concerned that we ensure all sides were touched, that we were not seen to be favouring one side or the other, that we were there to promote the peace process as a whole. That was the overriding aim of the whole trip." The second goal, for US domestic consumption on the verge of election year, was the projection of the image of the President as global statesman promoting peace in the spiritual and ancestral home of 44 million Irish-Americans. "That was one of the main reasons he wanted to go," said Ambassador William Crowe, with a military man's characteristic disregard for political subtlety. "He wanted to convey an image to the American people that he's involved, that his heart is in the right place and that he is appreciated overseas." This worried London, and indeed some Americans, because of the implications for the President's schedule. "The likelihood was some people were going to say to him, 'Ain't no votes being seen to shake hands with Unionists, lots of votes being seen with your arms around Nationalists.' So we were slightly concerned," said one British official. Sir Patrick Mayhew summed up Unionist anxiety: "There was a great sensitivity among the pro-Union community that the President should not come here and even inadvertently give aid and comfort by seeming to show favour to Republican Nationalists." The British Government's apprehension was made all the more acute by those who began attaching themselves to the planning of the trip within the Administration.

The President's visit to Ireland unsurprisingly tugged at the heartstrings of Irish-Americans in the Clinton White House, all of whom wanted a slice of the action. As well as Gearan and Brophy, there were Kitty Higgins, Cabinet Secretary, and Vice President Al Gore's Chief of Staff, Jack Quinn, who led the visit's Washington-based co-ordinating committee. Lucie Naphin, one of the trip planners and who had family ties to the west of Ireland, said: "I'd worked on numerable foreign trips for the President but I never had to deal with a personal love for a country like I did with this trip. It was really hard for me. Part of the role I had to play was to say, 'Hold on guys, let's forget who our descendants are and where we come from. We need to focus on what the President needs to do.'" But the Irish clique's involvement had alarm bells ringing, not only in Belfast and London, but among some attached to the White House as well. "There was a predisposed 'buy' before we got there, based on the fact the majority of the domestic political people who would be involved in Irish issues in the US would be Catholic as opposed to Protestant," said a source.

Higgins travelled on the first of two reconnaissance missions to the UK and Ireland on September 26-8, known as the site survey. The group also included Reefe, Hall, Friendly, Naphin, Ambassador Molly Raiser, Chief of Protocol at the State Department, Martha Pope, senior aide to Senator George Mitchell, and Fred Dohse, a military officer from the NSC. Naphin, as trip scheduler, and Friendly, who was trip co-ordinator, personally briefed Clinton on "mechanical aspects" of his visit. The politics were left to Lake and Soderberg. Secretary of State Warren Christopher also had an input. Before the group arrived on its fact-finding foray there was disquiet among US officials in Britain over how the President's itinerary was shaping up. One described it as "not very co-ordinated," another that there was a dearth of good ideas for events outside Londonderry. Washington was suggesting that Clinton jetted into Derry first, visited the predominantly-Nationalist village of Rosslea in County Fermanagh and when in Belfast attended a political reception to which it was stressed Gerry Adams must be invited. A document circulating in the London Embassy and Belfast Consulate dated 22 September spelled out the reservations: "As it now stands the schedule fails to meet our crucial objective of not only demonstrating US even-handedness in the peace process but of actively reaching out to the majority Unionist community in Northern Ireland."

Events under consideration for Derry, the city on which most emphasis had to that juncture been placed (together with the involvement of John Hume) caused most anxiety. Stateside, thought was given to taking the President to the SDLP leader's country retreat at Greencastle on the County Donegal coast, overlooking Lough Foyle. Hume was fond of telling visitors the next parish west was Boston and Clinton would certainly have been made to feel at home amidst the busts of President Kennedy and the framed copy of Martin Luther King's 'I Have a Dream' speech, a gift from the late civil rights leader's wife, Coretta. (Hume and Clinton shared the same political heroes.) The Irish Government felt very strongly that Clinton must go to Derry as well as Belfast. One counter-balance suggested by Stephens was a stop-off, either on the way to or from Londonderry, at the Andrew Jackson Centre in the mainly Protestant County Antrim town of Carrickfergus. It pays homage to the seventh US President, who occupied the White House from 1829-37 and whose parents left the area not long before he was born in

South Carolina. However, it never figured in the final schedule owing to the heavy demands on Clinton's time and, to a lesser extent, because the balance was righted elsewhere. It was the second occasion the centre had been overlooked on a Presidential visit: Reagan had been invited to perform the official opening while in Ireland in 1984.

Two Foreign Office officials from London, Maurice Dalton, Deputy Head of Protocol, and desk officer Pauline Butler joined the site survey team in Northern Ireland. The pair were there to offer the NIO team logistical advice and were slightly concerned at how much the Americans planned to squeeze into Clinton's day. Dalton, the British side's senior member for the survey, was "as institutional as people get," according to an accompanying American. Also from the British side were two security personnel, one from the Foreign Office, one from the Metropolitan Police, and Mike Maxwell and Valerie Steele from the Northern Ireland Office. Two RUC officers, including Henry Ervine, accompanied them. It wasn't uncommon for Met. officers to work with the local force on visits, particularly by the Queen or other members of the Royal family, and there was the added bonus of the experience they had gained doing previous Presidential trips to London. The conspicuous 35-strong group was bussed from location to location, casting an eye over factories, business parks and tourist attractions. It was the British side's first real appreciation of the scale of the US operation, which even in the opening stages overwhelmed its own. "There was a mis-match of resources in terms of us and the Americans, who threw absolutely everything at this," observed one on the UK side.

The Americans arrived with a few fixed ideas that needed showcasing at well-chosen locations: the President wanted to give a speech, meet people from both sides and see politicians at a reception. And where he was to perform these usually mundane tasks was crucial, not just in terms of whose turf, Protestant or Catholic, he choose to do them on. "Whenever the President travels overseas it's indispensable we communicate a sense of place so that people in America not only know where he is by pictures, but by seeing where he is they understand why he is where he is," said a senior member of the US planning team.

One place which was eliminated following the site survey was a Clinton people event at one of Belfast's so-called 'peacelines' – grim high walls or iron fences erected in flashpoint neighbourhoods to keep the city's rival factions apart. Across the Atlantic the President's team had conjured up an image of a triumphant Clinton striding through an opening in some Berlin Wall-type structure, symbolically uniting flag-waving crowds on each side. In its scenario, Belfast's version of the Brandenburg Gate was considered to be Lanark Way, a road linking the Shankill and Falls. So regularly had it been used as a channel of attack by one side or the other that huge spike-topped double gates were eventually set in place to block the terrorist bolt-hole at certain times of day. In truth the Americans didn't take much convincing to scrub the idea when confronted by the eyesore, and on second thoughts agreed an event showing the 'peaceline's' bricks and mortar could backfire by actually reinforcing the division within Northern Ireland society. Said one British Government official: "In terms of effect it was hopeless. It would've been a public relations nightmare. It was a no no." The RUC, which was against the idea, was worried about the risk, however small, of ugly scenes between the opposing communities.

A ramshackle tin-roofed cottage on a windswept hill in the border village of Rosslea was reputedly from where Clinton's grandfather five times removed, Luke Cassidy, left for the States over 250 years ago. The site survey team was under strict instructions from the President himself to make the 80-mile trek. Clinton told the authors: "Americans know it is very moving to visit the land of one's ancestors, to reflect on their difficult decision to emigrate. I would have liked to visit Fermanagh." The Americans, acting through the British, turned to Gerry Burns to act as tour guide but the fact-finding mission began disastrously when the usually-meticulous council Chief Executive failed to rendezvous with the visitors as planned at an agreed landmark. Burns had been in Belfast on business and returned home that evening to Enniskillen and a crisis. His telephone had been made red hot by a stream of frantic calls from the NIO, fielded by his daughter, anxiously enquiring where he was. They'd even phoned the editor of the local newspaper, Denzil McDaniel, to ask for help as the manhunt intensified. Burns, blood pressure soaring, realised he had made a wrong entry in his diary and drove like fury for Rosslea, only to pass the survey team bus returning in the opposite direction. He tailed them to an Enniskillen hotel and set about rescuing the situation. "I had allowed something to happen inadvertently and I could not blame anyone else. It was my fault. I apologised profusely to Valerie Steele who was very understanding." One American said the NIO official had earlier gone "three shades of purple" when Burns hadn't appeared. Burns arranged to meet them next morning but he had another problem – he'd no idea where the remote cottage was. For a second time that night Burns set out on the journey to Rosslea and with help of a priest eventually found the cottage, but as darkness had long closed in he, like the survey team, wouldn't see it until morning.

By then, to the concern of the Americans, the secret of their arrival had filtered out. "You don't cough in a place like Rosslea but everybody knows. Many of them were in pinstripe suits and carrying briefcases, not the usual scene to be found on a Fermanagh hillside," recalled Burns. He said they were happy with what they saw. "This was an old broken-down cottage which had no sign of habitation for centuries. They were dancing around highly excited." The group only got inside after clawing back a rusty iron door and removing several planks of wood. The floor was grass and what little light there was fell through a single, dirty window. There were two small rooms at either end of the main living quarters that measured 14 feet by 10, and there was a large fireplace. Burns said: "In terms of it being a country cottage there was no question about authenticity. I asked would they want it thatched and they said, 'No, no, it's to be left untouched.'" Those from Washington were snapping their cameras, taking notes and firing all manner of questions, like were the Cassidys Catholic or Protestant and were they genuinely Clinton ancestors. Burns wasn't sure but by that stage, having recovered from the embarrassment of the missed engagement, was in relaxed enough mood to crack a joke. "If you look above the fireplace you'll see a message scrawled in the stone. It says, 'Gone to Hope, Arkansas. Couldn't pay the rent.' They thought it was absolutely hilarious. I found their enthusiasm surprising. The place was not all that presentable but they thought it was wonderful. I got the impression the Foreign Office people were not as enthusiastic." An accompanying British official said: "Gerry discovered the cottage but I think he regrets it ever since. It was dilapidated and there was no way you were getting a cavalcade up the lane, but the Americans were delighted." Burns suggested they also take a look at Ballycassidy, a few miles north of Enniskillen. Unknown to him, SDLP leader John Hume had made the same recommendation to

Clinton. "When I saw him he spoke of his Irish roots," said Hume. "I mentioned to him Ballycassidy – townland of the Cassidys. He was very interested and I said, 'When you come to Northern Ireland you will have to go to Ballycassidy.' He was keen."

The romance of Clinton discovering his roots, though, was rapidly overtaken by sheer logistical unfeasibility. Five helicopters would have been required to transport the President and his inner circle to Fermanagh, difficult terrain in potentially hazardous November weather. The remainder of the vast entourage would have got there after a 90-minute road journey and a hike up a damp hillside. The prospect didn't appeal at all to the RUC who would have had to secure a route through five of the Province's six counties, and the White House Communications Agency was stumped as to how it would install telephone lines to a location not even wired for power. One senior American planner said: "There was nothing there and no reason to go that far. It was not a runner." An expedition to Rosslea would have eaten into too much of the President's valuable time on a trip that aspired to greater things. Consideration was given to Clinton flying to the village during the southern Irish leg of the trip but the Dublin Government and US Embassy staff there were against it. "Our parochial interest was having him here as much as we could get him here for," said one American source in the Irish capital. There was a feeling in Washington too that the press would have been cynical in its coverage of such an event. Explained Naphin: "We didn't want to put the President in a position where people were going to make a mockery out of it and prove us wrong."

On their return to Washington, Naphin and Friendly presented a report for Clinton and showed him the photographs of the Cassidy homestead. It was the first of two Cabinet Room briefings the President had with all those involved in the planning of the trip. Clinton shook his head and muttered "humble beginnings" as he glanced over pictures. "We spoke to the President and said, 'If you really want to go we can make anything happen', but there were other things that were much more of a priority," explained Naphin. "He said if it's not going to work it's not going to work. His feeling was maybe after I'm done being President I can go." Added Friendly: "Originally it was something he would've liked to have done but he understood the constraints."

Clinton's political friends were delighted Fermanagh was axed as a result of the site survey. "It was fortunate he didn't end up doing that," said Senator Chris Dodd. "Thatched cottages and all that garbage would've been seen as gilding the lily. Had he done it it would've detracted from a trip that had nothing to do with ethnicity, lineage and grandparents." The White House had trouble reaching a definitive answer to the Clinton ancestral riddle. It was something it couldn't prove but not disprove either. It was deluged with research material, both posted in and hand delivered. Alliance Party leader Dr John Alderdice did an old friend Cahal Cassidy a big favour by taking voluminous material to a meeting with Administration officials. Mark Gearan looked over it and other papers. "This wasn't a pander to an ethnic group. The President's proud of his ancestry but it wasn't that clear. My view is if we tortured it it would've been off-key." Another US official summed it up. "Logistics were probably 85 per cent of the decision and 15 per cent was the uncertainty about the genealogical claim." (In Dublin Clinton popped into a pub called Cassidy's. Embassy staff learned of its existence by flicking through the telephone book.) The outcome was greeted with bitter disappointment in the lakeland county, which had been dreaming of enormous tourism spin-offs. "The visit of a President of the United States would've been of immense importance not only in investment but in terms of the marketing of the whole county," contended Burns. "If Clinton had appeared, the amount of publicity that would've been engendered Fermanagh couldn't have paid for in a decade." People in Rosslea itself felt let down. A local community organisation expressed its disappointment in writing to Kathy Stephens. "The excitement and anticipation of both young and old in this area has been dealt a sapping blow," wrote Patsy McPhillips, the group's secretary.

Though the decision as to whether the President would overnight in Northern Ireland would be taken at a higher level, the site survey team addressed its practicalities. Blighted by 27 years of violence, the region had a dearth of spacious, top quality hotels, so the options were limited. As the size of the Presidential entourage was around eight hundred, including the White House press corps, it was clear from the outset there wasn't a hotel big enough that could host the party *en bloc*, the preferred choice. The Europa was the only downtown option and, most importantly, it would convey the right message if selected. Said one of the US survey team: "The symbolism of the President staying in a place which had been bombed a number of times sent out the message this is a safe place to be, which was different than people thought. And part of the reason it was different is because, at least hopefully in our mind, the role that Bill Clinton had played in trying to help the peace process along, and that if someone of his stature could stay in a place that had this kind of history it spoke volumes." Consul General Stephens backed the overnight option too, believing a stay at the Europa would be a vote of confidence in the process second to none.

Some on the British side put up a security obstacle, provoking an embarrassing squabble on the tour bus between Belfast and Fermanagh when the RUC officers flatly contradicted their advice to the Americans. "The security guys in Northern Ireland weren't particularly ecstatic about the people who worked in the Foreign Office," commented one American on board. "The security officer who came from London made this emphatic statement that we couldn't stay at the Europa for security reasons and it was interesting to watch the guys from the RUC basically tell him he had no idea what he was talking about." The Americans figured London was using security as a smoke-screen for political objections. Word of the dispute filtered back to RUC Assistant Chief Constable Tim Lewis, senior linkman with the US Secret Service. Lewis' boss, Sir Hugh Annesley, had issued him with firm instructions that the force's advice was to be based strictly on security considerations. "I was aware of discussions about what was or wasn't politically appropriate but thankfully it wasn't an area we had to become involved in," said Lewis. Added a force colleague: "The White House wanted him to stay at the Europa. There was opposition to it but that opposition stopped when we said we can make it work." The advance party visited Hillsborough Castle, residence of former Northern Ireland Governors, which Washington saw as being the NIO's preferred alternative to the Europa, particularly as Sir Patrick Mayhew would stay there too, thus underscoring the fact Clinton was in the Province as a guest of the British. The castle would have been a possibility for a political reception as well. But the Americans were adamant the President wouldn't be staying there. Said one: "The British wanted him to stay at Hillsborough. They put on a very nice show. It's a beautiful residence, but it sent out exactly the wrong message of what we were coming to do." The British, however, claimed they took the Americans to the castle only so they could eliminate it from their plans. "We showed them Hillsborough if only to rule it out because we knew that it was never going to be big enough," said a source. "We knew that the Americans were not going to come. They told us pretty plainly they didn't want to be seen in the pocket of the Secretary of State because that wouldn't have reflected terribly well back in Boston."

Relations between the Americans and British on the site survey were cordial enough. It was an opportunity for each side to sound one another out without giving too much away. "This was not the stage where people were going to get into really difficult discussions about who was really in charge," said a Washington official. "You don't leave your host feeling as if they have been improperly treated because you have to depend on them for a lot of the basic infrastructure of what you are going to be doing." The British saw the exercise as an opportunity to work their own location suggestions in Belfast and Derry onto the US list. Those from Washington went to numerous sites only out of courtesy, knowing straight away they were outside the realms of possibility. "It was apparent there were some differences," said one of the Americans involved. "The British Government preferred the more formal state visit model and the American Government wanted to be more free-wheeling, more kind of daring. We weren't quite on the same page." The site survey ended with a half-hour airport wrap-up meeting between Reefe and Dalton, the respective delegation leaders, as the Americans prepared to move onto Dublin to inspect possible locations there. After it ended Martha Pope, a former Sergeant-at-Arms in the Senate, paid Reefe the compliment of saying that, as someone accustomed to listening to speeches from politicians, she'd never seen someone talk so much for so long but say so little. Pope took part in the site survey as she'd already had some appreciation of the sensitivities of Northern Ireland through her work with Mitchell when he was economic envoy. "I leaned on Martha a tremendous amount," said Naphin.

Soderberg was in Belfast for two days in the week after the site survey, accompanied by Ambassador Crowe, to gauge local feeling about the Clinton visit and the state of the peace process generally, which was then stuck fast in the decommissioning quagmire. Crowe, who considered some in Washington to be out of touch with political realities in Northern Ireland, labelled the consultative exercise "operation educating Nancy".

A DUP trio of deputy leader Peter Robinson, Nigel Dodds and Ian Paisley Jr, the leader's son, warned the Clinton aide it might seek to sabotage the trip if it leaned too heavily in the direction of Nationalists. "We took a very firm line with her," said Paisley Jr. "We told her to expect protests on the streets, expect us to lead a very active campaign. We didn't threaten her. We just told her the reality of what was going to happen." The party was poised to print and distribute hundreds of leaflets-cum-posters, including one showing Gerry Adams alongside Timothy McVeigh, the man who planted a bomb which killed 168 people at a federal building in Oklahoma in April 1995, above the banner headline: "Clinton – is there any difference between these men?" They would also have issued a rallying call to supporters to converge on Belfast City Hall, where it was planned Clinton would switch on Christmas tree lights, and wave Ulster and Union Jack flags throughout the festivities. Said Robinson: "I think if we wanted a demonstration to happen it would've happened. There would have been a greater danger of that had he gone for his original itinerary which was all Nationalist." Robinson, MP for east Belfast, forcefully argued for the need for balance and advocated an event in his almost exclusively Protestant constituency. "Some of the proposals being put forward for the visit were frankly ludicrous," recalled Robinson, who was full of praise for Crowe. "He had a feel for what the President was walking into. I got the distinct impression he was quite happy at the points we were making. I'm not saying he was pro-Unionist but he certainly had an understanding that was more balanced than any of the other Americans."

Leader Ian Paisley raised the spectre of Clinton visit protests by party members, like the Lord Mayor of Belfast Eric Smyth, during meetings with Administration officials on a visit to Washington at the end of October 1995 and claimed it brought results. "Clinton was fed with Boston propaganda about Ian Paisley being a reprobate and then he realised he had to make peace with him because he wanted the Lord Mayor to accept him as a guest at his Christmas tree. He had to pull in his horns," said Paisley. A document, written by Americans planning the President's visit, cast the DUP as the "potential thorn" and advised "conferring closely" with it to establish what would and wouldn't be satisfactory to Paisley. "This way, if we still decide to do something that won't satisfy them we will know about it well in advance and the decision will be a fully informed one," it said. In a clear need to be more inclusive, the White House afforded Paisley and Robinson talks with Vice President Al Gore. "I'm a Presbyterian," he was reported to have told them. They presented him with a six-page document which condemned the Clinton Administration's role in Northern Ireland and urged it to be more even-handed. One top White House official remarked: "I was amazed. Paisley was charming, delightful and told little anecdotes. Not the sort of firebrand you read about in the press." Paisley and Robinson came out from the White House and said that for three years the Administration had sought to sideline the DUP but now it needed to listen for fear of the President's trip being tarnished by demonstrations, or at least the threat of them.

Ulster Unionist supremo David Trimble was in the White House at the start of November for a meeting with Gore. Clinton dropped in on the hour-long talks. Trimble had had to fight to ensure he got to the President through forceful lobbying of Stephens, Crowe and the British Government. "We had a bit of a tussle," he said. It all stemmed from an undertaking given to his predecessor, James Molyneaux, that the next time a UUP leader was in Washington he'd meet Clinton. But Molyneaux had stepped down on his seventy-fifth birthday that August and his replacement, Trimble, had first of all been offered discussions with Lake, maybe Gore. The Upper Bann MP said as much time during the Clinton talks was spent mulling over the upcoming trip as on progress towards the twin-track agreement. "What we had been told before we went to the White House about the planning concerned us," said Trimble. "It seemed too closely orientated to west Belfast, with no balancing. We were trying to interest him in suburban towns – Carrickfergus, Lisburn – partly to get him onto our patch, areas represented by Ulster Unionists." The party's American specialist, Jeffrey Donaldson, who was with Trimble, made a supporting argument and recalled: "When we talked to the President there was no sense of, 'This is my ballgame. I'll decide.' They were completely open to the suggestions we had and they wanted to ensure the visit was even-handed."

Just before Trimble made his first journey to Washington as head of the Province's largest party, the American trip team were back in

Northern Ireland on what was known as a pre-advance. Their number had swollen from about a dozen on the site survey to nearly 40 and included members of the US media who, to the astonishment of the NIO, were given a say in event planning, a reflection of their fourth estate status. Venues for Clinton's appearances had to be sizeable and accessible enough to accommodate the large travelling press pack. "There's an adage in doing this work," said one American, "If the press don't cover your event, your event didn't happen." Brady Williamson came on the pre-advance, which took place from 24-26 October, but the American delegation was again lead by Paige Reefe of Presidential Advance. David Watkins became his counterpart on the British side. "Watkins understood better than anyone where we were coming from and what we were going to get done, though he didn't necessarily agree with it. We parried and thrusted with each other," said one of the visitors. While the site survey was all about scouting places, the pre-advance dwelt on tightening up the President's schedule. Out went some events in Londonderry, for example, where planners had been too free and easy with the President's precious time. In between the site survey and pre-advance, Dohse and Naphin had been ordered to Belfast by Soderberg unannounced, where they linked up with Stephens to scrutinise locations with a view to working in some more political balance. Tony Lake summed up the planning process: "The people who did the logistics of the trip were working with the people who did the substance in order to make sure the logistics served the substance. I don't recall any arguments but it certainly did require, especially on Nancy Soderberg's part, constant and painstaking management to make sure that almost to the minute there was balance."

In part due to the secret trip and feedback to the site survey from Hall as well as Stephens, the US team was more attuned to local political sensitivities second time around. It readily accepted the need for greater balance, a subject that figured prominently at a get-to-know-you dinner attended by the British and US sides at the Stormont Hotel, Belfast, during the pre-advance. Alongside Watkins, who like Reefe gave a short address in the course of the evening, was Chris MacCabe from the political section of the NIO. Said a British Government source: "We needed to establish beyond doubt in their minds that they weren't coming in here to do everything the way they wanted and nothing we wanted and the issue of balance needed to be nailed down." The NIO pushed for an event in east Belfast as a counter to going to the Mackie factory in west Belfast, something the Americans had given thought to in the four weeks since they were last in town. "We ended up acceding to this event in east Belfast because it took care of an agenda of theirs which they believed for their own purposes was important," said a US team member. A lot of the time was spent discussing whether the British or the Americans would host a reception in honour of Clinton in Belfast, a troublesome issue which went unresolved that night. "We agreed to disagree and greater minds would litigate it out," said an American. The British saw the dinner as critical in establishing a working relationship that, according to a Washington source, matured from initially being wary.

It was when the Americans returned home from the pre-advance that the White House began to grasp the full potential of the Clinton visit. "There was really a great deal of enthusiasm," reminisced Press Secretary Mike McCurry. "The excitement about President Clinton coming became apparent to our advance people. It was very clear there was a real hunger on the part of the people to see a US President come and make a statement about the importance of peace. Word got back we should see this not only as an important moment for Bill Clinton but for the people of Northern Ireland as well."

IV

A chill warms on the Shankill

*I know the road was on the map for bad reasons but
this put it on for good reasons. I think people on the
Shankill thought he was for the Nationalists but once
they heard him speak and everything I think their
views changed.*

Violet Clarke, Shankill Road shopkeeper

Dockyard cranes and chimneys were what Clinton first glimpsed of Belfast before the gentle rounding of a downhill bend on the M2 gradually revealed more of the cityscape, like the green dome of City Hall where he would later attend a Christmas tree lighting ceremony. He put his speech away as his convoy accelerated along deserted downtown streets and switched attention to the first of his busy day's engagements. "This is the Protestant side of west Belfast," Consul General Kathy Stephens told him as they crossed from Catholic territory towards the Shankill.

Press Secretary Mike McCurry, travelling several cars back, was uneasy. "You could tell the motorcade had crossed the line. There was a noticeable chill in the air on the Protestant section. It was very, very eerie." In the President's vehicle, Stephens continued with a commentary she'd rehearsed on numerous journeys made in planning the President's trip, the last 48 hours earlier with a local civil servant rhyming off facts and figures just on the off chance the President, who bored easily, sprang an awkward question. Stephens still considered herself a stranger, having only been in the country four months. Clinton's visit, though, had put her on a steep learning curve and banished the horrible memories of her previous overseas posting to a Yugoslavia in the stranglehold of civil strife.

Born in Texas and raised in Arizona, Stephens' interest in politics began early – at the age of ten she kicked the backyard fence in a fit of frustration that as a woman she felt she could never be President. Typecast as a sports jock, she left an unfashionable college with a bachelor's degree in Asian Studies. Her first job was as an outward bound instructor. She sat a five-hour Foreign Service entrance exam while in the Peace Corps, where she taught boys' school in Korea for two years, and was one of 200 successful applicants from 20,000 hopefuls. Fresh from a three-month induction course, she was disappointed to be assigned to Trinidad in 1978 and 18 months of mostly visa work. Next to China and two years of life in a grim Canton hotel "with dog-sized rats," but where the fascination of witnessing a nation emerge from Chairman Mao's Cultural Revolution was intoxicating. Weekend leave in Hong Kong, where she'd developed her Far East interest while studying for a year, helped too. South Korea followed and with it the transition from consular officer to political officer. She was six years in the dictatorship-turned-democracy before applying, as a mother-of-one, to Harvard while in the midst of a divorce. After gaining an MA, Stephens spent 1990 in Washington learning another language, Serbo-Croat, before taking up a position in Belgrade, Yugoslavia. It was her unhappiest posting and lasted little more than a year. With the country disintegrating around her, she was an advocate of strong Western military intervention. Whilst unsettled colleagues were resigning, Stephens got a transfer home to the European bureau of the State Department in 1992 to manage US bilateral relations with the UK and Yugoslavia and other issues. By the time of the Downing Street Declaration the following year she'd become immersed in the Irish issue which stood her in good stead when she moved across to the NSC in the summer of 1994.

The easy-going Stephens seized the chance to escape the potential burn-out of White House political life when the Consul General's job became vacant 12 months later. Conventional wisdom was that it was a risky career move and several people counselled her against taking it. Stephens was over-qualified for the post but the idea of being her own boss in a region now high on the Administration's agenda – and with a Presidential visit pending – appealed to her. It was one of Washington's oldest outposts. Established in 1796, the Belfast Consulate was, according to Clinton, "one of our historic overseas posts, a symbol of the value we place on enduring ties and our commitment to strengthening them."

There was no question of Stephens being unacceptable to people like Lake, Soderberg or Crowe, who she'd helped coach through his Senate confirmation hearings for the Ambassador's job. Before taking up the position she took time out from official business in Belfast with Soderberg to check out schools for her son and view the impressive Consul's residence at Ardnavally, set within the seclusion of Belvoir Forest on the city's southern fringe. When it came to organising Clinton's visit, Stephens had substantial clout with the White House because of her tenure at the NSC. "No harm to Val Martinez, her predecessor, but he would have been up shit creek without a paddle," said an American diplomatic source. "Kathy had credibility with the White House which was very important when talking about itinerary, objectives, the need for balance." Added a White House official: "Kathy did a fabulous job. She gave really good advice." Stephens had earned the right to be at Clinton's side as they drove into Belfast.

The President's cavalcade, by now reduced in length because some cars had peeled away and gone directly to the Mackie factory, swept left from Northumberland Street and onto the Shankill Road, the blue lights blinking on the front police cars and motorcycles. Clinton's limousine – there were in fact two in his convoy, one was a decoy – slowed to an intentional halt outside number 167, Violet's Fruit Shop, its colourful wares on display outside. Brady Williamson jogged back from an RUC escort car, weaving through officials and Secret Service agents overspilling the narrow footpath, and popped his head into the backseat area of Clinton's polished black vehicle. "Mr President," he said pressing some coins into Clinton's large palm. "Here's two pounds. You're going to go into this shop and buy some fruit and flowers." Williamson then retreated to the background to be joined by Lake who smiled, put his arm around the fixer's shoulder and squeezed in jolly bonhomie.

Waiting to greet the President in the doorway was a flushed store owner, Violet Clarke. Her apprehension was luckily short-lived –

an aide from the White House only informed her she'd be serving a special customer a matter of minutes earlier. "She tapped me on the shoulder and said, 'Whenever the President stops, you go out and bring him into the shop.' I said, 'What, me go out and greet the President?' I was shocked. I wished I had washed the windows, combed my hair and put on some lipstick." The 41-year-old had reckoned the people pacing around her shop since opening time were merely seeking refuge from the November cold and hadn't attached any significance to it when she and scores of others were evacuated from buildings and streets to facilitate security checks. "I'm Violet Clarke," she said shaking the President's hand as on-lookers, many surprised he'd even stopped, applauded and cheered. "Welcome to the Shankill Road." Clinton introduced himself, then Hillary, and vanished from the spectators' view into the shop. Few aides followed to avoid a crush.

Seven years earlier a masked gunman from the Irish National Liberation Army, a small but savage Republican splinter organisation, had crossed the threshold and murdered Protestant man Freddie Ottley, the shop's last owner, with a shot to the head. Violet Clarke had lost an uncle in a shooting but Clinton's presence was proof, she supposed, of a new era for the long-suffering people of the Shankill and Northern Ireland. "I know the road was on the map for bad reasons, but this put it on for good reasons. It was the biggest day of my life. I just wanted it to last," she later said. The President made small talk, telling her of his long flight from America as he picked out four apples and a batch of oranges from the top left-hand shelf. An aide brought in a bunch of mixed flowers from a stand outside, while another told her to go behind the counter and go through the motions of attending to the Clintons. The shopkeeper at first refused to accept any money, but the President insisted on paying. He then was introduced to her co-workers and three coalmen from a delivery yard out back, one of whom addressed him in the vernacular. "What about you, mate?" he asked of a puzzled Clinton.

In the months afterwards Violet Clarke's shop would attract a steady trickle of tourists. A home-made sign placed in the window reading 'President Clinton shops here' also helped to draw in the curious. "It's the sort of thing that only happens once in a lifetime but I wish I had it all over again," said the smitten shop owner. "I think people on the Shankill thought he was for the Nationalists but once they heard his speeches and everything I think their views changed." To this day she cherishes the coins he gave her, storing them in a cigarette case for safe keeping.

The Americans had only let the British in on what they term an OTR (off the record) event the night before in a conversation over a beer in the bar of the Europa Hotel between Hall and Watkins. Watkins said he was happy as long as the RUC was happy. Hall, who along with Williamson had taken up residence in the hotel on 14 November, had been combing the Shankill, and indeed the Falls, for stops ever since the notion of doing something at the 'peaceline' had become unfeasible. The rule of thumb was a common sense one, but one not made easy in one of the city's most tribal heartlands: steer clear of contentious backdrops that could be caught in the most oblique of camera angles. The surroundings were as important as the building to be visited. What they didn't want on the Shankill, for example, was Clinton stepping out of a shop next door to a Loyalist office and onto a red, white and blue painted kerbstone with 'Up the UVF' daubed on a wall behind him. A stop on the Shankill had initially been ruled out. "We had rejected it at first," said a senior White House source. "We thought it would be too inflammatory to put him there for security reasons. It was a little unpredictable."

The US planners had wanted Clinton to come into contact with 'real people' before he gave his keynote speech. Said a White House planner: "You can be the President of the United States and be in your bubble the whole time but it was very important to give him a chance for human interaction and see the 'peaceline'." Logistically Clinton could have easily stopped on the Falls first, though not now that it was the designated spot where he would encounter Adams. Meeting the Sinn Féin leader right away would have got the trip off on the wrong note, though some in Washington had naively suggested that Adams meet Clinton at Aldergrove and possibly even share the car ride in. McCurry said it was the President who wanted to stop on the Shankill Road first. "Clinton was presented with the question, what do you want to do? We said, 'We're not certain you're going to get a good response.' We knew there was real scepticism in the Protestant community about whether Clinton was there on behalf of all the people or one community. I think that guided the decision to go to the Shankill first."

Knowledge that the President's motorcade was to pull up at Violet's and Clinton go in was, until the last conceivable moment, confined to five Americans on the ground – Hall, Williamson, Stephens and two members of the Secret Service detail. RUC Assistant Chief Constable Bill Stewart was only informed the morning of Clinton's arrival, but wasn't too phased. The stop was on roads the force had to seal and secure anyway. A British Government official said: "I suspect the Americans were nervous we'd say, 'No, you're not stopping.' But it didn't bother us, particularly because we knew there wasn't a high threat."

What real risk to Clinton there was was deemed to come from abroad and had been heightened by an event 26 days earlier in the Middle East. Israeli Prime Minister Yitzhak Rabin had been assassinated by a gunman who shot him in the back at a peace rally in Tel Aviv. All ports of entry into Ireland were monitored for the two weeks leading up to the President's trip. "The assassination of Rabin sent a shock wave through their organisation but it was not largely destabilising," said Assistant Chief Constable Tim Lewis. The RUC and Secret Service were agreed the nature and level of threat to Clinton was relatively small, but it didn't prompt complacency. "In any society where there are guns and where people have access to guns there is concern," added Lewis. "The worry was more about some unstable personality as opposed to a group." One of his senior colleagues contended any "lone nut" was, in his personal estimation, more likely to come from the Loyalist paramilitary community as opposed to the Republican one. A member of the Washington team said: "We never had a sense of a direct threat to the President but in an environment like Northern Ireland where there are bad people and weapons you couldn't rule out the possibility of some sort of foolish stunt."

The motorcade's course to the Shankill had been altered once in the planning stages on the recommendation of the Secret Service before someone at the NIO leaked the revised route details to the *Belfast Telegraph* the week of the visit. The risk assessment, however, wasn't deemed great enough to alter the plans again, particularly as no mention was made of the intended walkabout by Clinton. The Americans were privately furious with Mayhew prior to the leak, accusing him of effectively signposting the route with his advance drive through, which included stopping on

Northumberland Street to chat to a senior police officer when a pressman suddenly showed up. "We were not at all thrilled because the last thing you want to do is advertise the route. We have this thing with the Texas Book Depository [from where Lee Harvey Oswald is said to have fired on President Kennedy]," said one US official. "The Secret Service went bonkers. It didn't go down well at all but it wasn't a show stopper." The episode caused the one real moment of friction between Watkins and Hall during their weeks working together.

Out of Violet's fruit shop, selected because it was relatively roomy as much as anything else, Clinton marched along the footpath and set to cross the Shankill Road for the first of what his aides refer to as grip-and-grin exercises. "Where's Hillary gone?" he asked members of his entourage as he made to do what he does best, work a crowd. The First Lady had been left trailing in his wake. "How does it feel to be in Belfast?" shouted a reporter. "Oh, we're delighted to be here," came the reply. Clinton was up ahead dipping into the crowd. "Wherever he finds hands, he'll shake hands," said a White House official. "He loves people, so you put him in a place where there are as many people as possible. For 20 or 30 seconds he stares into those eyes of yours and you think you are the most special person in the world."

To avoid as much advance publicity for the stop as was possible and given the lateness of the notification, no crash barriers had been erected. The RUC and Secret Service struggled to keep Clinton from being swamped by a thinnish crowd of men, women and children vying for physical contact and press photographers hungry to snap one of the day's first images. "The crowd was polite but small. Not the sort of frenzy we saw later," observed a White House staffer in tow. "Back up, back up right now please," shouted plain-clothes agents as the crowd – which had been scanned using hand-held metal detectors – surged forward, straining the white police tape beyond which they were forbidden to stray. The President was undeterred. 'What's life like?' he asked members of the public. Community worker Billy McCarroll got close enough to lay a hand on the President, though his cameras made it appear he was part of the professional press corps. "It gave the road a bit of a lift. It meant something that he stopped on the Shankill first." Said McCurry: "It was electric." Live television and radio broadcasts captured the scenes, helping to win over the cynics. (14 countries took live pictures.) "Word spread incredibly quickly," added McCurry. "By the time we left Mackie there were a lot more people out in the Protestant streets. There was a very positive reaction because people said he stopped and talked to people on the Shankill first."

Clinton bent down to console a 19-year-old invalid who was sobbing after falling in the commotion. Michael Mullan, a Catholic from the deprived Twinbrook housing estate, remembered: "He said, 'Are you afraid of me not talking to you?' I was too shocked to say something. Somebody was holding me up." He and more than a dozen others formed a cross-community contingent that had been brought to watch the President by a charity which deals with the disabled, PHAB. They had gathered at a point further away when an American tipped them off as to exactly where Clinton was going. One of PHAB's staff, Richard Long, said: "We thought the President was just going to drive up the road but he stopped. He said he was proud to be on the Shankill and it made us proud for him to be there because it was a one-off. His personality just swelled out of him. He seemed sincere and genuine."

Clinton was back in his car by the time he reached a boarded-up gap in a row of shops several hundred yards further up from Violet's. It was the cue for Stephens, back at the President's side, to recount the tale of one of the most horrific acts of the Troubles. Number 273, a family-owned fishmongers, had been demolished 13 months earlier by a prematurely-exploding IRA bomb which killed nine customers and passers-by, together with one of the terrorists who planted it, Thomas Begley. The target had been offices above Frizzell's, where it was wrongly assumed Loyalist paramilitary leaders were in session at the time. The event was referred to in US-authored briefing materials for the Presidential entourage as being "widely viewed as having turned many people away from supporting violence." (They also wrongly put the death toll at eight.) The bombing, together with revenge killings, made October 1993 the worst for terrorist murders since 1976. Twenty-seven people died. A week after Shankill the Ulster Freedom Fighters exacted retribution in the village of Greysteel near Derry, spraying the Rising Sun bar with gunfire that left seven dead, six Catholic and one Protestant.

There was never a question the cavalcade would pause at the scene of the Shankill blast and Clinton make some gesture in memory of the dead, who included a child of seven. Said one American planner: "The message we wanted was the ceasefire and the benefits of the ceasefire in bringing the communities together and overcoming sectarianism. The message of the bombed-out fish shop wasn't the image we wanted at all."

In setting foot on the Shankill at the outset, Clinton immediately signalled this was a trip that would deliver in its attempt to be inclusive. David Ervine, once jailed for possessing explosives but now an articulate spokesman for the UVF-affiliated Progressive Unionist Party (PUP), was a face in the crowd and watched from a distance as the President milked the applause and cheers. "I was delighted the people came out to see him," he said. "I have to admit to being a bit nervous on the day. Here was a very important day in Loyalism's life and I was fearful some idiot would ruin it." Former Belfast Lord Mayor, Hugh Smyth, a man Shankill born and bred, said: "Whoever actually took the decision to have him come deserves a medal because it showed his impartiality." Ervine, Smyth and Jackie Redpath, a community leader who headed the Greater Shankill Development Agency, were among those the Americans had sounded out about the visit. Smyth, who knew the President would be passing through the Shankill but wasn't aware he'd be stopping, would tell those sceptical of Clinton's trip to wait and see.

The warm reception Clinton received in the cradle of Loyalism would have been unimaginable at the outset of his Presidency. If his campaign pledges hadn't raised too many eyebrows – they served only to reinforce the stereotypical suspicion that America was Irish Nationalism's most powerful friend – then Clinton's decision to grant Gerry Adams his first visa aroused a deep sense of bitterness. The anger spawned outrage when the Sinn Féin leader – loathed all the more on the Shankill, if that were possible, for having carried Begley's coffin – was feted at the White House. The fury was highlighted by the actions of one Shankill community worker.

Jack McKee, a fundamentalist preacher who ran cross-community projects, slit his thumb with a carpet blade and spilt blood on two Stars and Stripes flags he'd ripped from the wall of the centre he ran and delivered them by hand to Val Martinez, then the city's US Consul General. "I was in a fit of rage and had to express my feelings at the hurt of the people in this community at the very thought of Gerry Adams sitting in the White House with Clinton," explained McKee. "When I handed them to Val he knew they were coming from someone who was genuinely hurting and who represented the feelings of the people on the Shankill."

But taken in isolation the treatment of Adams wasn't enough to break the quickening pace of developing contact between Washington and Loyalists in the 1990s. The interaction had come on in leaps and bounds from when Ulster Defence Association paramilitaries attended a Boston conference on the Northern Ireland conflict in 1975. Out of it grew a relationship, established by strategists like Andy Tyrie, Glen Barr and John McMichael, with New York human rights lawyer Paul O'Dwyer, a County Mayo immigrant born nine years before the Easter Rising of 1916. Years later the man dubbed "the grandfather of Irish-America" had a hand in drawing up the key UDA policy documents, *Beyond the Religious Divide*, which was promoted in the US capital, and *Common Sense*.

O'Dwyer and McMichael, who was assassinated by the IRA in 1987, became particularly close, with the American staying with him a number of times when he visited Northern Ireland. Given O'Dwyer's Nationalist credentials, McMichael had to offer protection as he travelled about the country. A decade later, when McMichael's son Gary led the UDA-linked Ulster Democratic Party (UDP) on its first trip to the United States, the two fought back tears when they met in New York. "He talked about the times him and my dad had together," recalled McMichael, "and how it hurt him that I was over in America and my dad wasn't able to be there." However, America was never a natural constituency and the overwhelming majority within Loyalism preferred it that way. Said Barr: "I'd argued for years we should have somebody based in the United States. I was urging the paramilitaries to make available the resources to place somebody on Capitol Hill. Others were doing it very effectively, but we'd nobody." It wasn't until President Clinton put Ireland on his agenda that Loyalism reacted by putting America seriously on theirs.

Kathleen Stephens' predecessor Martinez had been a familiar face on the Shankill, making inroads through informal talks with personalities who were emerging as leaders of the political flanks of Loyalist paramilitarism, the PUP and the UDP. In that respect he'd grasped a baton handed over in August 1993 by the man he in turn succeeded, Doug Archard, who'd married a Shankill youth and community worker, Claire Curry. "She plugged him into a whole network and Doug played a critical role in advancing people like Jackie Redpath and encouraging Americans to listen to them," said one source who moved in their circles. Archard would bring political adversaries around his dining table at a time when it was unique. "He turned Ardnavally into a place where people could meet," recalled one of his diners. "You would meet more interesting people around Doug's table than you would at Hillsborough or the NIO. He had that ability to transcend differences." Both Martinez and Archard had made it part of their brief to engage with parties across the spectrum, though it was arguably the Loyalists who benefited most. "Martinez had no axe to grind," said the PUP's Ervine. "You weren't going to pull the wool over his eyes in terms of the nuances of Northern Ireland. The level of trust we were able to achieve with him was important." Martinez, a Catholic not unaccustomed to strolling from Mass on the Falls Road for meetings on the Shankill, was the subject of an unofficial Loyalist death threat after the first Adams visa and it was precisely because of contacts he'd forged that it was never executed. At a time when communication between US representatives and paramilitary figures on both sides of the divide was officially banned by Washington, Martinez's liaisons with Loyalists intensified in the summer of 1994 as the IRA ceasefire beckoned. He believed it was vital to build upon his relationship of trust and provide a crucial avenue of communication to the White House.

Around then Bill Flynn had established himself as another significant conduit, due in part to Presbyterian cleric Roy Magee, the most important of the insurance magnet's intermediaries. "It was Roy Magee who made sure I saw all the real people," said Flynn. "I always liked him for walking with me into these areas and seeing to it that no harm came and that I understood what was being said. We became very close friends." Magee first encountered Flynn in the Europa in early 1994 and recalled: "He wanted a foothold in the Loyalist camp and my analysis was the Loyalists could only gain by getting involved. I think Flynn's role was clearly defined by the White House and he was the one the Loyalists could relate to." Magee, nicknamed Reverend Ceasefire for helping to guide Loyalist paramilitaries towards their truce, introduced Flynn to the UDA leadership. At the same time the multi-millionaire American was, again via Magee, meeting those from the other main paramilitary group, the UVF. All talks were convened in the utmost secrecy.

Flynn's position assumed such respect amongst some Loyalists that he was made privy to the ceasefire declaration before it was made public in October 1994. So important had the US become that the announcement was timed to ensure the optimum morning news exposure across the Atlantic. Flynn spent two hours with Loyalism's political and military leaders at the Europa on the eve of the statement, which had gone through numerous drafts. "We were mostly enjoying the fact it was all happening," remembered Flynn. "There was one sentence in the ceasefire agreement that I wish the IRA had put in theirs and that was where they apologised for the damage they had done to so many. I thought that that was incredible for fighting men to say." A decision by one of those present in the hotel's first floor bar to invite Flynn to the announcement at a north Belfast community centre sparked a row in the ranks. Billy Hutchinson of the PUP explained: "The invite shouldn't have been given. He was kept in a back room for the simple reason that people would've believed the American influence was more than it really was. He came in at a very late stage when decisions had already been taken."

On the back of the declaration, Flynn's money and influence came into play. He sponsored modern-day Loyalism's inaugural visit Stateside under the banner of the National Committee on American Foreign Policy and did all in his power to guarantee the visitors got a fair hearing. Said one Loyalist: "Flynn was the one who said these people need to be heard. He said, 'You have listened to Gerry Adams, now listen to them.'" The NSC had also made an approach to the Loyalists, requesting that their trip include Washington. The six-man team comprised of, on the PUP side, former UVF commander Gusty Spence, who made the Loyalist ceasefire announcement, Ervine and Hutchinson, while McMichael was joined by UDP colleagues Joe English and Davy Adams. The rank and file had already been briefed on the American strategy. Glen Barr, who withdrew from politics in 1981, revealed his involvement in a secret, three-day conference involving Loyalist paramilitary commanders in the run-up to the ceasefire. "I was always a great believer in getting the blackboard up and setting out scenarios. They understood the need of getting up off their arse and getting out there and courting people. I've no doubt that set the scene for what the UDP did later."

The fact a ceasefire had been declared wasn't alone enough to ensure automatic entry to the United States. The decision to allow the six in came from the White House just hours before they were due to leave for New York, but almost never materialised because of a bizarre mix-up involving Davy Adams. Magee, who collected the visas from Martinez and rushed them late at night to each of six homes, revealed: "They weren't going to let Davy go because their computers showed he had a record . But they'd mixed him up with a jailed relation of Sinn Féin's Gerry Adams." The week-long, three city tour – Boston was the third venue – helped sell America on the worth of the Unionist case and the Loyalists on the value of America. "It was a real eye-opener," said Hutchinson. "Quite a lot of Irish Americans reached out to understand where we were coming from."

In February 1995, former Lord Mayor Hugh Smyth again portrayed Loyalism's acceptable face in a ground-breaking short tour of North America with his Dublin counterpart, John Gormley. The unlikely double act carried a message of hope to places like Washington and Boston where Smyth, a PUP member, had been for the first time three months earlier as part of a Belfast City Council trade delegation. "It was like going into the lion's den," said Smyth. "It was steeped in Republicanism, but I was a shock to them. They were amazed when I told them Protestants were deprived of facilities, good housing and employment, just like Catholics." Smyth, who would become a frequent visitor to the US, said his greatest regret politically was that he and other supporters of the Union hadn't gone out sooner. "I admire what John Hume's been able to do for Derry with the help of America. Had we gone ten years ago we could've shared in the wealth."

Loyalism consolidated its position in March 1995 when McMichael and English chose to attend St Patrick's Day festivities at the White House. It wasn't an easy or popular decision, given Gerry Adams was to be there. English said the hardliners were extremely difficult to sway. "There were a lot of people sceptical about us joining in what were Nationalist celebrations but at the same time there were enough far-sighted people to say away you go." The PUP spurned the opportunity, as did the Unionist parties. Before going, UDP leader McMichael explained his rationale. "The Loyalist position is going by default. While Gerry Adams has the world stage to put forward the political objectives of Sinn Féin and the IRA, Loyalism has remained at home under a self-imposed veto.

It's time the message is put across that there are two parts of the community in Northern Ireland." The UDP pair were introduced to Clinton at the event, though English has clearer memories of bumping into one of his screen idols, Paul Newman, who incidentally offered Clinton the use of one of his properties in Ireland during the Presidential visit. Nancy Soderberg told the pair: "You guys are pretty gutsy for coming here."

The entire Protestant political family, however, decamped to Washington two months later for the Washington Investment Conference where it was the Loyalists who made the biggest impression. They worked their charm in the event's fringes, in the bars and restaurants, making new friends of old enemies. Said a top White House official: "They're some of the most forward thinking people in this whole process." As a sign of their progressiveness, the PUP's representatives held behind-the-scenes discussions with Sinn Féin at the investment conference. " This was an important engagement and we were very positive about it. We have had contact with the Loyalists for some time and I think they have been mutually beneficial. There is a better understanding. We do know each other's analysis and we have exchanged views," said Mitchel McLaughlin.

At the conference Hutchinson first met a retired businessman who'd made $2bn from the sale of his computer software company and who would unlock the door to Boston for the reformed terrorist. John Cullinane was introduced to Hutchinson by Mo Mowlam, then the Labour Party's Northern Ireland spokeswoman. Cullinane, a friend of the Kennedys and whose office wall is adorned with a personally inscribed picture of Jacqueline Kennedy, was intrigued upon learning Hutchinson sent his children to a north Belfast school where Catholics and Protestants are educated side by side. Before long the PUP politician was taking up Cullinane's offers to sell the Loyalist case in Boston, where he'd end up running marathons with a friend, Belfast SDLP councillor Alex Attwood. Cullinane was keen to promote the political careers of both. "Cullinane is key to our future in America," explained Hutchinson. "If he withdraws his support we'll feel the cold. We would bounce ideas off him and can go to him and say we need 'x' amount of money and he would throw it on the table." Hutchinson's Boston fixer was Joe Costello, who worked for the Kennedys. "He is key because he makes things work," said Hutchinson, who became so at ease in the city that one colleague quipped: "If the ceasefire breaks down Hutchy will have a safe house in Boston."

Also attending the Washington Investment conference was community worker Jackie Redpath who could legitimately lay claim for being among the first to articulate the grassroots Protestant position to Americans. Born in the Woodvale district, Redpath, a history graduate, became friendly with Consul General Archard and saw rich pickings in America. Archard supported an educational trip to the US by Redpath in 1991 and put the Shankill on the itinerary of visiting American political and trade delegations, setting a precedent that by December 1996 would even result in a Kennedy treading the Shankill Road in the shape of Congressman Joe. Redpath took flak from close quarters over the frequency of his American travels and those he was mingling with. Said another community worker: "He was getting a lot of stick from his own community but Jackie stuck it out. There was a joke going about the Shankill. What's the difference between Jackie Redpath and God? God's everywhere, Jackie Redpath's everywhere but the Shankill Road. He was far-sighted enough though to see you have to bring powerful people on board."

Redpath made a big impression on the Connolly House group – O'Dowd, Flynn, Morrison and Feeney – at their initial meeting in a south Belfast hotel in 1993. While others on the Protestant side snubbed the offer of talks, Redpath was willing to exploit every opportunity to kindle US interest. "I think Jackie Redpath influenced me more than any other single individual in the north of Ireland," said Flynn. "He described conditions on the Shankill Road when all I'd heard about were conditions on the Falls Road."

On the other side of the coin, Redpath was important in explaining the advantages of dealing with Americans to Loyalist politicians, whom he held sway with after helping coax the UVF down the road to peace. He became associated with the American Ireland Fund, a charitable group set up in 1975 which allowed the great and the good to channel millions of dollars into projects promoting reconciliation on both sides of the Irish border. Its Board of Directors ranged from former Speaker of the House of Representatives Tom Foley to the Northern Ireland-born Hollywood film star, Liam Neeson. Redpath's high society coming-out party was a Fund dinner in Boston in the spring of 1995. "That was my first big introduction to Irish-America. People were fascinated because I don't think they'd met anyone from the Protestant tradition before. I was overwhelmed by the level of interest," said Redpath, who was at the event along with Mayor Smyth and fellow Shankill activists Joe Stewart and May Blood. Together they made such an impression that they brought home money for an educational trust. One of those who witnessed Redpath in action remarked: "He's articulate, intelligent and very persuasive. In America I've never yet seen him fail to capture an audience." Redpath's standing was such in US Government circles that Ambassador Kennedy Smith would ask a dinner guest from Belfast: "Do you know Jackie Redpath? He's famous, isn't he?"

The Fund's Irish Advisory Committee is chaired by the former head of the Northern Ireland Civil Service, Maurice Hayes. He was influential in introducing figures in corporate Irish-America to those on the ground like Redpath who were working on a sub-political level. Hayes threw dinner parties to bring the sides together. "It was a lot about personal vouching. People coming in from the US wanted to know if the people they were talking to were worth seeing and people here wanted to know if they were being taken seriously," said Hayes.

Founders of the Fund and the most important players Redpath fell in with were publicity-shy Boston aristocrats, the Dunfey brothers, who owned an international hotel chain. Jack, Bob and Jerry had been big shots in the Democratic Party since JFK first ran for office. They were Irish Nationalists whose ancestors hailed from Kerry but whose altruistic bent had them dabbling in conflict resolution in South Africa, Central America, the Middle East and Northern Ireland, where a fourth brother, the late Walter Dunfey, had led a fact-finding mission way back in 1972. The spark that ignited their interest in the Troubles was the civil rights crusade of the late 1960s and the parallel they drew with Martin Luther King's movement. They fundraised for Hume and for the Falls, but came to promote the other side as well. After establishing links with Redpath, they pumped money into his Springboard cross-community training programme, the *Shankill Voice* newspaper and other projects. "They have backed up their interest with financial support. It's not phenomenal amounts but significant amounts," said Redpath. It was the Dunfeys who picked up the tab when the six

Loyalist politicians ventured into Boston in November 1994. They'd pledged to bankroll the mission when Flynn telephoned them from the Europa where he sat with the Loyalists the night before the announcement that they were ending their terrorist campaign. "If you're going to be solving the problem you have to be dealing with people on both sides," said Bob Dunfey. "We took the Loyalists to Boston College, the second most prominent Catholic college in the United States, which made them a little suspicious. They were absolutely convinced that a hundred per cent of the Irish-American community were supporting the IRA or Sinn Féin or both, but they soon found out it was different." The Dunfeys counted among their acquaintances George Mitchell, who was a member of their philanthrophic club, the New England Circle, and Clinton, who had used Jack's offices during his 1992 election campaign. The Dunfeys accompanied the Presidential party on the visit to Ireland, but weren't on the Shankill Road to witness the first leg of Clinton's triumph in an area which had benefited from their activity.

As Clinton's cavalcade departed the Shankill Road, the excitement subsided, but only briefly, as other important visitors would follow later in the day. A delegation headed by Commerce Secretary Brown and Education Secretary Riley would follow in the President's footsteps and stop on the road, touring the Argyle Business Centre. Brown, who had been to the Shankill before, and his assistant, Charles "Chuck" Meissner, who was charged with the Northern Ireland portfolio, had done their part in burying the myth that the Clinton White House was partial to Nationalism. "They were key in terms of convincing people America was even handed. They were straight down the line and worked very hard," said Billy Hutchinson.

Five months later Brown and Meissner would perish on another economic mission to a war-torn land. They were among 35 American corporate and Government leaders killed when a US Air Force plane ploughed into a mountain range near Dubrovnik, Croatia, in poor weather. Their loss was felt deeply on the Shankill, and indeed the Falls. Redpath gave a special reading at a memorial service in Belfast for the two men. "Meissner was determined to ensure west Belfast was seen as including the Shankill," he said. "He was someone willing to put the slogging hours in. Seldom have the deaths of two men of such international stature been mourned so locally."

V

A factory lock-out crisis

*We would have had serious problems if Adams had
shown. Mackie boys are tough. A lot are from the
heart of the Shankill. Somebody could've hit him
with a brick. I was thinking of the children we were
going to have there if people started a riot.*

Pat Dougan, Chief Executive, Mackie International

Martha Pope stood tapping her feet in agitation. For the
umpteenth time she looked at her wrist watch. Her charge
Mitchell was running late for an appointment and he was AWOL
on the shop-floor of an engineering plant in west Belfast.

It was 29 June 1995 and Clinton's economic envoy had gone to
an early-morning meeting at Mackie International to hear of, among
other things, an ambitious dream for a new university campus on
the 'peaceline'. The company's boardroom provided the perfect vista
of an inner-city wasteland known as Springvale where the University of Ulster hoped to plant a seed of learning. A few years earlier,
Mackie had relocated from the site to a purpose-built plant close by.

The shrewd boss of Mackie, Pat Dougan, employing the maxim
that you don't get something for nothing, bartered the use of his
premises for time with the influential former Senator. The presentation washed down with coffee, Dougan and his visitors bounded off

for the machine rooms on a whirlwind tour that began with a time limit of ten minutes but ended after thirty. Almost immediately Dougan lengthened his stride so he and Mitchell opened up a gap on the stragglers. "They'd moved way ahead," remembered Professor Wallace Ewart, the university's representative. "It was very much a tête-à-tête and Pat did not want to be disturbed. I tried to indicate to him that time was running short and got a typical two fingers back."

During their brisk walkabout, Mitchell told Dougan his mother had operated a loom back home in Maine. He even had some of the garments she'd woven. (Researchers tasked by Dougan later discovered it was actually on a loom manufactured at Mackie she'd worked.) Dougan, who had got wind of the President's visit while attending the Washington Investment Conference, used his time with Mitchell wisely, promoting the plant as a venue for a Clinton stop-off. "It was in my head that we had a fighting chance," he said. "I had visions of Kennedy standing on the Berlin Wall and as our factory was on the 'peaceline' I was going to build that theme up. I'm an opportunist. I could see the picture." The Chief Executive's tour finished in a steel-beamed warehouse known to the workforce as the shed. It was where Clinton ultimately spoke but where Pope was lingering, her thoughts temporarily distracted by the environs and Clinton's upcoming peace mission. Remembered Dougan: "Martha was going bananas. She was giving me Dixie but I'd done my job and got Mitchell involved. She said, 'Where have you been?' I replied, 'I was trying to convince Senator Mitchell to bring the President here.' She said, 'I was just thinking that this building would be ideal for it.'"

From the moment the President's trip became official, seven days later, Mackie was a permanent fixture on the schedule. It was one of the few constants in an itinerary that altered frequently in the coming months. Said a British Government official: "Mackie was sewn up even before we knew there was a visit." The only moment of doubt would arise dramatically in the hours leading up to Clinton's arrival and then it was Dougan who threatened to pull the plug, not the Americans.

Dougan, born in Dunloy, County Antrim, was an orphan who upset the odds in his climb to the top. Raised by an aunt, he became one of Northern Ireland's most flamboyant businessmen. By his own admission he was an anti-establishment maverick who revelled in the role, and he was also Mackie's saviour. The company's roots went back to the mid-nineteenth century. When founded under the name James Mackie and Sons it fed the machinery needs of a booming flax and linen processing industry in Ireland. (Dougan's brothers had in fact gathered potatoes on the Mackie family's estates.) The factory nestled between Catholic and Protestant neighbourhoods in the shadow of Black Mountain. Its manufacturing output peaked in the 1950s when it employed 5,000 mainly-Protestant workers.

But within three decades Mackie was moribund and the London Government took a political decision to keep it afloat in the unemployment blackspot of west Belfast. As injections of capital would only borrow time, the then Northern Ireland Economy Minister, Richard Needham, coaxed his friend Dougan out of early retirement to stop debt-ridden Mackie from going to the wall. "We went to the most extraordinary lengths to save Mackie," stated a Government official. "We rescued it more than twice with a rate of assistance that was way above our normal, but finance is no use without decent management and we asked for Dougan." The British Government was by no means at one over the bail-out which heralded Dougan's arrival. Recalled Needham: "Myself and [then Prime Minister Margaret] Thatcher had a big fight over the money. Civil servants were terrified of the Public Accounts Committee at the House of Commons. Mackie was the single most important issue I was confronted with. It had been bombed out. It could be an example of bringing the two communities together and was one of the great engineering power houses of Ireland. If there was any way of saving it it had to be saved."

Dougan had come to the fore thanks to the record results he'd achieved at two mid-Ulster concerns, Sperrin Metals and Powerscreen International. By the time he inherited the Mackie hotseat, the firm had made headway in correcting the woeful religious imbalance of its workforce. Dougan repaired dismal management-worker relations, making employees feel partners in the company's future. A trade union official who witnessed the ups and downs over 30 years of service, Ronnie Lewis, said: "Pat was like a breath of fresh air. If it wasn't for him we wouldn't be here. Mackie would have went under." Added a London Government minister: "If we had more people like Pat Dougan the Northern Ireland economy would be moving quicker."

Pope mulled over the merits of Mackie for the Presidential visit with a colleague in Senator Mitchell's office, David Pozorski. Born in Chicago, the Harvard and Yale graduate had bridged the gap between Martinez's departure and Stephens' arrival, acting as Consul General in Belfast for a couple of months. Pope and Pozorski sold the Mackie concept to the White House who saw to it that a factory once synonymous with discrimination against Catholics was on the September site survey trip and then the October pre-advance. "Martha had visited Mackie without specific reference to the Presidential visit," said a senior member of the US planning team. "She was the one who said 'this could be the right kind of idea,' so we specifically put it on the agenda." Those among the President's men who mattered most could picture the potential of Mackie the instant they viewed it and ignored British protestations. One American said: "When we saw Mackie we discussed the pros and cons but within 15 seconds I was in love with the place. It was a place that could send out the kind of message that Bill Clinton would want to send out." The British, though, took some convincing. "We had reservations," said an official. "There were obvious things that were delicate, like is it on the left of the 'peaceline' or to the right? Is it a Protestant company, as it used to be, or is it not? It was an exercise in expanding our imagination. It seemed to us there were other places for a speech. City Hall was one possibility, Queen's was another." But they were fighting a lost cause.

The Americans were magnetised by the factory's location, the strides it had taken to overcome its anti-Catholic bias and the challenge of transforming a shed used to test prototype machines into a theatre fit for an address by a world leader. At one point the Clinton planners toyed with the idea of using Mackie's 'peaceline' location as the trip's big photo opportunity. "We had this idea of him walking to or from the Mackie plant through the 'peaceline'. The visual of him walking through would've been a good picture," said a White House source. "But it didn't work for a variety of reasons. One was the picture simply wasn't there." Admittedly a few on the US side initially shared British doubts about Mackie. "I didn't think it was going to work physically because of the long nature of the hall but the White House guys came in and they could just see it. They said

The Shankill Road warms to Clinton on his first walkabout of the day. A face in the crowd (top left with moustache) is the Progressive Unionist Party's David Ervine. "I was delighted people came out to see him. Here was a very important day in Loyalism's life," he said. (*Belfast Telegraph*)

The show-stealers – Catherine Hamill and David Sterrett introduce the President at Mackie International. "Those children represented the best argument for the peace process that I know," said Clinton. Looking on is Mackie Chief Executive Pat Dougan. (*White House*)

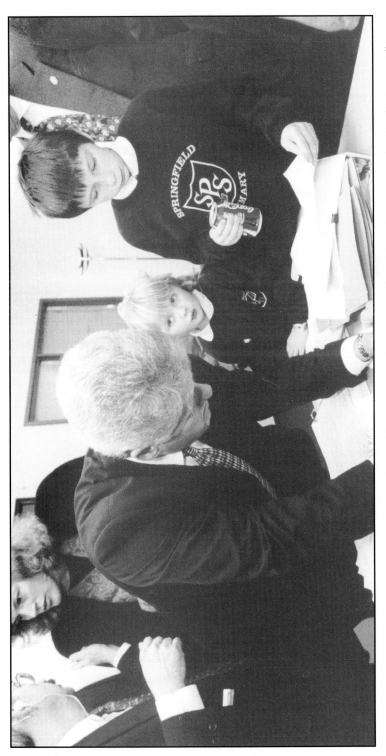

The eyes have it. Catherine Hamill is under Clinton's spell backstage at Mackie as he signs her letter of peace. "This is a lovely statement," he wrote. "Thank you for joining me." Behind Clinton, Consul General Kathleen Stephens and trip-planner Brady Williamson discuss the next move. (*White House*)

Ceád míle faílte − "a hundred thousand welcomes" to the Falls Road from Gerry Adams. "Everything about this visit came right down to how we handled the radioactive question of when, how and where we dealt with Gerry Adams," said a US trip organiser. *(REX Features)*

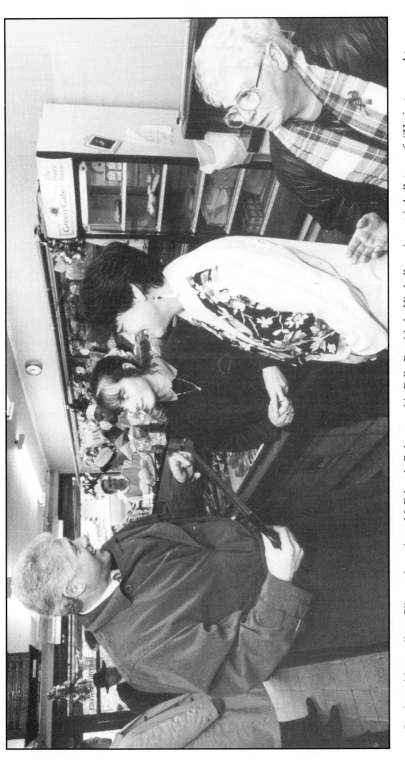

Service with a smile – Clinton drops in at McErlean's Bakery on his Falls Road halt. His bulky raincoat is bullet-proof. "He just seemed to be so big he filled the place," said Liz Hartley who is pictured (second from right) presenting a plaque with her daughter. (*White House*)

The Planners − above, Professor Brady Williamson, 'Mr Tricky Trips', greets Clinton at Aldergrove Airport. *(John Harrison Photography)*. Below right, diplomat Blair Hall was Williamson's right hand man. *(John Harrison Photography)*. Below left, Derry trip co-ordinator Ed Emerson, wearing scarf, waits with Clinton at the Guildhall. *(Guildhall Press)*

Above, the Clintons salute the crowds in Guildhall Square, Derry. "I was honoured to share a dais with John Hume and I know that added to the warm greeting we received," said Clinton. Derry Council Clerk John Keanie (at podium) looks on. *(Crispin Rodwell).* Below, hanging on his every word... the Guildhall crowd mesmerised by the President. "The President loves to be warmly received and he was absolutely overwhelmed," said Clinton aide, Susan Brophy. *(Crispin Rodwell)*

Lay your hands on me... Clinton is mobbed as he greets well-wishers in Derry's Guildhall Square. The President later said to his wife: "They tried to pull my wedding ring off."(*Crispin Rodwell*)

they could make it work and damn if they didn't," said one. British minds were taxed imagining the possibilities. "We thought it was an odd location. We had difficulty seeing how the room could be configured in a way that would go down for a major Presidential speech," said a source.

Dougan was unrelenting in his single-minded furtherance of Mackie, bombarding influential Clinton Administration figures like Soderberg with telephone calls. She was behind the idea. He also sought to sway allies within the British Government and was coldly-calculating in his damning indictments of other venues that vied for the President's presence. "I was lobbying like hell, left, right and centre. I took the attitude that if the enemy was all around you start to pick them off. If there were birds coming in overhead that were going to shit on me I shot them down before they got in," he said. "I was determined that the President came here. I started at the point that there was nothing to lose by trying because if I failed it hadn't cost a penny." His efforts won restrained acclaim from sparring partners within the Northern Ireland Office. "It's a tribute to Pat," one mandarin stated. "I think he made a very big impression on one or two significant American advisors."

Mackie's one major hurdle along the way arose out of a period in its past when Lummus Industries Inc., a US manufacturer of cotton machinery, bought a controlling interest in 1990. Loans totalling $10.5m were made to Mackie under guarantee from the US-based Overseas Private Investment Corporation (OPIC). When Dougan took over he acted to free Mackie from the burden created by the borrowings. But the deal to sever the OPIC debt, which was done with the help of influential figures like Congressman Joseph Kennedy, came back to haunt him during the planning of Clinton's trip. The White House asked its Embassy in London to run a routine check on Mackie's background and received back a memorandum which included a reference "an odour" from the company concerning the OPIC arrangement. Dougan was convinced the British had conspired against him, though they denied it. "The NIO had done a dirty tricks job. The OPIC thing came from them. They were determined to have Clinton go somewhere else," claimed the factory boss. Mitchell's office got word of the communication and moved quickly to clear the air. Said a source: "OPIC didn't think there was anything questionable about the deal. In fact it felt

Dougan had cut Mackie a good one." A memo from Pope was sent to trip co-ordinating supremo Jack Quinn at the White House and that was the end of the matter. The British felt full disclosure was a prerequisite. "We were anxious the Americans had the full story. We weren't trying to blackball Mackie. The last thing we wanted was the President to go somewhere and then, two weeks later, the media and the Americans ask, 'Why did you let him go?'"

At one juncture Dougan sought to strengthen Mackie's hand by bringing on board the University of Ulster, which was trying to convince the White House that Clinton should accept an honorary degree. He suggested the ceremony could be performed at his factory, only a stone's throw from the planned new Springvale campus site. The arrangement was seen as cutting both ways, with the university believing it could use the occasion to get Presidential approval of the project to which the British Government hadn't committed funding. "Pat was exploring all opportunities," said Ewart. "I think his thought process was, if there's a University of Ulster at Springvale connection why not try and focus it all on Mackie." The university was actively courting American support for the £100m scheme which had already been lauded by Commerce Secretary Brown, Senator Mitchell and Vice President Al Gore. University staff had performed a masterstroke at the Washington Investment Conference, getting to Quinn, Gore's Chief of Staff, and winning him over. To their astonishment Gore included in his speech backing for the "exciting project." University Vice Chancellor Trevor Smith attempted to persuade Ambassador Kennedy Smith of the value of Clinton accepting a degree at Mackie. "It would renew the Administration's endorsement for our campus proposal," he said in a letter written on 2 November. Ultimately the plot foundered because the Americans were loath to have Clinton abet the academics in their bid to attain British Government approval. "We shouldn't be telling them how to spend a hundred million pounds," internal American correspondence stated.

Ten days before the visit the Americans sent in the site officer responsible for running the Mackie event. The man picked for the task was a United Airlines jumbo jet pilot, Jamie Lindsay. He'd started working part-time for Clinton during the 1992 election campaign when his union, the Airline Pilots Association, backed the Arkansas Governor's run for the White House. "I convinced our union president to let me and seven others go out on the road in uniform and campaign for him," he said. "Once Clinton got elected they asked us to keep helping him and I guess I was the only one dumb enough to stick around." The former US Marine, who'd learnt to fly at the age of 14, had been seconded to the Office of Presidential Advance for a trip to Latvia and for events in France marking the fiftieth anniversary of D-Day. A White House source said: "Jamie is a striking character. He may not be the most diplomatic of people but he's got lots of energy, is very committed to working for the President and is very good at his job." Added another official: "Lindsay is a funny guy and likes to be a manly man. He can rub people both ways."

Lindsay, who sported a small *de rigueur* handlebar moustache and had a picture of his vintage aeroplane, 'Sidekick', on his calling card, pounced on the opportunity to go to Ireland. "I could think of no trip that I'd rather be on because it was going to be so spectacular," he said. His blue-collar credentials made him the ideal man for Mackie. "The only thing I knew was that there was a Protestant gate and a Catholic gate," the upstate New Yorker later remembered of his first visit to the Springfield Road factory. "I just said to myself, 'I work for the President of the United States and to hell with it.' I was going to do what I had to do." From the outset sparks flew between Dougan and Lindsay. They were men of action, a couple of no-nonsense communicators not afraid to trade profanities. One Mackie worker privy to the verbal fireworks said: "Jamie just didn't take any crap from anyone. He's the only man I've ever seen matching Pat Dougan word for word." Another added: "The relationship was fraught. Pat told Lindsay, 'This is my factory.' Jamie said, 'From here on in it's not.' They took lumps out of each other." But Lindsay liked Dougan and at once appreciated that the Chief Executive cared passionately for Mackie and that much of his angst sprang from an obsessive determination to protect the company and its employees. "I didn't know whether he could manage a two-car funeral but this was a leader of men. His workers were his heart and soul. With Pat you knew where you were and once he realised we weren't trying to put Mackie at risk, which took a while, we didn't have a problem," said one member of the Presidential trip unit.

Lindsay, aided by a member of the White House Press Office, lived at the site and mingled hourly with the 350-strong workforce.

Each to a man told him it was a company where you left your religion and politics at whichever gate you entered. Trouble brewed when it became obvious to staff that the Americans intended inviting politicians to hear Clinton's keynote speech. Worse still, Washington would possibly stage a handshake between the President and Gerry Adams on the premises. From the trip's inception there were those at the White House who exerted influence to get a rendezvous between Clinton and Adams in west Belfast. "It was a question of how to work it out," recalled a top Administration official. "There had to be a way for him to connect with the President while he was there. Adams was very much in the peace process at that point and he was a folk hero in a certain part of the community." The challenge was how to fashion the encounter in an understated manner that gave the appearance of being uncontrived. Said Tony Lake: "There was a lot of work and discussion among ourselves into how to do it in a way that wouldn't set Unionist teeth on edge and yet would satisfy Adams and Sinn Féin that they were getting equal respect. That was the most difficult bit of negotiation of the trip." Adams wanted the President on his patch. Mike McCurry said: "Adams had said, 'I want the President to see my neighbourhood.' He said, 'I want him to see the Falls Road', and that it was very, very important to him that Clinton be physically present in the neighbourhood that had suffered so much."

The prospect of Adams stealing the show sent shockwaves through Mackie and reverberated through those in the planning team on the ground in Belfast. Dougan said: "The workers were quite excited about the trip but that was not the problem. Their problem was who was coming." With the rumour mill in overdrive, the Mackie boss determined the best way to establish the facts was to convene talks between a work's committee, consisting of union officials, and the US advance team headed by Williamson. Shop steward Lewis recalled: "We didn't want Mackie turned into a political roadshow. That wasn't on. We'd been hearing Adams was coming and if he was we would find it hard to take part in any of it." It wasn't that the staff were more intransigent over Adams' attendance than other politicians; he just seemed at the centre of the Americans' attentions.

Williamson and Blair Hall sat back at the boardroom discussions and let Lindsay do most of the talking. One of those there said: "Jamie banged his ring down on the table and said, 'Damn it fellas, I'm a dues-paying member of a union too and I know what unions are like.' He laid out the plan in a way these guys liked. They naturally reacted to it." The visitors assured the union representatives that any political dimension to the President's visit would be discreetly low-key. Said one: "We told them we weren't reserving a front-row seat for Gerry Adams. That sort of dissipated the problem from our point of view." In fact they already had Adams' seat selected. It was in a position that television cameras couldn't cut to during Clinton's speech. A Mackie representative recalled: "The assurance was given that Adams wouldn't be allowed to turn the shop floor into a media circus. The Americans had talked the work's committee round to allowing Adams onto the site. They said they would place him out of the way. The issue wasn't about Adams coming to Mackie as much as shaking the President's hand – that was the real problem." The Americans walked away from the table believing they'd left some room for manoeuvre. "We still thought after that conversation it might theoretically be possible to have a handshake on Mackie grounds – not in the hall or not in front of the television cameras – and technically it would've been within the agreement but maybe emotionally it wouldn't," said one. But the Mackie side interpreted the arrangement differently, believing there would be no contact between Clinton and Adams period. The confusion resulted in high drama the morning of the President's arrival.

As the finishing touches were being put to the stage set close to midnight on Wednesday, 29 November, Lindsay dropped the Adams bombshell. He pulled aside a public relations consultant hired by Dougan especially for the visit, Tom Kelly, and informed him the White House had sanctioned the handshake at the plant next morning. Kelly had worked in public affairs on Capitol Hill and been involved in 30 Democrat political campaigns across the States. Mackie workers had taken to Lindsay and had clapped him off the Presidential rostrum earlier in the day after a ceremony in which he was presented with a citation honouring him. Kelly said: "I think the award played on his mind all day. He knew what the Americans were going to do and eventually he decided to give us an opportunity to do something about it rather than have it sprung on us." The Americans hadn't yet determined on the circumstances of the handshake. They had a number of scenarios in mind, including positioning

Adams along a rope line Clinton would work on exiting the hall, or having the Sinn Féin leader bump into the President as he emerged from a side door surrounded by a group of schoolchildren. The news was going to be presented as a *fait accompli*, if it were disclosed in advance at all. Kelly telephoned Dougan at a south Belfast hotel where the Mackie board was hosting a pre-visit reception. Dougan exploded and ordered Kelly to sort it out. "It's not happening," Dougan yelled before hanging up. "Our main problem at that stage was not about Adams. It was more about what the workforce would do," recalled Kelly. Throughout the trip's build-up Mackie bosses were aware of the very genuine risk of a staff walk-out in the event of Adams appearing, or worse, the potential for unrest. "We would have had serious problems if Adams had shown," said Dougan. "Mackie boys are tough. A lot are from the heart of the Shankill. Somebody could've hit him with a brick. I was thinking of the children we were going to have there if people started a riot."

A full-blown spat erupted at the spot where Clinton was due to give his keynote speech, involving Kelly, Lindsay and two other members of the American advance team. Williamson was on the other end of the phone from the Europa and berated Lindsay for having revealed the plan. "We were having an argument," said Kelly. "We were trying to come up with a compromise but the Americans were very adamant." The four failed to hammer out a solution and with time running out they opted to kick the problem up the line to their bosses. Lindsay went to the Europa, Kelly to the Forte Crest Hotel where the Mackie board was about to go into emergency session. Lindsay's pang of conscience had put him in the dog house with his superiors. He apologised to Williamson but told him he couldn't be party to breaking the spirit of the agreement with Mackie workers, despite the prospect of it costing him future White House attachments. (He went on to work on the Clinton 1996 re-election campaign before leaving.) At 1.00am Dougan had an extraordinary showdown with Williamson over the telephone. "I was frustrated the whole thing was going to be ruined by a simple handshake," recalled Dougan. "I said to Williamson, 'Forget the whole thing, there's nothing happening. Now you sort it out.'" The Mackie Chief Executive abruptly ended the call by playing his ace. In an act of daring brinksmanship he vowed to shut the factory gates on the Clinton motorcade. "You must be joking, Patrick? Think of the publicity," responded the disbelieving Williamson, holed up in the US staff meeting room at the Europa. Dougan snapped back: "Think of the publicity we'll get if I leave Clinton sitting on the Springfield Road and he can't get through the gate. That'll go round the world. It'll be brilliant." Ronnie Lewis said later: "I was proud of him."

The Americans, faced with the trip's first showpiece spectacle being plunged into chaos, contacted Soderberg in London with the Presidential party. Williamson was joined in the room at the Europa by Hall. Stephens, who'd gone home to Ardnavally, was alerted when a caller phoned to say: "All hell's broken loose. Dougan knows." Lindsay drifted in and out of the staff meeting room at the Europa but was *persona non grata*. "I kept saying, 'I'm sorry. I feel really badly about it, but I feel I'm being loyal to the President. You better straighten this out because you've got a mercurial leader of Mackie and his employees dug in.' I believe my actions were completely justifiable," said Lindsay. A flurry of tense telephone negotiations began. Adams, who given Mackie's history, wasn't in any respect enamoured about going there in the first place, was roused from his sleep. He'd already supplied Soderberg with his own list of more preferable locations. Williamson, although unhappy with Lindsay's move, took the problem in his lawyerly stride and set about putting it right. "He deserves a medal," said a colleague. The trip fixer rang Dougan back. The senior Americans had mis-read – or chose to ignore – the depth of his opposition to Mackie being used as a backdrop to a political occasion and Williamson told him Adams wouldn't now be coming after all. Said one American embroiled in the crisis: "It doesn't matter whether Dougan would have shut the gates or not. At that point we weren't interested in seeing who'd the bigger pair. The question was, how do we make this work and what are the alternatives?"

Across at the Forte Crest Hotel, the board of Mackie had swung fully behind Dougan's uncompromising stand. Chairman Roger Looker, whose family was steeped in British military tradition, said: "There was a fair degree of frustration. We didn't want this to be a political event. It was meant to be an underlining of what can be achieved when Protestants and Catholics work together. The more political the event became the more that was going to be obscured."

Williamson, Soderberg, Stephens and Lake all spoke with the Sinn Féin President in the course of the morning. A leading White

House official said: "Adams was upset about us not being able to resolve this. Tony Lake got on the phone and talked to him and said, 'Look, we're dealing with it and we're going to try and work something out.'" Lake then told Soderberg to dig them out of the situation, of which the President had by now been made aware. A US source said: "There was a whole series of conference calls with the basic line being, it's a political imperative the President see Adams to reward him for the ceasefire. The Belfast end of the circuit was saying, 'it's a matter of balance; why don't we just do it at Queen's University, isn't that enough?' Nobody was disagreeing with each other. We were just trying to come up with the modality of how best to maintain what we considered was the golden mean." The most obvious solution, which Adams advocated, was a handshake when the President stopped on the Falls Road after leaving Mackie. It wasn't as straightforward as it sounded. The White House was wary. "We were initially reluctant to do it on the Falls Road because nobody would've believed it was natural," said a senior Clinton aide. "It would've looked too planned and it would've looked like a public rally for Adams. But the more we talked it through among ourselves, and the more Adams talked us through it, ultimately we were persuaded. The gist of all our dealings with Adams were the same from day one. He's very astute and pushes for the maximum he can get. We say no, he pushes and ultimately we come to a middle ground."

A draining three hours was spent salvaging the visit's curtain-raiser. It concluded with Hall being assigned to link up with Adams next morning for his appointment with the President, at a bakery on the most infamous street in Northern Ireland. "Adams had hit a home run and knew it," remarked one of the negotiators. But before Hall could finally retire for the night he had to bring his boss, Ambassador Crowe, up to date on developments. Crowe, formerly President Reagan's most senior military advisor as Chairman of the Joint Chiefs of Staff, was "used to hearing bad news in the night," as one of his staff put it. He was vehemently opposed to the Falls handshake but wasn't empowered to halt it. In the end he trusted Hall's and Stephens' judgement. "He didn't like the idea," said one American close to the negotiations. "He didn't have any opposition to the President meeting Adams during his time in Northern Ireland. The concern was that Adams on the Falls Road was too much."

After little or no rest, Lindsay, Dougan and Kelly arrived back at Mackie International by dawn where a fresh problem with a more obtuse Sinn Féin dimension was about to rear its head. The stage had been constructed to American specification by a Mackie employee, Robin Patton, and wired for state-of-the-art lighting and sound by military men from the White House Communications Agency. "These guys are the best in the world," said a member of the advance team. "Their job is to control the quality of lighting and sound for the President of the United States so he doesn't sound like he's at a high school prom." The standards they applied were mind-boggling. "We light Clinton from entrance across the stage to exit so it's just one constant. It's uniform light and everything is shadowless," explained an American. The power of the bulbs is fixed to capture Clinton at his best, blanching out his ruddy complexion in front of the cameras. (Mrs Clinton has a weaker light setting, but when both are on stage together the light is set to the President's level.) Clinton also likes to be photographed from his left and the media are usually marshalled accordingly.

Three identical slogans, capturing what the President's team felt was the spirit of the event, were fixed to the blue set so that each lens trained on Clinton could pick up the message in the background. The US planners, together with Mackie, had agreed upon "Northern Ireland Welcomes President Clinton. Peace." However a White House communications staffer, Joshua King, decreed it too bland and unimaginative when he turned up to monitor progress late on the Wednesday. "That's nice," he said. "But it's something a nine-year-old could've thought of. How about 'Towards a Lasting Peace?'" No-one on the American side knew he'd inadvertently seized on an Adams book title and Sinn Féin slogan. Without conferring with the Mackie team the change was arranged. Next morning Patton pointed out the alteration to Kelly. "I looked up and said, 'Jesus, that's very familiar sounding.' Josh King felt the agreed slogan wasn't exciting enough. There was no malice aforethought in the new message. It was just a phrase locked in his subconscious but the Americans were determined it should stay up." Kelly complained to Lindsay who laughed at the irony of it all. Dougan learnt what had happened and went to the stage. "He came down guns blazing, ready to rip Lindsay's head off," said one of those present. "But he knew by the look on Jamie's face he wasn't trying to pull a fast one." Dougan again ranted down the phone to Williamson who, realising the potential for embarrassment, ordered they revert to the original phrase. The hammers were out as the first of the invited guests began arriving at the factory gates.

The manner in which the Americans dealt with the invitation list for the President's address reflected their deft handling of this political hot potato. Williamson sought advice from Kathy Stephens in the planning of the ticketing arrangements. Rather than send invitations to individuals, they gave out blocks of numbered and colour-coded tickets, not just to political parties but to groups as diverse as the Northern Ireland Tourist Board and the British Army. It was then up to the various organisations to decide which among their number got a ticket. Most allocations had a blend of gold, blue and red tickets, which translated into exactly how close a person sat to the Presidential podium, known bizarrely as the 'blue goose'. The number of tickets the political factions received reflected their electoral strength. The Ulster Unionist Party, for example, got 20, Sinn Féin 15 and the Progressive Unionist Party five. "That was our first attempt to address this very difficult problem," said a US planner. "One of our goals in using the ticket system we devised was the United States in effect wasn't going to pick who was in the audience. The idea was that these were the people of Belfast."

However, Nationalist community groups operating in the shadow of Mackie felt snubbed at not being invited. One of the organisations, the West Belfast Economic Forum, voiced its anger in a letter signed by its Director, Ruth Taillon. "I wish to express concern at the under-representation of the Nationalist community at Mackie. It could be very damaging if this community feels that it is being effectively excluded from this event." Stephens responded that 13 groups from the vicinity had been invited. Many Nationalists, while delighted Clinton was coming to west Belfast, were disappointed at the venue chosen. A nine-page letter from Sinn Féin to Soderberg on 22 November cited Mackie as having a long association with discrimination against Catholics.

The RUC was responsible for handling the arrival of a thousand-plus invited guests and press. Senior police officers in west Belfast had been involved in planning meetings at Mackie. As at the other locations, there was generally a good camaraderie between the RUC and Secret Service, despite a *faux pas* by a policeman who quipped to an American counterpart: "We've had the Queen here umpteen times and she's never been shot. You haven't a very good track record." One agent told Dougan: "The RUC is the smoothest operating police force I've ever worked with." A check on residents surrounding Mackie was conducted by the RUC the week of the visit and the factory grounds swept twice in the 24 hours before Clinton's arrival: once by the local force, once by the Secret Service. The route of the motorcade was also double-checked. Only a few select guests were allowed to bring their vehicles inside the Mackie compound, much to the annoyance of one disgruntled Mayor who had his official car turned away at the gates.

The guests began assembling three hours before Clinton's appearance. Each had to walk through an airport-style security arch which scanned for weapons and explosives. Dozens of these were deployed at Presidential events in the 48 hours Clinton was in Ireland. One RUC officer on duty at the gates of Mackie said: "The women's bra straps and workers' steel toe-capped boots were sending it haywire and when it triggered it meant the person had to be body searched." Before long the queue stretched several hundred yards and the Secret Service was told there would be difficulty getting people screened and inside in time. The RUC suggested doing away with the X-ray device and assigning additional officers to carry out the type of body searches that made the Americans fear lawsuits. The Secret Service reluctantly agreed. "It got so bad with 15 minutes to go, and there were still 150 people outside, that I was allowed to order body searches," added the senior officer. "It was done fairly quickly and efficiently and everybody was good humoured. We managed to achieve the impossible and get everybody in with minutes to spare."

At 10.36am the President's car, licence plate number 599 363, rumbled through the 'Protestant gate' of Mackie after the first stop of the day on the Shankill Road. Clinton's vehicle – a small Stars and Stripes fluttering on one front wing, a flag bearing the seal of office on the other – halted at a rear exit door to the factory shed. The President was ushered into an inner sanctum of specially-constructed holding rooms where he was presented to the MP for west Belfast, Joe Hendron of the SDLP, and his Ulster Unionist counterpart for north Belfast, Cecil Walker (part of Mackie's periphery strayed into his constituency). Clinton addressed both in first name terms. "You almost got the impression he'd known you all his life, he was so affable," remarked Walker later. The President said he was aware of their joint excursions to the US to drum up investment in their areas. Hendron, who'd sat beside Clinton for dessert at the Speaker's St Patrick's lunch in 1994, hid an anger he would only disclose in public 18 months later. He was seething that this greeting was happening out of view and felt, as always, he was playing second fiddle to the man he had ousted at the 1992 General Election. "I was the MP for the area and yet all *they* were worried about was Gerry Adams," he said. "Like everybody else at the time, everything was set up to keep Adams on board. I felt like pushing past the Secret Service and going and meeting Clinton at the door but that isn't in my nature."

Clinton then came face to face with the man who'd threatened to lock him out. Dougan was cordial. Earlier one of the American planners had sidled up to him and said: "You're some guy. We've been fighting with Washington to have the Adams handshake at Mackie stopped for three days." Dougan mentioned to Clinton that Mitchell's mother had woven clothes on a Mackie loom. "Yes, George was telling me," said Clinton as a flock of aides began grooming his hair, brushing down his jacket and straightening his tie. "It was amazing the detail they went into," said Dougan. "I remember saying to myself, 'I better go and look at myself in the mirror.'" He was with his wife Mary and his ten-year-old granddaughter Tiarna. Pulled from the stage and waiting in an ante-room to be presented to the President and First Lady were Lewis and two schoolchildren who were about to be beamed across the globe and steal the President's thunder.

Nine-year-old Catherine Hamill, a pupil at St John's Primary, a Catholic girls' school, and 11-year-old David Sterrett, who attended the Protestant Springfield Primary, had heart-rending tales of life growing up on the streets of Belfast. Lindsay had arranged for the children of the two schools nearest the factory to pen letters to Clinton two days earlier, mirroring an official competition run by the Belfast Consul's office for older pupils. The best from each school would be read for the President. The Mackie boss had no qualms about putting them on stage. Dougan had a great sense of community spirit and an affection for the schools, feeling it was almost Mackie's obligation to provide its pupils with jobs when they grew up. Children from both were in the audience at Mackie, the cries of their laughter a pitch higher than the chatter that percolated through the diverse gathering assembled for the President. "The thing that was so extraordinary about Patrick Dougan was, when I broached the subject of the children introducing the President he didn't even blink," recalled Lindsay. "He said, 'Yes', like that. That's a rare individual, a manager who didn't have tunnel vision and feel it was his right and his right alone to introduce the President at his factory." Dougan also had his own ideas on the event's format. He had managed to twist enough arms to win reluctant US approval for Northern Ireland Economy Minister Baroness Jean Denton to say a few words on stage ahead of Clinton. "They were determined there'd be no British influence," he said. The Americans were therefore relieved when she was struck down with flu. "It broke my heart not to be there," she said. The NIO rang Dougan and said they'd send Malcolm Moss, a colourless ministerial colleague, instead. The Mackie boss swore down the line at the official and hung up after the parting shot: "Moss is not going to be here. Do you understand?"

A Dougan hired hand, who was coincidentally against the children's writing idea, called at the schools on the Wednesday and collected the bundles of letters mixed with crayon drawings from the younger kids. An *ad hoc* gathering of eight Americans waded into them. It was an emotional experience. "We were reading them and they were tearing us apart," Lindsay said. "Secret Service guys were reading them, tough military guys were reading them and they were crying. I read Catherine's letter and said, 'This is it.' I gave it to everybody, and nobody was able to read it without crying." Catherine's teacher, Sinead McGovern, had told her to write about her family. "I remembered what mummy had told me about my daddy and I just started writing about that," said Catherine. She was but a baby of six months when gunshots cruelly invaded her world. Her father Patrick Hamill was aged 29 when two Loyalists burst into the family's home at Forfar Street in 1987 and gunned him down in front of Catherine, her mother Laura and elder sister Kelly. David's letter stood out for its stark simplicity. "David Sterrett's letter was all boy," said Lindsay. "There wasn't deep thinking. All he wanted to do was play soccer with his buddies and not get killed." The two schools were telephoned and told to present Catherine and David at Mackie early on Thursday morning. "I didn't see them until the day the President came," Lindsay stated. "David was as much of a boy as he was. The juxtaposition with Catherine was unbelievable. She had the eyes of an angel and looked like she came from central casting."

The youngsters were less tense than shop steward Lewis when they met Clinton backstage. "He was as nervous as a prostitute in church," remarked one American. David Sterrett was drinking Coca-Cola. He had phoned his grandmother and mother Georgina, who'd told him: "The President's only a man. Forget about everybody else and just read it for him." Lewis said: "The President immediately set about putting us completely at ease. He was asking the kids about their schools and me about what I did at Mackie. He seemed very interested." The President put the apples and oranges he'd bought on the Shankill on a table and said: "Help yourselves kids." Before being led out on the stage he asked Lewis if he were nervous. "No need to be, no need to be," said the President reassuringly.

Out front the late arrivals, the Clinton entourage, were shuffling towards their seats in the packed shed-cum-auditorium. Secret Service agents guarded the stage and whispered to their ties or cuffs. One with hands clasped in front of him was unable to conceal the large bulge under the right armpit of his jacket. There was a last minute flap over the prime seating arrangements. Sir Patrick Mayhew, first taken aback by running into Needham, was then peeved to discover Dougan had secured the ex-minister a better seat than his, bang plum centre of the front row, one along from Mrs Clinton. Needham went across and chatted to Commerce Secretary Brown. "A wonderful, charismatic, interesting man," he enthused. To the First Lady's left was the only woman apprentice at Mackie, Theresa McCullagh, a 21-year-old from Draperstown, County Tyrone. Five minutes earlier, Lindsay had unexpectedly ushered her to the front from three rows back. She recalled: "Mrs Clinton said, 'I believe you're the only girl on the shop-floor.' We talked for three or four minutes before the President came out about what it was like at Mackie. She was very friendly, very talkative, very interested in what I did. I said to her, 'I'm a bit embarrassed that I have to wear a blue boiler suit and bright thermal socks.'" Said one of the American entourage: "Mrs Clinton's ego was subordinate to what she knew was important and her being in the audience was just as important as the President being up on stage.

She sat down with the apprentice and was comfortable, charming and affable. Now, someone like Mrs Reagan would've wanted up on stage as the belle of the ball." Less content than Mayhew at the seating arrangements was the pinstripe-suited board of Mackie who'd breezed in and claimed seats at the front, only to be uprooted by Lindsay and replaced by workers in blue overalls, as per arrangement. "That's when I really appreciated Jamie," said Lewis. "He insisted this whole event was for the workers, that the President had purposely expressed he wanted to visit a workplace. I enjoyed the look on the board's faces when they got thrown off their seats." Just before his grand entrance, Clinton ran one of his car-ride speech alterations past Jim Lyons. "It was the reference to the Arkansas Governor who'd fought in the Civil War. It was a powerful image to the President and his question to me was, 'Is this so obscure nobody's going to really understand it?' I said, 'Absolutely not. Remember people in this society are among the most literate on the face of the planet. They'll know exactly what you're talking about.'"

"Ladies and gentlemen. The President of the United States accompanied by Patrick Dougan," an announcer boomed over a tannoy as the audience rose to clap Clinton on stage. He momentarily placed a hand of comfort on the shoulder of little Catherine Hamill, then waved and gave a thumbs up in the direction of a group of young Mackie apprentices perched on top of a huge machine to his right, under a banner proclaiming: "Peace. Jobs. Opportunity For All." He waved towards the school-kids and Mrs Clinton turned to Mary Dougan and said: "I'm glad to see the children here." Having memorised her briefing notes, the First Lady had sat down and immediately asked how her daughter was in South Africa. As the applause lingered, the President spun to his left and pointed out to Dougan the group of Congressmen who'd accompanied him on his trip. "I'd a pretty good view of him as he came on stage," said Republican Congressman Peter King from New York. "I saw a little apprehension. Not the apprehension of someone who's afraid he's going to be among enemies, but the apprehension of someone thinking maybe it's not going to be as good as I thought it was going to be. When he walked onto the stage in Derry he'd much more of a bounce in his step." Clinton even managed to work in a relaxed salute during the one-minute, whistle-punctured ovation and mouthed "thank you" on at least six occasions.

Dougan searched both inside breast pockets of his jacket before laying hands on his speech and moving to the podium, a mightily relieved man. He'd been up at four o'clock rehearsing his lines in front of the family dog. Clinton sat down beside Catherine Hamill and put his arm around her as Dougan began: "For people who know me in Northern Ireland I should say for my next trick." The President began flicking through his speech as Dougan introduced his "co-worker" Ronnie Lewis, seated to the right of the podium alongside young David Sterrett. With the podium a fixed height for the six-foot-plus Clinton, the diminutive shop steward had to stand on a step to get his head above the microphones.

Lewis had been asked to welcome Clinton on behalf of the workforce a week earlier. The night before the visit he'd turned to Lindsay for help with his speech. "What way will I introduce him? Do I say, 'Good morning, Mr President?' The American replied: 'No. Say, "Good morning, Mr President and Mrs Clinton." Now, that's all I'm helping you with.'" Lewis' anxiety hadn't been allayed when he went home, sweated over his speech and read the finished product to his family. "Daddy, that sounds crap," his daughter told him. A fitful night's sleep later, he was so preoccupied by it that when he arrived at Mackie that morning he banged his forehead by walking into a glass door. "I was seeing stars an hour before going on stage. Somebody had to tell me, stop rubbing the bump on you're head, you're making it worse. Everything was going wrong. We got training in the unions about how to do speeches but they never prepared you for something like this." Lewis mounted the step behind the podium gingerly – he'd almost knocked over a glass of water set on its ledge during a dummy run – and adjusted his reading glasses before starting. "This is truly a great occasion for our company, west Belfast and Northern Ireland in general," he said as Clinton scribbled notes on his address. "Both Mackie and Northern Ireland have faced some very tough times over the past 25 years and now both we, and I'm glad to say Northern Ireland, are on the up and up," added Lewis. As the applause rang out at the end of his address the President was one of the first on his feet and gave the shop-steward a congratulatory handshake. "Great speech, Ronnie. Thank you," he said.

Dougan was next and he began by paying tribute to a recently deceased lifelong friend, Paddy Duffy. "I would have dearly loved him to be here today," said the Mackie boss. His address, complete with stumble here and there at the outset, pointed to the recent success and stability of the company, announcing agreement in principle to create two hundred new jobs. (When the expansion was formally announced the following August it brought 94 jobs.) He also included a plug for the University of Ulster's Springvale project. At the front Ewart smiled approvingly for he'd suggested it. "We are engineers, not politicians, but we have the right to expect the decision makers and leaders in all our communities to learn from the examples which we set while we go to work here in Mackie," Dougan concluded. Clinton grinned and nodded in agreement. Dougan recalled: "I was thinking how far I'd come. From being a north Antrim orphan to standing next to the President of the United States. I felt extremely proud of that achievement." Speech over, the Mackie's supremo then introduced the two young stars-in-waiting, stooping to pull across a box for them to stand on behind the podium.

Catherine Hamill and David Sterrett, who was a head taller, peered from over and through the microphones to read edited extracts from their letters, which held the President transfixed and the audience spellbound. "My name is David Sterrett," began the elder of the two, both dressed in their school uniforms. Behind them, Clinton leaned forward in his seat to listen even more attentively. Without lifting his head the boy went on: "I live in a mixed area with both Catholics and Protestants. We play football and races together. I want to thank you for coming to Northern Ireland to help the peace process. I think that peace is great because there is no shooting or bombing. It means I can play in the park without worrying about getting shot." His mother, watching on television at home nearby, cried. Then Catherine, blond hair tied with a yellow ribbon, strained her neck nearer the microphones and began the 28-second soundbite which would be replayed on news broadcasts in Ireland and the US for the rest of the day. "My name is Catherine Hamill. I live in Belfast. I love where I live. My first daddy died in the Troubles. It was the saddest day of my life. I still think of him. Now it is nice and peaceful. I like having peace and quiet for a change instead of people shooting and killing. My Christmas wish is that peace and love will last in Ireland forever." Laura Hamill sat in the audience clenching the hand of Catherine's teacher. "I kept saying to Miss McGovern, 'I can't believe that's our Catherine up there.' I was so proud. It was overwhelming." Lindsay later apologised to her for not having made the box Catherine was standing on bigger so she was more visible. He had edited both letters to the President. Catherine's actually began: "My mummy is only a housewife. Is your wife a housewife?" As the applause erupted, the two children raised linked hands and uttered the first few words of a sentence of introduction to the President. But the clapping grew louder. Catherine pulled down David's hand, tucked her hair behind her ears and waited for the acclaim to die down before continuing: "And now, ladies and gentlemen, we'd like to introduce the President of the United States." The two then spun around, leapt from their perch and returned to their seats. Ambassador Sir John Kerr remarked: "It was a wonderful piece of theatre but Clinton would have a text to match the occasion." Clinton put his right arm around Catherine, gently squeezed her shoulder and pressed his cheek against her head. They shared a bond. Both had lost fathers they never knew. Clinton aide Susan Brophy, watching with the Congressional delegation, said: "He was clearly touched by the children. He likes kids, likes talking to them, hearing their stories. The little girl was just incredible." The President rose and shook David's hand before applauding both children as he stood with his back to the audience. Clinton later informed the authors: "In part I was moved by their personal histories, but more so by their words. Those children and the young people of Northern Ireland, they represented the best argument for the peace process that I know." Backstage the President's closest friend, Bruce Lindsey, was in tears. "There wasn't a dry eye in the house," said Jamie Lindsay. "The only thing louder than an Irishman's laugh is a little girl's cry for peace and that to me was the loudest message that came out."

The audience got off their chairs as one as the President turned and took his place. "This is one of those occasions where I feel that all that needs to be said has already been said," he began as the guests settled back in their seats. "It is good to be among the people of Northern Ireland who have given so much to America and the world." Clinton read from hard copy, the more difficult local place names and surnames broken down in syllable form. He doesn't like using an autocue. He was so familiar with the text he looked out to the hushed audience as he delivered most of it, hands clasping either side of the podium. The spit and polish of the address, a *tour de force*, had been applied by Vinca Showalter, a member of the President's speech writing team. Its artistry was sublime, the craftsmanship no better exemplified than by the line: "In the land of the harp and fiddle, the fife and the lambeg drum, two proud traditions are coming together in the harmonies of peace." Never before had a political speech in Northern Ireland resonated with such eloquence. Its delivery too was on a par of its own. "John Major should hire whoever wrote it," remarked one member of the press. Mayhew listened in admiration. "All his speeches were remarkably well constructed," he said. "All of them I thought bore a big input from him personally and a very mature and accurate understanding of the nuances that needed to be made. He didn't put a foot wrong. I was enormously impressed." So was Mark Gearan, standing with Showalter behind the set. The two picked up Clinton's own additions. "I think he enhanced it, and Vinca would agree," Gearan said afterwards. Soderberg had fleshed out the message to Showalter in numerous brainstorming sessions in Washington. Stephens had also contributed. Clinton had gone through it on the flight from the United States, the night before in London, on the plane journey to Belfast and during the car ride from Aldergrove.

Clinton asked Congressional members, Republican and Democrat, to rise and take a bow before the audience. In a reference to the easing of the US budget crisis, which had permitted him to travel, and the bi-partisan support for his peace mission, the President said to laughter: "We've sort of got a truce of our own going on here today." A few weeks earlier, the trench combat had began encroaching on the Ireland trip. "Republicans in Congress weren't co-operating with regard to sending a delegation over," said Congressman King. Susan Brophy called him and he and fellow-Republican Jim Walsh put their names to a letter on 13 November, attempting to drum up support for the visit on the Hill. It wasn't that members were disinterested, but Speaker Newt Gingrich had minds locked on the domestic budget crisis. Federal Government had been shut down for a period and at one point it looked like Clinton would have to cancel the Ireland trip. "Your presence would add to what we hope will be a great show of strength for a tiny nation which very much appreciates the help Congress has provided so far," wrote King and Walsh. Old rivalries were buried for the trip. "There was a lot of partisanship going on in the US at the time that did not carry over into the visit," said Walsh. "It was a very closely-knit delegation once we were over. Quite honestly I wanted the Republican Party, my party, to be involved. Traditionally the Democratic Party has taken the lead in Irish affairs and I thought it was about time our party, especially as we were now the majority, played a role."

Clinton waved a finger and shook a closed fist to emphasise his key messages during the speech. He complimented those who'd hauled Northern Ireland to its new dawn. But missing from the roll-call of Anglo-Irish political figures was DUP leader Ian Paisley. His exclusion was noticeable. "He wasn't included because we didn't think he'd taken risks for peace," said an American source. Paisley, watching the speech on television as he did some constituency work in his Ravenhill Road offices across town, later tried to put a brave face on the calculated snub. "I was very glad he didn't mention me. I compliment myself that I wasn't mentioned among a gallery of rogues," he said. However the blow smarted and Paisley had to be coaxed out of reciprocating the snub at Queen's University that evening.

It was one of the DUP chief's former cohorts who failed to unsettle Clinton with two muted interjections towards the tail end of the President's address. When Clinton said that those who renounced violence were entitled to be full participants in the democratic process, Cedric Wilson's subdued cry of "never" was lost in applause. And when the President rammed home the point and in the next instant said that those who showed courage to break with the past were entitled to their stake in the future, Wilson let out another slightly muffled "never." The eyes of Secret Service agents scoured the crowd and VIPs at the front turned around to look for the culprit. Remarked Congressman Walsh: "It was just a solitary voice but it showed how difficult it was to put those feelings to rest." Wilson, attending with a son and daughter and who had clapped the President on stage, afterwards explained: "It was a natural reaction that just came out of me." By Wilson's standards as a self-styled, placard-waving serial protester it was his most abject cameo. Wilson, who ran a nursing home along with his wife, had coined the phrase 'Ulster Says No' in opposition to the Anglo-Irish Agreement and had once been fined for participation in an illegal protest march against it. When news photographers spotted him entering Mackie they asked him what he was up to. "It was the last thing on my mind to do," he recalled. "I have no regrets but I took a deep breath before doing it. It was an occasion of great magnitude. I wanted to lodge my protest but not disrupt proceedings. That wouldn't have been appropriate."

An inquiry was instigated to discover how he had obtained three gold-coloured tickets. His presence showed the perils of the American's approach to the distribution of invitations. The Lord Mayor of Belfast, Eric Smyth, who eight hours hence would welcome Clinton to the City Hall, was one of the few who condoned Wilson's stunt. "I wish I'd had the guts to do it," Smyth said on congratulating him. Wilson, by his own admission a Jekyll and Hyde character, had scuppered his business organisation's chance to meet the White House press corps at the Europa that night. At the end of Clinton's speech their overseer, Sam Myers, dressed down the offender: "Mr Wilson, you've blown it. You'll not be speaking to anybody from the corps. No-one challenges the President like that, not even members of Congress."

The outbursts failed to take the shine off Clinton's speech. He caught the second interruption, for immediately afterwards, when he said that leaders must make compromises and "risk the backlash," he smiled ironically and gestured towards the direction of the heckler, without departing from the script. The President's 24-minute address, laced with ten bursts of applause, pointed to Northern Ireland's bright future as opposed to its dark past. "I believe you can summon the strength to keep moving forward," he said. "After all, you have come so far already. You have braved so many dangers, you have endured so many sacrifices. Surely there can be no turning back. But peace must be waged with a warrior's resolve – bravely, proudly and relentlessly – secure in the knowledge of the single greatest difference between war and peace: in peace everybody can win." There was an international dimension to it, with Clinton drawing parallels to sister struggles for political settlements in South Africa, the Middle East, Haiti and Bosnia. "We will stand with those who take risks for peace in Northern Ireland and around the world," he said. Clinton also said the region could learn from America's strength from cultural diversity.

The address drew a one-minute standing ovation which would have stretched longer had the President not come off the stage and down into the audience. Before doing so he embraced David Sterrett and Catherine Hamill and shook hands with Dougan and Lewis. The Mackie chief said: "Thank you for coming. I appreciate it. I wish you well." It was no accident that the first person the President greeted in the front row was a machinist in overalls. The gentle strains of a harp began to fill the hall. Dougan was at the President's side, Lindsay up ahead telling people not to ask for autographs. Mayhew had wanted to join in, but the Americans prevented him. "It wasn't my decision but I was happy with it," said Dougan. "Brady Williamson said, 'No, this is a day for the President of the United States and Mackie.' No-one else was to have any part of the show." When Clinton reached Needham at the rope, the former NIO man light-heartedly remarked: "I thought you made a better speech than Mr Dougan." The President replied: "Yes, well I am a professional at it." Needham thought the event remarkable: "It was one of the greatest days of my life. The whole thing was so unbelievably professional. Could you imagine the Northern Ireland Office doing anything like that?" People three rows back surged forward to touch Clinton as he inched up the line. Someone yelled out: "Four more years."

Clinton was almost buried under an avalanche of schoolchildren who streamed down the tiered seating. They almost knocked their teacher off her feet in a heady rush of exuberance. Dougan worried someone would be hurt in the crush. "Don't push," Clinton cried out. It's not every day the planet's most powerful man is ignored by so many.

Finally retreating behind the scenes, the President was re-united with the two children who had moved him on stage. The lights had made them both hot and restless. He took David Sterrett's letter and wrote on it: "David, this is a very fine statement. Keep speaking out, Bill Clinton." Catherine Hamill, aided by Lindsay, wriggled her way through the entourage to Clinton. He hugged and kissed her. The President admired a golden harp pin which her mother had attached to her jersey for good luck. Within a week they'd be sharing the limelight again, this time at a Christmas tree-lighting ceremony in the White House. The *Daily Mirror* paid to fly out the five-member family. (The Sterretts went later but their trip didn't capture the same media attention.) Standing in the Oval Office, Catherine wore a T-shirt with a picture of her and Clinton on it and the President autographed an issue of the *Irish Times* with their photo splashed across the front page. "To Catherine. I was so glad to be with you on this day. You did a fine job. Bill Clinton." Baby Brendan slept through it all. Clinton had wanted to see Catherine's original letter, but her stepfather Manuel had lost it in the taxi-cab journey. Escorted by Lindsay, the west Belfast youngster had the run of the White House for five hours. "She hung over the desk in the Oval Office like it was the kitchen table," said her mother Laura. "Don't worry," said a Clinton assistant. "It's been a long time since kids relaxed in this room." Her visit made front page news. "Billy and the Kid" screamed the headline in a New York tabloid. Catherine and the President began exchanging letters. After she sent him a St Patrick's Day card in 1996, he wrote back: "In the last few months you have touched many lives throughout the world and we are very grateful for your friendship. While I realise the past month has been very difficult [the IRA ceasefire had collapsed] please know we will continue to do all that we can for a lasting peace in your land. We are keeping you and your family in our thoughts and prayers. God Bless."

Backstage at Mackie, the President posed for pictures while guests marvelled at his speech. "The thing that gave me most satisfaction is that I feel the speech influenced the whole trip," Dougan later said. "I didn't know a speech could have so much drawing power but I feel people went to see him later at City Hall because they'd listened to what he said. All our guys went down with their families." John McGuckian, chairman of the Industrial Development Board, a British Government-funded jobs promotion agency, was among those who got a photograph with Clinton. "The visit transformed during its being," he recalled. "Mackie had an impact. When he arrived people were cynical, but then there was an understanding he wasn't here to take sides or instruct anybody. I don't think there was a day in the history of Northern Ireland when everybody was at one to the extent they were then."

Clinton made time for more workers unable to get into the main body of the hall before leaving. One pressed a religious tract into his hand and the President put it in his pocket. He then left the event which almost never was, praying that the Adams meeting on the Falls would not be the trip's undoing.

VI

A cavalry charge to the Wild West

Our hope was that the visit would kick start a process ready to collapse. What President Clinton got was a warm embrace from people saying, 'You are the cavalry.' It was probably the first popular event that could bring together the hopes and expectations that had been opened up by the cessation of the previous August.

Gerry Adams, President, Sinn Féin

Gerry Adams got out his pocket transistor radio and offered one of its two earpieces to his American handler for the morning, Blair Hall. The President of Sinn Féin took the other as they listened in silence to a live broadcast of Clinton's keynote speech at Mackie. The US diplomat glanced at Adams out of the corner of an eye as the President told an audience half a mile away: "You must say to those who still would use violence for political objectives, you are the past, your day is over." Typically, Adams displayed no emotion. "By and large it was a balanced view of the situation," he later said of the address. "If I'd been writing the speech it may've been a different speech. It wasn't an Irish Republican speech."

Adams listened for allusions to a detailed text which Sinn Féin had sent to Soderberg eight days earlier. The party felt "the gravity of the current situation" warranted the President focusing on the need for speedy movement towards unconditional all-party peace talks. "Both [British and Irish] Governments have explicitly set inclusive and comprehensive negotiations as their goal but these have not yet begun," the Sinn Féin draft stated. "That failure is frustrating and threatens to dissipate the momentum towards a lasting peace." There was no hint of a crisis in anything Clinton said. Sinn Féin's correspondence to Clinton's aide had identified the need to gee-up London as central to the trip's purpose, from its perspective. "We look forward to it and believe it can play an important role in positively influencing a peace process where potential for forward movement has all but dissipated as a result of the British Government's bad faith engagement."

Adams, who'd met Hall in a ground-floor coffee shop at an Irish language centre, didn't appear to be showing the strains of a night's heavy negotiating for the meeting with the President. "Gerry Adams always looks tired because he's always burning the midnight oil," said his press officer, Richard McAuley, who was present along with one of Adams' bodyguards. Adams had used Caife Glas in Culturlann MacAdam O'Fiaich at 216 Falls Road for previous American encounters. Soderberg, George Mitchell and countless Congressmen had all passed through its doors. Said McAuley: "We were the only four people there that morning and we sat and had a yarn with Blair for a while. He'd a link with the Secret Service and would occasionally speak up his sleeve as the President's progress was monitored." Sitting round a vinyl-covered table, they enjoyed mugs of coffee and Danish pastries as they patiently waited for a signal which would usher them to the designated spot on the Falls Road where Clinton would go walkabout.

In an ideal world Sinn Féin would have had the President come to Adams rather than the other way around. It suggested that Clinton call at the Irish language complex or two other locations. The request formed part of the wish-list sent to Soderberg along with the speech proposals on 22 November. Its letter to the National Security Council staffer declared: "We are proposing that the President meets Gerry Adams at a reception hosted by community organisations in one of the following venues on the morning of Thursday, 30 November – Conway Enterprise Centre, Conway Mill; An Culturlann Cultural Centre, Falls Road; Clonard Hall, Clonard Street. All proposed venues are a maximum five minutes' drive from Mackie."

From the outset, however, the Americans had privately ruled out taking the President to any venue where Adams could be a *de facto* host. An internal memorandum spelt out their concerns: "It is important people events do not get hijacked. This should be fairly easy provided [the] Belfast [planning team] is kept informed. We should make sure to stay on top of any planning of these type of events so they do not become a Trojan horse for any group to sneak their agenda into ours."

Halting on the Falls Road was always the US option. "We wanted to put the President on the ground," said a senior trip planner. "The question was, where did he stop? If he went too far down the Falls Road it would have been too near the Sinn Féin press centre and the mural of [dead IRA hunger striker] Bobby Sands. So really, the shops right at the corner of Springfield Road were the only place for a stop on the route after leaving Mackie." Adams hadn't figured in the Falls equation at that point. As President Clinton told the authors: "The purpose of stopping in the Falls Road was to meet people from one of the Catholic neighbourhoods most affected by the conflict, just as I had stopped in the Protestant neighbourhood of Shankill."

The British had no steadfast objections to a Falls walkabout, given that it was to be balanced against the earlier one on the Shankill Road, but neither event would have featured in its favoured itinerary. "We saw it as inevitable," a Government official claimed. "When the Americans told us there were to be unscheduled stops we had two questions. One was, were the RUC content? The other was, was it to be Falls as well as Shankill? When they said yes to both we'd no problems."

The Sinn Féin President, who'd been tepid on meeting Clinton at Mackie in the first place, was more than satisfied that his sought-after handshake was to occur in well-known surroundings. "A lot of people gave me credit, wrongly, for being the man who brought the President to the Falls Road," said Adams. "The Americans could have chosen anywhere but they choose the area where I had grown up. It's where I've lived, it's where I've written about and it's a place with which I'm extremely familiar. Had they done the meeting up at Andersonstown or somewhere else it would have had the same effect, but it happened in a place where I had an affinity with."

Unaware of the full extent of American attempts to bring Adams to the Mackie plant, the British had surmised he would be on the Falls Road when Clinton stopped. "We thought that was blindingly obvious and it didn't cause us the slightest anxiety," a source contended. "Remember, Paddy Mayhew had already shaken hands with Adams. It wasn't an issue." True, London wanted an encounter used to embed Adams further in the democratic process, but the British would have much rather seen Clinton and the Sinn Féin chief meet solely at the Queen's University reception for political leaders – and ideally shielded from the glare of the media. Said Northern Ireland Secretary Sir Patrick Mayhew: "I was not in the business of boosting Mr Adams' stature and standing but it was a matter for the President. I was certainly not going to regard this as a matter of such moment [that] we ought to say, if that's what you're going to do you're not going to come." In Washington, British Ambassador Sir John Kerr had lobbied against the idea of meeting Adams separately from other leaders at Queen's. "We wanted Adams in no way singled out for special treatment," he recalled. "There were people worried he would somehow be presented as the hero of the hour."

Blair Hall and the Sinn Féin President left An Culturlann as Clinton was finishing his speech at Mackie. They walked down towards the Springfield Road junction with the Falls, where large crowds had earlier gathered to watch the President on his journey to the factory. The footpaths were now thronged, the crowds anticipating that he'd get out of his car on the way back. Adams' presence firmed up that view.

As Adams and Hall neared the rendezvous point at McErlean's bakery, a Secret Service agent emerged from the crowd and told them the President was running late. They opted to kill time by strolling in the convent grounds at St Dominic's School, a place where local couples sometimes had their wedding photographs taken. Said McAuley: "Just the three of us went for a walk. We were talking about anything and everything. Blair Hall and us had a good working relationship. He's the sort of guy that if he's given a job to do and that job is engaging in small talk then he will engage in a small talk. If the job is hard negotiation then he'll be a hard negotiator. But that morning it was small talk. It was quite pleasant and very relaxed." McAuley hid in his pocket a camera that would bring the first shot of Clinton with Adams to the world.

The tranquil walk gave Adams further time to reflect on what would be the most public and powerful endorsement of his and his party's role in the peace process. "It was important for morale in the sense of self-pride for the Republican section of our people," recalled the Sinn Féin President later. "The peace process at that time had been stretched like a piece of elastic and was coming more and more to snapping point. Our hope was that the visit would have kick-started a process ready to collapse at any point." Since they were in an area of the city once dubbed the wild west, McAuley mused: "Clinton was the seventh cavalry coming over the hill to the rescue. The more successful the visit the more likely the peace process would actually be pushed through to a proper conclusion."

As Adams strolled in St Dominic's, others couldn't help but reflect on his personal journey. Denied an American visa by Clinton in 1993 because of his association with terrorism, he was about to be honoured as a peacemaker two years later by the President. "He made very rapid progress with the White House in a way that I know Sinn Féin were themselves surprised," confessed Niall O'Dowd. The party owed Clinton a great debt of gratitude – his earlier actions had already conferred respectability upon it in the eyes of the international community. An American President, like no other, could bring them in from the cold and ensure the parity of esteem it sought.

The US had become crucial to Sinn Féin's strategy at the turn the decade. It was a place to win friends who could carry influence in the political mainstream. "We identified a group of people that could not be tainted with the IRA and put them to work," said party strategist Mitchel McLaughlin. "The Irish-American lobby that emerged during President Clinton's campaign didn't emerge in a vacuum. It emerged because people in Ireland decided this was the moment." Added Adams: "While recognising the good work done by NORAID and other groups in the US, we saw the need to move the whole issue of Ireland more into the mainstream. Part of that was Sinn Féin opening an office in Washington as part of our efforts in that new climate and to build upon a diplomatic outreach." Mairead Keane, who ran the Washington office, was ideally placed to testify to Sinn Féin's rise. "Before the peace process you had links with Irish-American people who felt strongly about the issue. But once the peace process came and brought hope for a settlement, a wider body became involved and we were able to tap into its good-will."

With the time for Clinton's arrival on the Falls fast approaching, a White House official interrupted Adams' walk to suggest he take a car round to the back of the bakery. Said an American official: "Our concern was that with Adams walking through these crowds and with the RUC and all this excitement something could happen. But Adams said, 'Look, there's no way I'm going in a back entrance to meet the President. I know this crowd. It'll be fine.' So he just ended up walking through it. It was like Moses parting the Red Sea." The crowds clapped, whistled and cheered his entrance. "Here's our President," they shouted. Adams, Hall and McAuley took seats inside the bakery, where several women were enjoying a morning tea-break. The Sinn Féin leader, in a dark suit, collar and tie, asked staff to prepare a parcel of soda bread to give to the President.

Outside the RUC was engaged in one of its most sensitive policing operations ever, attempting to contain an ever-swelling crowd in arguably its most hostile area of operation, ceasefire or no ceasefire. "We were worried about this potential for conflict between the police and the crowd," said one of the Americans in attendance. "But there wasn't any kind of raw antagonism. It was more like some sporting event. Everything was very good natured." To help ease tension, many officers were in dress coats which conveniently concealed personal weapons. No rifles were carried by officers on duty, 150 of whom were deployed at what the force termed the 'big x' (the junction of the Falls and the Springfield). Officers from D division, who had dealt with crowd control during the Shankill stop, were drafted across to the Falls. "As well as bringing in more officers I had to relocate crash barriers," said an RUC commander. "It became evident a stop was imminent and crowds of eight hundred to a thousand people were gathering. We didn't feel under any threat and the absence of catcalls and verbal abuse surprised me. They were co-operative and kept at bay by me saying if they kept behind the barriers they'd get a clear view of the President. Any disruption and the stop wouldn't take place. The Adams meet had no part in my agenda. My job was crowd control." The situation was more intriguing to some in the Presidential party than the approaching Adams handshake. Jim Lyons said: "I knew what was going to take place, but frankly I was more interested in the what the police-crowd dynamic was."

Things threatened to turn nasty as the Clinton motorcade crawled past the high-fenced surrounding of Springfield Road RUC base just before noon and into view, the Secret Service agents jogging alongside the President's car adding to the dramatic effect. "The limo was meant to stop right on the yellow grid box-marking on the road but instead it turned left and parked right outside the bakery," said a senior police officer. With the prospect of their view of Clinton being impaired, many spectators started vaulting crash barriers and rushing closer. Chaos threatened. "The crowd thought they were being obstructed and began jumping the barriers," added the police commander. "It was over-exuberance but we had prepared for them closing in. It was more push and shove than fists flying." Officers grabbed a firm hold of each other's belts to form a human chain around the President. Some Americans panicked at the prospect of newsreel footage of Clinton in the middle of an ugly mêlée. As the crowd surged at police lines a Secret Service agent told an RUC officer: "Think CNN." Lyons observed: "Here was the RUC charged with keeping back Catholic crowds that surged forward. At several points the crowd sort of penetrated the RUC and got very close to the motorcade. There were some Americans around me asking, 'why aren't the RUC doing more?' But I knew myself they weren't doing more because they didn't want to provoke difficulty. I thought it was a remarkable job by the RUC, just a remarkable job."

Adams, hands clasped in front on him, was standing in the bakery doorway as Clinton's car pulled up. Brady Williamson tapped him on the elbow in a signal for the Sinn Féin leader to step forward and welcome the President as the limousine door swung open. Out got Clinton in a trench coat few realised was bullet-proof. (Mrs Clinton had gone her own way to south Belfast from Mackie.) The two Presidents smiled as they shook hands. Recalled Adams: "That it happened on the Falls Road was good. This was a battle area, a place which had been the victim of deprivation and discrimination. If there were a lot of negotiations between the US and the British about where this event was going to happen, or whether it was going to happen at all, it turned out in a way that was more spontaneous and more human." It was hard to tell who looked happier as the pair dwelt on the handshake. "*Ceád míle fáilte*," said Adams, the traditional Irish greeting of a hundred thousand welcomes. Clinton told Adams he'd read his book, *The Street,* that morning. "Now I know where you get your inspiration from," remarked the President. (It would be two more years before a British Prime Minister would shake hands with Adams as President of Sinn Féin and then Tony Blair opted to do so behind closed doors at Castle Buildings in the Stormont estate.)

McAuley drew the instamatic camera from his pocket. He and a local photographer had dreamt up the contingency plan. "I thought everybody else would get the shot but it was always on my mind that things could go awry." Hall considered blocking the lens but didn't, and the Sinn Féin press aide snapped his exclusive. President Clinton's official photographer dashed around the corner too late, and locally-deployed newsmen couldn't get a clear shot in the confusion. Not unintentionally, members of the White House media corps were too far back in the cavalcade to act. Said McAuley: "The fact CNN or nobody got the picture was just one of those things. Two guys with video cameras were in the crowd. One got the handshake, the other didn't. For somebody to have planned for the press to have been cut off would've taken enormous planning and I don't think they would've had the ability to do it."

Indeed, Sinn Féin and the White House had discussed allowing the media to take its first pictures of Adams and Clinton beforehand. (Photographs which were taken privately in Washington the previous St Patrick's Day haven't been released.) Washington didn't want saturation coverage however. Clinton spokesman Mike McCurry pointed out: "We did it as impromptu as the White House ever does anything. When the White House wants to stage a photograph we can make sure that every lens in the world gets it. This one wasn't done in that fashion so it would not be the dominant picture of the trip. We did not want it to be the dominant picture of the trip but it served a very important purpose. I think it helped Adams internally within Sinn Féin. I think he was out on a limb himself and I think having Clinton stop in his neighbourhood and shake hands with him was a big deal in many ways."

Next day the picture was splashed across the front page of the *New York Times* and countless other newspapers, provoking contrasting reactions in Washington. "There was certainly no delight around here that Adams had his moment with the President on the front page of the *New York Times*," said a high-ranking diplomat at the British Embassy. "It was a bit of a stunt. The thing that really narked me was, why did they to choose that image when there were so many others, like the Christmas tree lights?" At the Sinn Féin office, Keane was delighted. "It was absolutely brilliant," she said. "It was what people in Irish-America had wanted to see. Here was President Clinton's commitment to the peace process encapsulated in one picture."

If Clinton needed moral support for his actions, he needn't have looked further than the group of Congressional representatives travelling in tow. "High noon on the Falls has to be Gerry's finest hour," said Congressman Peter King of New York. "To meet the President right in the heart of Irish Republicanism, on his own turf, has to be his and Irish Republicanism's greatest achievement." King, who had witnessed their first handshake at the Speaker's lunch in Washington, had been trapped in the crowds as he got off the Congressional bus and missed the Falls encounter. "I'd felt for twenty-five years the greatest challenge Irish Republicanism had was to break loose from its own narrow environs and get the rest of the world on its side. It had to generate support and to generate support in the United States, which is supposed to be Britain's closest ally, is a great achievement and to be able to manifest that achievement on the Falls Road showed how far the Irish Republican movement had come." Added Senator Chris Dodd: "I don't know what the President's own thinking might have been but my assumption was that he wanted to reinforce the notion that Gerry Adams deserved great credit for having taken the step he did. At that point the ceasefire was very much in place and I think to reward those who had chosen that route was critically important. It was a very important moment to send a message to those within Adams' ranks who may've questioned whether or not he'd made the right stand."

There was a foreseen chorus of condemnation from Unionists over the handshake, but it didn't derail the President's visit. What upset a good many most was the setting and the stage-managed feel to it all. Clinton himself though had no qualms about meeting Adams on the Falls or indeed later at Queen's. "Meeting Mr Adams was an appropriate part of the visit," he told the authors. The British Government thought the Falls handshake could be turned to its advantage. "We actually saw there being merit in it," one official commented afterwards. "We knew, whether we liked it or not, the President was going to meet Adams. When we reflected on it for any length of time we saw it as being a step forward, because it was going to make it harder for Sinn Féin to back away from the peace process."

Adams loitered on the footpath as President Clinton entered the small bakery. "He just seemed to take over the whole place when he came in," said Liz Hartley, who worked at the nearby Irish language school, Meanscoil Fearste. "You couldn't see anything else only him. He just seemed to be so big he filled the place." Clinton's bulk had been increased by his protective raincoat. Hartley and her 14-year-old daughter Alison presented him with an Irish-language plaque in front of a bun counter, as uniformed shop assistants giggled nervously behind it. "There were about a dozen women and a couple of children inside. He shook hands with them and spoke to them all individually. I don't think I was ever as excited about anything else in my life. Alison wasn't a bit enthusiastic. I suppose when you're fourteen you don't give a damn but it was the best day of my life," said Liz Hartley. Clinton listened closely as the Hartleys told him they were there representing Irish schools. (Adams was originally going to present the plaque but on reflection felt it was better coming from them.)

Back on the street Mayhew and Kerr found themselves the focus of attention for all the right reasons. Far from being cold-shouldered they were welcomed. Clinton's arrival, it seemed, had temporarily caused enmity to be cast aside. "We went on across the crossroads as the President diverted to meet Mr Adams," remembered Mayhew. "I didn't particularly want to be present on that occasion so we went along the street. They'd have shaken hands with anybody. They even shook hands with me." Kerr was busy telling people, "I'm not an American, you know," such was his disbelief at their reaction. He later said: "I'm just a jaded old bureaucrat, but it got to me. It was quite dramatic to be on the Falls because in the previous five years I'd lived in Brussels, travelling around in a bullet-proof car with an armed guard because I was supposed to be on some sort of IRA hit list. So it was rather nice to be walking around these streets."

As Clinton re-appeared from the bakery, Adams was struck by the reception the President was receiving. "What President Clinton got was a warm embrace from people saying, 'you are the cavalry,'" he recalled. "It was probably the first popular event that could bring together the hopes and expectations that had been opened up by the cessation of the previous August." Clinton's interaction with the public impressed the Sinn Féin President. "President Clinton engages with a lot of people in a very good way," he observed. "The Secret Service were going bananas as he walked about talking to people." The President went into a chemist's shop next door to McErlean's. "When he arrived on the road we knocked on the window and called to the President," said shop assistant Joanne Shaw. "He waved back and actually went, 'I'll be over.' He was very friendly when he came in, not off-handish or anything. It was great that he'd made a point by coming to the Falls. It gave us all a little hope, showed he was really interested in doing something for peace."

Customer Evelyn Meredith planted a kiss on the President's cheek in the crush. "I just automatically put my hand around him and kissed him. I said, 'It's great that you came.' But the security men, they nearly died." It wasn't long before the Secret Service were back on top of things. As Clinton walked towards McDermott's Bar and was offered a pint of Guinness, an agent tipped it onto the street.

Still the crowds came as Clinton's motorcade moved off again, turning from the Falls onto the Grosvenor Road and past the Royal Victoria Hospital at a snail's pace. "There was a real buzz. It was a carnival atmosphere," remarked an RUC officer on duty. "People just kept spilling out of the Royal. I don't know who was left to look after the patients." Watching from a hospital window was Dr Ian Carson who had more interest than most in the progress of the visit, for the Royal was where Clinton would be brought in the event of a medical emergency.

As was the norm when Clinton travelled abroad, local medical facilities were double-checked and placed on standby. At the Royal a helicopter landing pad, operating theatre, intensive care bed and staff were reserved for the President. "I had to ensure that a full staff presence was available for that twelve to twenty-four hour period," said Carson, the Royal's Medical Director. "We were given a limited amount of information – his height, weight, blood group and something about his current medication or his current health. But very little. Only a sentence or two." The drill was as follows. In an emergency Clinton would be stabilised in situ by a team of critical care nurses travelling in a black van with the Presidential entourage. Once at the Royal, Clinton's personal physician, Dr Connie Moriano, who moves but a heartbeat from her charge, would have been consulted by RVH doctors performing any surgery. "Medical decisions that needed to be taken would have been taken by our team. His advisor would give advice," said Carson. "Afterwards he would have been cared for by White House nurses before he was fit to travel home. I told our staff the day started as soon as he arrived and ended whenever he flew out. It was quite obvious from an early stage it was a tension-free visit, which made the staff a little more relaxed."

As Clinton headed for east Belfast, Adams linked up with Niall O'Dowd and Bruce Morrison. "I think Gerry was relieved," said Morrison. "Gerry's life is a series of difficult political objectives to be achieved against all the odds and I suppose the handshake was no different." They walked to Springvale Enterprise Park where a lunch had been organised for US Commerce Secretary Ron Brown. (The venue would later be hit by a rocket following the collapse of the IRA ceasefire.) Adams greeted Brown like a long lost friend. "Ron and Chuck Meissner were in and out of this community more often than British ministers," Adams claimed. The Sinn Féin President felt he and Brown, a civil rights activist, were on the same wavelength. Recalled Adams: "One of the first times we met he said to me, 'Can you tell me what you want?' I said, 'I can tell you what I don't want, and that's to be asked to sit at the back of the bus.'" (Adams was referring to racial segregation that once prevailed in the American south.)

Following lunch, Adams, other senior Republicans, and the Irish-Americans had a pre-arranged meeting in the front parlour of a terraced house in Kashmir Road. In the middle of the euphoria engulfing Clinton's visit, the IRA administered a private dose of reality. The ceasefire was in danger of crumbling. The President had only borrowed it time. O'Dowd said: "In the midst of all the pageantry this was a very depressing meeting. I remember being very annoyed and quite deflated. I mean, this thing had more lives than a cat but I was definitely convinced we were in deep trouble." In truth it was nothing O'Dowd or Morrison hadn't heard before. Adams had cried crisis so many times in the months before the visit that he'd stopped issuing statements to that effect. "We decided we would stop doing that, which may have been the wrong thing, but we never stopped warning privately," said Adams afterwards. Mayhew and other British ministers knew the IRA was still targeting individuals and continuing to train members. "It wasn't the first discussion of that type," said Morrison of the clandestine talks. "We'd had it in July of 1995 and repeatedly. It was not the sort of bad news that was different. Gerry Adams' fundamental message was if something doesn't happen quickly that puts this foolish decommissioning thing aside and gets some activity that vindicates the ceasefire it's not going to last."

Still, many without Morrison's insight on the streets of Belfast and Derry on 30 November dared to believe there was no going back.

VII

Leader of the west goes east

I admit our strongest card was the requirement for him to have a balanced itinerary. I've no doubt it was this issue that required him to come to east Belfast.

Peter Robinson,
DUP deputy leader and MP for east Belfast

That Bill Clinton detoured to east Belfast was in large measure thanks to the coercion of a handful of individuals in the trip's planning team who took issue with the dummy itineraries produced in Washington. The British Government and the various facets of Unionism had clamoured for political impartiality as to where Clinton went and who he saw, but the voices that carried most clout were those from within. They grasped that east Belfast represented balance, the special ingredient that was to prove so crucial to the visit's success. Five or six weeks before the trip Clinton was poised to shun the most overwhelmingly Protestant of Northern Ireland's 18 electoral constituencies. It wasn't wilful: the constraints on the President's time meant many propositions had to give way. While the First Lady or even the US Congressional delegation could have been sent into east Belfast as a sop, Washington about-turned in the face of the convincing argument that a Clinton stop-off on the Shankill Road wouldn't on its own be sufficient to balance the gesture to Nationalism in Derry and west Belfast.

The shift in White House thinking was gradual through the month between the site survey and the pre-advance visit and owed much to Belfast-based Kathy Stephens and her *de facto* Washington emissary on the issue, Martha Pope. "I think people like Martha and Kathy were very, very thoughtful in educating all of us on the importance of balance," said a highly-placed source within the White House. Pope, well schooled in Northern Ireland politics as chief organiser of the Washington Investment Conference and as Senator George Mitchell's lieutenant, came to comprehend that Protestants required more from the visit than five minutes on the Shankill Road. Her grandfather was a Protestant clergyman and she had ancestral links to the aristocratic O'Neills of Shane's Castle in County Antrim. (It was therefore a distant relation of Pope's, Lord O'Neill, who, as the Queen's representative, provided the official welcome for Clinton at Aldergrove.) Pope championed the cause of political neutrality at trip meetings she sat in on at the White House. "Martha's constant refrain, in a very gentle but firm way, was to admonish us to ensure there was balance," said one of those in attendance.

In tandem with Pope's input, Unionist politicians and the British Government, concerned at the signals coming out of Washington in September and much of October, were fighting their corners robustly. Northern Ireland Secretary Sir Patrick Mayhew summed up his pre-trip worries in an interview with the authors. "There was a great sensitivity among the pro-Union community that the President shouldn't come here and even inadvertently give aid and comfort by seeming to show favour to Republican Nationalists. There was anxiety about that." Clinton had a low approval rating among Unionists, according to a survey the Americans secretly commissioned in the build-up to the trip. Ambassador Crowe was, as always, susceptible to their apprehensions. "We had to make every effort that the President's trip would not suggest to one side or the other that he was partial. It had to be a very neutral trip and show that he was very genuine."

Once the White House had accepted the need to go somewhere like east Belfast, the hunt began for a suitable location. Other Unionist constituencies would have served the purpose equally well but were too far out of Belfast. Lisburn was considered at one point because its MP, James Molyneaux was head of the UUP at the time. Along with aerospace company Shorts, the other big east Belfast employer, Harland and Wolff shipyard, had been discounted. It was felt Clinton should do only one factory set piece and that privilege should be Mackie's. Shorts was checked out during the site survey. "We heard some weeks later that, taking into account logistics and the balance of his programme, they'd decided he wasn't going to come," said the company's President, Roy McNulty. "We weren't disappointed. It was just another decision that was entirely proper for them to take." Commerce Secretary Brown's party went instead. Harland and Wolff, famous for building the ill-fated *Titanic* in 1911, wasn't surveyed on the advice of the British Government. Also deemed unsuitable were church and community projects. Then there was the East Belfast Enterprise Park which had been brought to Stephens' attention by a community worker, Sammy Douglas.

Douglas, who met Clinton as a delegate to the Washington Investment Conference and who was head of the Greater East Belfast Partnership, pitched the idea of an invitation to the President at a meeting of the organisation's board. Its members included the area's MP and deputy leader of the DUP, Peter Robinson, his UUP counterpart, John Taylor and the leader of the middle-of-the-road Alliance Party, Dr John Alderdice. Douglas' suggestion came at a time when both Unionist parties were far from ecstatic at Clinton's Northern Ireland adventure. "I said we were always complaining about people coming to Belfast and ending up in the west of the city," recalled Douglas. "I didn't know where Robinson and Taylor stood on the thing but I argued we should be writing to these people and outlining the reasons why the President should come to east Belfast. We were trying to raise the profile of east Belfast and I reckoned if Clinton came you could get publicity you just couldn't buy. The whole world would be looking in." What caught Stephens' eye was that this could give Clinton the opportunity of meeting three of the Province's leading politicians in one fell swoop under the guise of the Partnership board.

Through Stephens, Pope and another member of Mitchell's team, State Department official David Pozorski, arranged to have lunch with Douglas and Robinson at the Stormont Hotel on 24 October. Robinson was there on Parliamentary business and slipped out for an hour or so. Pope acknowledged that Washington had made mistakes in the trip's planning that it now was anxious to right, assuaging Unionist and British Government fears of imbalance in the process.

It was music to Robinson's ears. He'd once told a press conference the Clinton visit had the potential of being a "NORAID tour," given the locations being touted in the early planning stages. Pope's news was a vindication of Robinson's effort. Before the President set foot on east Belfast soil, the MP would conduct a total of 14 meetings with Administration personnel in Washington, London and Belfast pressing for Presidential recognition of the Protestant majority, in his constituency of course. Of all the DUP politicians, Robinson was the one who commanded most respect among some of the key personnel on the US side. "He was the most rational, the one we felt we could do business with," said an American. Robinson's ace had been Washington's dawning realisation that the President's itinerary didn't make enough of a gesture towards Unionists. "I admit our strongest card was the requirement for him to have a balanced itinerary. I've no doubt it was this issue that required him to come to east Belfast." The MP saw political expediency as economic opportunity. "The purpose of getting him to come was to sell east Belfast as a place where there was a chance for investment. I wasn't particularly keen on encouraging him to make any political speeches."

It was on the high of the reaction to his Mackie speech that Clinton made the three-mile journey from west to east. The communication link between Clinton's limousine and the front RUC car crackled once more as the motorcade swept towards east Belfast. "The President wants to stop here," came the order from a Secret Service agent travelling with Clinton, who'd spotted more animated crowds gathered up ahead, close to Central Station, on the outskirts of the city centre. Among them were 320 children from St Malachy's, a local primary school twinned with one in the state of Maine. Its ten classes had made American flags especially. Said Vice Principal Sean Campbell: "The entire school was out and as the President came round the corner the kids started a specially prepared chant of 'USA all the way, President Clinton come our way.' The limousine unexpectedly slewed across the road and stopped. When the President got out his bodyguards looked very nervous. He'd a word to say to us all. He asked me how I was and said he was glad to be here."

The Shankill and Falls walkabouts, while masterly in creating the illusion of having been impromptu stops, had been programmed right down to the last detail, but halting in the Markets area, a working-class Republican stronghold from where numerous terrorist operations had been mounted down the years, was totally off-the-cuff. Assistant Chief Constable Bill Stewart looked at Brady Williamson with trepidation as the command came over the airwaves, but it was a decision both knew they had no option but to comply with. The local police chief was perturbed because the district hadn't been fully secured and he feared Clinton, fired up by a hero's welcome, might even stray into one of the roadside terraced houses. The stop caught the media on the hop, stuck as they were at the tail end of the convoy. Mike McCurry was with them and within minutes was reduced to tears. "There was a row of first grade or kindergarten students, roughly the age of my eldest son, looking just as cute and adorable as could be. The moment just overtook me. I started shaking hands and they looked up and said, 'Are you the President?' I said, 'No, but I work for him and see him every day and I'll say hello from you.' They got an enormous thrill from that. It's very hard to be away when I travel. I miss my three children desperately. So to see all these kids lined up, so excited the American President was there, was my best moment of the entire trip."

Up ahead Clinton, cocooned by his armed personal protection squad and still wearing his bullet-proof coat, was drowned in a sea of well-wishers who stretched out their arms to pat him. Some waved the green, white and orange flag of the Irish Republic. One of the President's men said: "This is where I thought, man, this has really got a grip on him. It was the drive over to east Belfast where I got the sense we were getting the right response, that the story wasn't just going to be, the Falls Road turns out for Clinton but the whole of Belfast turns out for him."

The President's eventual destination, East Belfast Enterprise Park, was less than two minutes' drive up the Albertbridge Road. Just as on the Shankill Road, Protestants took to the streets to glimpse him. By this stage though, support for Clinton was starting to over-take natural curiosity as the reason for drawing them out. Some businesses temporarily shut down to allow workers out to line the road. "Hey, we were the biggest show in town," said one of the US entourage. Mini-sized Union flags fluttered in the hands of some spectators, denoting the fact that the President had traversed from one political zone to another in the space of several hundred yards. The journey to the second major event was an indicator that the

President was winning over the majority community. "There was no lack of adulation on the Protestant side," contended Clinton aide Susan Brophy. "It was not as if this was an outpouring from people who had Nationalist tendencies."

Beret-clad RUC marksmen with high-powered sniper rifles slung across their chests monitored Clinton's progress through binoculars from roof-tops. They were under stern instruction not to spy through the telescopic sights of their weapons. The Enterprise Park, wedged between the intersection of two arterial roads, had been screened off using 15-feet-high sheets of metal which concealed decorative, wrought iron railings, glistening from a coat of black paint freshly applied for the President's coming. A gust of wind sent a section of the security screening crashing down just minutes prior to Clinton's arrival. "There was panic all over the place," said Alderdice who, like others indoors at the Park, was jolted into momentary alarm by the loud noise.

Constructed on the site of demolished public sector housing, the Park had been opened a year earlier, having attracted £900,000 in funding. Community-owned and run on a non-profit-making basis by a volunteer board of directors, it was split into 24,000 square feet of work units used by 27 small businesses which employed nearly 100 people.

Williamson was in position awaiting Clinton as he stepped out of the limousine just after midday, on being given the all-clear from the most senior of the Secret Service agents who clustered around the car. Helping the President shake off of his bullet-proof trench coat and straighten the jacket of his suit, the trip's top fixer explained the next moves. Clinton waved once in the direction of the tiered press gallery as he strode across the Park forecourt and, with entourage in tow, disappeared inside an office building for a private meeting with the six-member board of the International Fund for Ireland and its observers from overseas donor Governments.

The IFI had stumped up almost half of the start-up capital the Enterprise Park had required and it was the centre's link with the Fund which had helped seal its inclusion on Clinton's schedule. Once the decision to go to east Belfast had been taken, the difficulty had been to find a suitable location. The Enterprise Park was the solution. It was spacious, not far from the city centre and there was the IFI tie-in. "We wanted to do a business community event and we had to do an IFI event," said one of the US advance team. "It was sort of political touch base thing as well, with Alderdice and Robinson. It wasn't the highlight of the visit but we needed to provide some filing time for the press on the Mackie speech and we needed to get people over to Derry before the President went there." Douglas, who acted as a consultant to the Fund and had accompanied members of the advance team on planning trips to the Park, said: "It was very much what they wanted to see in terms of enterprise and there were real people he could speak to. I think the International Fund was one of the main elements because here's one of the best Enterprise Parks in Northern Ireland and here are American dollars creating jobs."

Clinton was the first President who included backing for the IFI in budget proposals sent to Congress. Under Republican Presidents Reagan and Bush, it was the legislative branch which had seen to it that the IFI wasn't starved of aid. Clinton's support was further demonstrated by his increasing the contributions. The Fund, established in 1986 to promote reconciliation through economic regeneration, principally in areas of greatest disadvantage in Northern Ireland and the border counties of the Irish Republic, was an offspring of the Anglo-Irish Agreement. A pledge of financial aid for the treaty from Washington had been obtained months beforehand and in a sense went a little way towards honouring President Carter's 1977 promise of economic assistance to bolster a peace settlement. Aside from the US, the Fund's revenue came from the European Union, Canada, Australia and New Zealand. In its first ten years, the IFI had used £320m to promote 3,400 projects and claimed to have created 26,000 jobs in Northern Ireland alone. However, it wasn't without its political critics. Unionists opposition was based not only on the Fund's origins – an accord that gave Dublin a formal role in Northern Ireland affairs. Later, when it eventually gained begrudging acceptance, they accused it of favouritism towards schemes in Nationalist areas of the North.

In Jim Lyons, Clinton positioned a close confidant as intermediary between the IFI and Washington in the summer of 1993. The pair's friendship had begun in 1977 when Lyons, a trial lawyer, was put in touch with Clinton, then Arkansas Attorney General, through a mutual acquaintance. "He was my friend before he became the President and I'd like to think he'll be my friend after he's finished being President," said Lyons. "He asked me to devote some time and some energy to this particular task and I'll do the best job for him that I can." Lyons, whose mother's family were Northern Ireland Protestants and whose father's ancestors hailed from the Republic, soon began working on Clinton's Gubernatorial, then Presidential campaigns. He'd turned down jobs in the Administration before accepting the position with the IFI, an organisation he'd never heard of. "We are kindred spirits," said Lyons, a jogging partner of the President's, who played cards with him when he was laid up in his White House private quarters with a knee injury which prevented him attending his own St Patrick's Day bash in 1997. Clinton had been a regular visitor to the lawyer's home and later, when President, he would throw open the White House to Lyons' parents who overnighted in the Lincoln Suite.

Although describing himself as one hundred per cent Irish, it took the President to stimulate a deep-seated interest in the issue. The lawyer, who Clinton turned to for professional advice when his Presidency was first shaken by the Whitewater financial scandal, was a key sounding board within the White House inner circle on Ireland policy. Said Susan Brophy: "Jim Lyons is a very close personal friend. More so than anybody, Jim Lyons is the biggest influence in terms of Ireland." Lyons certainly saw his brief in bigger terms than the Fund. "I think as American observer to the International Fund, under the circumstances in which we now find ourselves, we need to be constantly exploring how we can do whatever little we can to promote the peace process as well as do what is our basic job. Talking with the political leadership on both sides is important."

An audience with the President was something the IFI was quietly confident of attaining when Clinton's visit was announced in July and Lyons was of course well placed to see that it materialised. Washington trip planners were continually made aware that the IFI would have to be a major participant at one event. "It was always on the cards that if the President was going to visit Ireland there was going to be some involvement by the IFI," said a highly-placed Fund source. "The group preparing the itinerary were saying, he's going to Mackie but we need to get him into east Belfast. We'd a plum project in the Enterprise Park which gave them the kind of entrée where they were able to meet Peter Robinson and others."

Because of security arrangements, Fund chairman Willie McCarter and his board colleagues, together with other officials, had been cooped up in the administration building's boardroom for four hours without a seat, keeping abreast of Clinton's progress on television. Manhole covers had been sealed, the insides of lampposts checked for concealed bombs and building tops guarded. Said McCarter: "There was a great buzz about the place. I met President Clinton at the door and with Jim [Lyons] there there was some banter back and forward." On entering the boardroom Clinton greeted each of the Fund representatives in turn. McCarter presented the President with an IFI-logoed T-shirt commemorating the visit. It had been made at the American-owned Fruit of the Loom factory in Buncrana, County Donegal, and McCarter half hoped Clinton would wear it out running. (RUC officers and Secret Service agents had actually jogged a route inside south Belfast's Ormeau Park just in case Clinton wanted to go exercising next morning before departing for Dublin.) McCarter, managing director of the Fruit of the Loom plant which had been in his family for 55 years before the US take-over, also handed over a specially-labelled bottle of Tyrconnell Irish whiskey. (The President, who is allergic to malt and hops, would that night break the seal to celebrate the day's achievements and subject himself to a rare hangover in the process.) Clinton congratulated the Fund on its work, making reference to some difficult years, and vowed American support for it would continue. McCarter said: "It was very gratifying personally and it also helped raise the profile quite a bit in the States, Northern Ireland and indeed the Republic."

Mayhew, Crowe and Stephens were in a line-up in the empty car park as Clinton reappeared from the building. Williamson straightened the President's twisted jacket lapel as he made his way towards them. The MP for east Belfast was about to get the treatment Hendron had craved at the Mackie factory. To Stephens' left stood the bespectacled Robinson, beaming with unconcealed delight. "This is Peter Robinson," said the Consul General. Mayhew, who should have been handling the formalities, was lagging behind. Just in case Stephens' introduction was lost in the wind, the DUP man was sporting a name tag. "Welcome to east Belfast," he said, barely breaking his smile as he spoke. (Robinson and his wife Iris, a fellow politician, had once been dubbed "the Clintons of Castlereagh" by the *Irish Times*.) If Robinson was in the least put out that the last local politician Clinton had pressed hands with was none other than his *bete noire* Gerry Adams, or that the President had intentionally snubbed his party leader in his Mackie speech, then he was hiding it well. This was the same Peter Robinson who had sniped from the wings at the Administration's Irish policy so often in the preceding weeks that his office had received a rush of telephone calls from US officials eager to calm the waters. He had also grinned approvingly from the leadership platform at the DUP's annual conference days before the visit as delegates venomously denounced Clinton's involvement in Northern Ireland affairs. "You can disagree with someone politically yet be good mannered when welcoming them to your constituency," explained Robinson of his welcome, which wasn't so much warm as white hot. "He's a world leader and whether you agree with him or not you have to respect his position. Had I done something I think the American people would take it very ill, seeing it as an insult against the position of President as opposed to the individual," he added. In any event Robinson knew there would be ample scope for political point-scoring when Paisley had talks with Clinton later in the day.

As Clinton passed, the MP spied an old American thorn-in-his-side, Congressman Peter King, who had once slandered him during a live television debate. Robinson's new-found tolerance didn't extend to Adams' chief US-sponsor, who was among the group of politicians accompanying the President. The Congressman felt his icy glare. "I saw Robinson, he saw me," said King, " but I didn't want to do anything to create an incident with the President there."

Alderdice was next in line in the welcome party and, over a lingering handshake, thanked Clinton for coming. He had been to the White House for St Patrick's Day in 1995 and on meeting the President had, like almost everyone else, encouraged him to go to Northern Ireland. When his opinions were solicited by the American planning team, Alderdice too had pressed for east Belfast's inclusion on the tight schedule. "The White House realised if they were going to make any sort of useful contribution it was going to have to be a balanced visit," he said. "I wouldn't say one found it a very difficult selling job in the sense there was no negative feeling. It wasn't as though we were banging on a closed door but there was competition, there was a limited amount of time." Clinton and Alderdice's transitory encounter was the only public recognition the Alliance man received on the day, though he didn't feel cheated that other party leaders were getting the chance for substantive discussions that evening. Alderdice claimed to have fallen victim to his and his party's moderate outlook. "One of the endemic problems of politics in this part of the world is the more extreme you are the more you will find people will try to pacify you. I wasn't putting down some kind of demand in advance of the trip because my expectation was it would be a day of events and if he chose to meet some people so be it."

John Taylor shunned his moment in the spotlight and decided to stay away from East Belfast Enterprise Park, but he wasn't missed by the Americans. "Where Clinton was going wasn't in my constituency, it was Peter Robinson's," the MP for Strangford later said haughtily. "If he had been coming to my constituency I would have held time free." Taylor said he was on business on Northern Ireland's biggest day for years. However one of those involved in organising the event claimed: "Taylor voted with his feet." Added another: "Initially there was a requirement to have the DUP, Alliance and the UUP represented in the line-up but Taylor pulled out because he'd a minor role in the proceedings." It was Robinson who escorted Clinton as he paused briefly to meet the Chairman of the Park's board of directors, Peter Thompson, and then over to one or two of the centre's tenants who'd been selected for him to call with. Robinson had been through two dry runs of what was expected of him. "The degree of organisation would've been equivalent to fifty Royal visits. They said, 'We want you to be on the left side at this point, the right side at this point', all so that he could be protected at the various stages. Every last detail was arranged beforehand."

Standing apprehensively by glass display cabinets outside unit number 26 was Sonja Gorman, owner of Holly Handmades, a firm that made children's ornaments. Clinton instantly put her at ease. "I had a wee struggling business and I couldn't believe this was happening," said 28-year-old Gorman. "He kept holding my hand, shaking my hand. He was a very warm person, a very genuine person." Added Robinson: "He was a star performer. He has a tremendous ability on a one-to-one basis talking to people. You could see the interaction with people along the way. You could feel the buzz as we went around." Off to the President's right Williamson tugged at Lyons' elbow and pulled him out of the line of sight between Clinton and the banks of camera crews. The tactile Clinton took charge of the situation, clasping Gorman's hand for a third time, and called for his official photographer to capture the handing over of a green-coloured clock showing a clown with the words 'time for peace' inscribed on it. The President beckoned Lyons over to admire the gift. Recalled Gorman: "I said, 'We call the clown Oscar', and he had a big red nose. It was the bitterest, coldest day and the President said, 'I feel I look a bit like the clown at the minute.' I was dumfounded but I felt honoured that I'd met him."

Next Clinton and his entourage trooped around a corner for an appointment at a second business, Renaissance Ironcraft, which produced a range of designer furniture. The encounter between the President and its owner Franklin Hunter, 57, took place out of view of the media. The Americans had taken a dim view of an outburst by Hunter days earlier, when he told them he wanted to use Clinton as a sales tool. "I think it was their way of getting back at me by keeping the cameras away, but it was nice to meet him," said Hunter. "The thing that impressed me – and I've often wondered about it – is how could a man who'd never met me before exude such genuine warmth? That's the one thing that's stayed in my mind." Hunter presented the President with a shamrock-shaped iron candlestick, identical to one which he'd hammer out later for the Irish Prime Minister John Bruton. "We had a six-foot-tall seat, the back of which was shaped like a flame," he remembered. "As he went to leave I said, 'Mr President, we call this the hot seat. Will you sit in it for us?' When he sat on it he said, 'I've sat in the hot seat many times before.' His staff found it funny." After posing for pictures, it was on to more serious business.

A polite ripple of applause spread through an invited audience of Government and business representatives from Northern Ireland and the United States as Clinton, again given directions by the ubiquitous Williamson, stepped onto a lavish blue-and-red set created inside the empty shell of a building adjacent to Hunter's premises. These two business units, fortunately vacant, gave ample space for a stage-managed discussion on the local economy. An RUC officer pulled back a rope separating the 150 guests from a U-shaped table to let a windswept Nancy Soderberg and Mike McCurry through to take their seats. Clinton walked around the table shaking the hands of each of the nine participants before taking his chair, obligingly pulled back by Williamson, and removed prepared notes from his pocket. Joining Clinton at the table was Senator Mitchell, who sat down beside Margaret Alton, owner of a children's clothing business. "He introduced himself and said, 'Don't worry about the President. He's very nice, just a normal person and he'll put you at ease.' I thought that was very good of him," she said. The backdrop to the President proclaimed, 'East Belfast Welcomes President Clinton', above a Stars and Stripes design. But despite the best efforts of the US advance team in creating a perfect setting, the discussion lacked sparkle. That it flopped was no reflection on Clinton who, despite looking tired, was as ever the star performer in the public eye.

At the front, to the right of the President, Robinson was at a podium preparing to address him. Clinton wriggled in his seat to make himself comfortable and sipped at a strawberry-flavoured cold-cure drink as the MP prepared to deliver one of the shortest speeches of his career, 34 lines in total. The Americans were privy to its content in advance, Robinson having faxed it to them. "President, this is a special day for east Belfast," he began. Advised to keep it brief and bereft of party political colouring, he made just the one reference to the bigger picture. "Any group or organisation that might consider resuming a campaign of violence, or seeking to benefit from the threat of doing so, will receive no sympathy or support from this community." Mildly put by his standards. Clinton, a man who liked to quote the scriptures in his statements, chortled admiringly when Robinson added: "In biblical times the wise men came from the east. In modern times the wise businessman will come to the east." His remarks were well received. "Peter Robinson made a very nice statement. By that point he'd worked through his initial scepticism over the visit," observed a US official.

It was then Peter Thompson's turn. The President's microphone picked up a "thank you" when the chairman of the Park's board told him how much his presence was appreciated. The Park's official opening that summer had been a damp squib and Thompson, like the tenants, felt Clinton was more than making up for it. Thompson had had to redraft his introductory greeting a number of times. The Americans, who strictly controlled the duration and content of a participant's remarks, had called all the protagonists together in the run up to the event. Said Thompson: "At one of their meetings they said, 'Peter, would you like to give us your speech.' So I read it out. I suppose it took five minutes. They said, 'That's marvellous, but could get it down to 45 seconds?' They did control things, but did it very nicely." Thompson, a member of the Alliance Party, was kept abreast of attempts to woo Clinton to the Enterprise Park by Alderdice. "We reckoned it wasn't because of the tremendous job East Belfast Enterprise Park was doing that he was coming. He was coming for reasons of balance and we just happened to be the lucky people," he admitted.

Some board members were annoyed that they were forced to play second fiddle at the event to the IFI, whose staff had had a private audience with Clinton. One insider said: "Some board members were very disturbed and said, 'If we're not going to meet him we don't want the visit.' They ended up in the audience at the round table discussion but some of them were very upset."

After his short address, Thompson handed the proceedings over to David Blevings, the Park's manager, seated to the President's left. He and Sammy Douglas, who was also at the table, were charged with co-ordinating the seminar. Blevings was drained. He had occupied a ringside position during the weeks of planning and had had to solve many of the day-to-day problems. Each Park tenant was vetted and those who came and went duly noted. The night before, Blevings and an RUC constable had covered the exterior glass doors and windows of the administration block with vinyl sheeting. Security personnel had late in the day discovered the President could have been spotted inside from a nearby rooftop. It was Blevings' office which was put at Clinton's disposal for a brief rest period after he met the IFI board. A sign on the door read POTUS (President of the United States). Blevings said: "There was a lot of pressure on me because I was the man on the spot who had to liaise with whoever. You had to be there on demand but I was quite happy to wear that. It's not every day you get the chance to met the President of the United States." Clinton nodded approvingly during Blevings' opening comments, but as the talking laboured back and forth across the table for 15 minutes he began to fidget in his seat.

Of the nine people around the table, three were women. The US planners had insisted that all the participants should not be male and asked for the inclusion of representatives of small business from beyond East Belfast Enterprise Park. What each participant had to say about themselves and their company had been well rehearsed. The Americans hadn't been prepared to leave anything to chance. Franklin Hunter, who had been scheduled to take part, was dropped when he informed them he was a preacher who spoke spontaneously. Sammy Douglas told Clinton: "The eyes of the world are focused on Belfast this morning. We are daring to believe that Northern Ireland will become the top region in the United Kingdom for investment and we want to thank you for your help." Clinton looked interested though not engrossed by what he heard. He rested his head in the palm of one hand every so often and gave the impression of listening closely. He also scribbled the odd note. To many it was incongruous for the President of the United States to hear of "flexible lease terms", the "sales and servicing of sewing machines" and the "recycling of toner cartridges for laser printers."

Blevings felt afterwards that the event had been an anti-climax and the format hadn't really worked. "He was listening, which surprised me because I would've thought he'd much bigger things on his mind. It put East Belfast Enterprise Park on the map, but it wasn't interesting." Peter Thompson, who watched and listened from the front row of the audience, was left with the impression Clinton had used the event to recharge his batteries. "I think he was on automatic pilot. The Americans had led us to believe the President would command the thing and he would make it go, but he didn't do that." US Government officials later admitted privately the discussion was too stilted and that they'd envisaged it being more lively. Then again, they argued, it was never designed to grab the headlines anyway. "We weren't hoping to make news. This wasn't the news-making event. The Mackie speech was what we wanted to finish the morning events with." Lyons, however, felt the occasion was nonetheless meaningful. "Left to his own devices the President probably would've been delighted to just walk down the Falls and the Shankill all day long. But it was important that he understood firsthand and saw firsthand the kind of things that the American contribution had been underwriting."

Clinton concluded the discussion by first giving thanks to Congress for supporting the IFI and then finishing on a lighter note. "When I read my notes about what all of you do. I saw that Lynn McGregor is the owner of a company called Altered Images and I thought to myself, she could become an overnight millionaire in

Washington DC." Senator Mitchell came away from the table even more convinced of the importance of economic development in Northern Ireland's future. "I thought they [the participants] confirmed my own convictions that economic development is an essential foundation to the peace process. People have to have a sense of hope and a feeling of opportunity if the process is to work and that means economic growth and job creation."

The President rose from the table and went to work the rope. He'd been directed to glad hand the Park's board on row one. Vice chairman Bobby King wanted more than a cursory hello. "There was very little being said to him the whole way down the line and I thought, this guy's going to be past here in a minute flat. So he reached me and I said to him, 'I'm going to Florida on Tuesday. Any chance of a lift on Air Force One?' He said, 'No way. I'm outta here on Saturday.' We all laughed about it." Former Lord Mayor of Belfast, Ulster Unionist Reg Empey, who was standing next to King, looked aghast. As Mitchell made his leave one of those who'd taken part in the round table event approached. "I said to him, 'I was speaking to a fellow yesterday who spoke highly of you. He's a man you can do business with.' Mitchell replied, 'Who's that?' I said, 'David Ervine of the Progressive Unionist Party', and Mitchell's response was, 'Yes, I'm impressed with some of these people.' I suppose I mentioned Ervine because people like that need affirmation." Before Clinton departed for Belfast City Airport and a helicopter ride to Derry, Douglas presented the President with a picture of the Newtownards Road from years gone by. "I was able to chat to him for a few minutes," said the community worker. "The picture showed a newspaper hoarding that said, '*Titanic* sinks, hundreds dead', and the President said, 'Oh yes, the ship was built here in east Belfast.' And for some reason I said, 'I must tell you, Mr President, the captain was an Englishman.' I didn't mean to say it, it just came out. But he saw the funny side of it."

First Lady Hillary Clinton, meanwhile, was over in south Belfast. Said a member of the American planning team: "She basically wanted to stay with the President, stay with his programme, except for maybe one event. We looked at a couple of possibilities, hospital things, abused women centres." Blair Hall, along with an employee of the US Consul's office, scouted a women's drop-in centre on the Ormeau Road run by a spirited community worker, Joyce McCartan.

The working-class Banbridge mother-of-eight had carved a life out of adversity, being awarded an honorary degree and an MBE for her community work. Her 17-year-old son Gary was murdered by Loyalist terrorists in 1987 and 17 other relatives had their lives cut short by the Troubles. "I think through need and issues that arose during motherhood she started fighting for things," said a colleague. McCartan established the drop-in centre in 1990, providing two full-time and seven part-time jobs. Over time its aims advanced from being a place where women could take knitting classes to a centre promoting job creation in the inner city. Hall was immediately impressed by McCartan's gusto, but was concerned that the venue, which doubled up as The Lamplighter café, was too small. Mrs Clinton's own advance team arrived after him. "When Hillary's team came through they really liked Joyce," said an American source. "They weren't bothered by the location because Mrs Clinton just wanted a kind of small chat with women in the community to hear what their lives were like and so forth. She herself decided that she didn't want to do health-care issues."

McCartan, who passed away after an illness within six weeks of the trip, aged 67, appeared nonplussed at the attention which descended on her centre during the planning phases of the Clinton visit. "Mrs Clinton's aides came over and said that Hillary wanted to meet women from both communities," recalled McCartan's assistant, Janice Archibald. "I remember thinking Joyce was trying to put them off. I think she was embarrassed to bring Mrs Clinton to our place. I think she thought somebody in such a high position wouldn't want to come to a community group on the Ormeau Road. She said, 'Why don't we get her to go up to the offices of the Northern Ireland Council for Voluntary Action', which are nearby." But McCartan's reservations had probably as much to do with the cramped surroundings, which caused her guest list of 40 to be whittled down by three quarters by the Americans. She certainly needn't have worried about a First Lady hung up on airs and graces. "Mrs Clinton was very good at putting them at ease," said a British official who accompanied Lady Jean Mayhew, the wife of the Northern Ireland Secretary. "Her attitude was very much, I'm here to listen, I'm here to learn. She was very natural and very good at breaking the ice."

Mrs Clinton and her entourage arrived at 11.40am and stayed an

159

hour, longer than planned. She and McCartan's guests sat around three sides of tables which had been pushed together into a square in the café. Its walls were decorated with pictures of old Belfast. "No matter what our background, we all want to make the world a better place for our children," Mrs Clinton told them. They drank tea from a stainless-steel teapot which was given to the First Lady as a gift. (The makers of one brand of tea later telephoned to enquire if it was their brew they'd supped around the table.) McCartan's husband Seamus said: " Joyce was overjoyed and I was very proud of her. I told her at the time she was taking too much on and wasn't well enough but she was determined to go and see Hillary Clinton. It was a great honour for her and the family. I never realised just how much she was doing and how well liked she was."

VIII

Paying homage to Hume

*I encouraged the President to go to Derry but it
didn't take much lobbying. John Hume is widely
respected in America for his efforts to bring about a
peaceful solution that is fair to both communities.
A visit to Derry was likely from the start.*

Senator Ted Kennedy

Ed Emerson, the President's lead advance man for Londonderry,
said: "That's not him." He was providing a running commentary for the city's SDLP Mayor, John Kerr, as helicopters appeared
one-by-one out of an overcast sky. The adrenaline had been pumping among a delegation of dignitaries watching from the first-floor
business lounge at the City of Derry Airport ever since word had
come over Emerson's earpiece. "The President has left Belfast. Over
to Derry. You're in charge now."

Emerson, the Derry equivalent of Brady Williamson, had become
known to some as 'easy Ed' because of his laid back manner. But
he abruptly stamped his authority on the room as John Hume became
even more restless. "Right, let's go out onto the tarmac," exclaimed
the SDLP leader as the first helicopter came into sight. "I'm the
boss here," snapped Emerson. "If you want to meet the President
you'll do as I tell you. It doesn't matter who you are." One who
witnessed the scene said: "You've got to remember, anything Hume

says in Derry goes. It's gospel. It was unbelievable then that he'd been ordered to go and sit back down." Hume, however, didn't have to contain himself for long.

Clinton's army-green helicopter – United States of America emblazoned on its tail – was buffeted by high winds as it battled to hold its line for touchdown on a runway near the banks of a choppy Lough Foyle. It was phase two of the visit. According to those on board Marine One, Clinton had recharged his batteries with an upright doze in his cramped seat.

Twenty-seven years after watching a Catholic civil rights march in Derry erupt in violence on television, Clinton arrived in the birthplace of the Troubles. He was in Northern Ireland's second, Nationalist-dominated city to pay homage to Hume, schoolteacher-turned-statesman. "Derry was always a given because of John Hume," explained Emerson. "He was the centrepiece. We were going to pay homage to Hume." The Americans, as ever conscious of the necessity for political balance, had planned an event to appease the city's dwindling number of Protestants. But it was axed less than five minutes before it was to have happened – a snap decision which left a bitter taste long after the President had gone. "The negative aspect of his itinerary was Londonderry," complained Ulster Unionist leader David Trimble later. "Local Unionists were excluded. Whether Clinton was fully aware of that I don't know. Londonderry was not good but the question of responsibility should start with the SDLP because they would have had significant influence."

Clinton's landing proved as awkward as the Americans had anticipated. Concern had been expressed about the tricky, 40-minute helicopter jaunt by US Marine Corps pilots. During the site survey some highly-skilled aviators had cautioned against it, given that the final approach to the landing strip – exposed to the elements at this time of year – was extremely testing. The airfield wasn't big enough for Air Force One and until the morning of 30 November a smaller, fixed-wing aircraft was considered as an alternative. The runway had been marked out for a plane and helicopters. "The Air Force and the Marine Corps have very strict regulations. If the weather didn't meet them then the President didn't fly. If he doesn't fly we weren't putting him in a car 140 miles over the mountains and back to Derry," said one senior US planner. Said a Derry City Council source: "There was quite a bit of concern about the weather and how it would effect his travel. That was always an axe hanging over our head."

A 'plan B' would have been drawn up if it looked like the weather would rob the city of a Presidential visit. However, alternative arrangements, which would have seen Clinton remain in the greater Belfast area throughout the day, never had to be finalised because the US military had called on the most sophisticated weather forecasting technology available. Data from satellites was poured over for weeks. "At the end of each of our countdown meetings the Air Force guy got up and gave us a weather report. As we saw it looked like the weather was going to be O.K. the concern over 'plan B' receded from view. If we'd have gotten a bad weather forecast we would have had to firm it up," said an American official.

Difficult as the President's approach appeared, his journey wasn't nearly as hair-raising as that of the occupants of one of three support helicopters. Nighthawk Three, carrying Congressmen and White House staffers, flew with doors wobbling in the wind. "The back door, for whatever reason, wouldn't close, which was good news, bad news," recalled Congressman Jim Walsh. "Good news in the sense that I could see the beautiful landscape, but bad news in that all the mist and diesel fuel were being sucked in and people were getting sick." Those on board, including Nancy Soderberg, were each equipped with ear plugs and huddled up to keep warm. "It was as cold as hell, a miserable flight, but we got there," added Walsh. Dignitaries watching them arrive, from their airport lounge vantage point, had been waiting there since mid-morning. "The building had been torn apart the night before by men in white boiler suits and rubber gloves," said airport manager John Devine, who'd turned down a request to close the airport to facilitate the President's travel arrangements.

Two white-capped Marines in knee-length dress coats marched in rigid fashion to the double doors of Marine One, the last of the aircraft to land. As its giant rotorblade spun to a gradual halt, a White House aide stepped forward and shouted to one of the soldiers: "Don't open the doors until the carpet's rolled." Two airport workers, unmistakable in fluorescent green waistcoats, moved in and unrolled a length of red carpet from under the helicopter's single step out to where a 150-strong crowd had gathered. Emerson, in leather coat and checked scarf, pointed to the spot where he wanted the VIP party to line up. It was still shuffling into position when Clinton caught them unawares. Not standing on ceremony, the President ducked out from the doors, which hadn't been fully opened by the fresh-faced military honour guard. (His impetuosity to get to the crowds would be a feature of his time in Derry.)

Clinton buttoned his overcoat, waved and turned around to help his smiling wife off the helicopter by the hand. The gloved Marines held a salute for the First Couple and Mrs Clinton stepped aside to allow the President to stride ahead and receive the hand of welcome extended by the Lord Lieutenant of County Londonderry, Sir Michael McCorkell, his chest bedecked with military medals. Kathleen Stephens, last out of the helicopter after Ambassador Crowe, bumped her head as she stooped to get out. Tony Lake had given her his seat so she could brief the President about Derry. Mayor Kerr welcomed Clinton with the Irish words *ceád míle fáilte*, just as Gerry Adams had done on the Falls. Mrs Clinton, working her way down the line behind the President, had met Derry City Council Town Clerk John Keanie before, although she took reminding. "We shook hands at the big tent in the White House during the Investment Conference," Keanie informed her. The First Lady laughed and replied: "Did you get soaked? I hope your suit wasn't ruined." Recalled Keanie afterwards: "I had said to her in Washington, 'I hope the next time we shake hands we will be in Derry,' and here we were. It was remarkable."

One down from Keanie, Hume jigged from foot to foot. He clenched his fist as he emphasised to Clinton the momentous significance of the occasion. Hume, who'd been cautioned not to hog the President's time, later summed up the importance of Clinton's coming to the city. "It was hugely historic. He had to go to Belfast and Dublin, the capitals, but he made a special point in coming to Derry."

The President, under Emerson's direction, made for the crowd of well-wishers who'd been roused into a cheer by a hand-waving gesture behind Clinton's back from Kerr. Said Devine: "Clinton wasn't meant to go over but somebody said to me that he can't resist a crowd. I'd gone across to the people before he arrived and said, 'Look, if you want him to come across and talk to you you better make sure he hears you.'" It was no accident that the President's glad-hand started with a boy in a Secret Service baseball cap.

Special agent James McGettigan had earlier placed it on nine-year-old Mark Sheridan's head to indicate to the President where to start working the line. The child's father, Peter, was the RUC officer in charge of security in Derry for the visit. "I thought they only put the hat on his head because it was my son," he said. "But then I heard one of the agents tell his counterpart on Marine One as it was coming into land that the President should start working the crowd at the young fella in the baseball cap. I watched the President after he finished the official greeting and he looked up nonchalantly, went straight over to my wee fella and tipped his cap and said, 'I like your hat.' That was the way it was done."

The crowd, consisting of families of RUC personnel and the 50 airport staff, was peppered with tiny children, many hoisted up on the shoulders of their fathers. Police relatives went to the airport as they felt safer than going to the main event in Guildhall Square. Added Sheridan: "The people who met Clinton at the airport were screened. They kept it for police and airport families so the White House knew there wasn't going to be some lunatic there." Clinton looked tired but was in no rush as he made his way along the crash barriers on a person-by-person basis, concentrating in particular on the children, repeating "hello" and "thank you" with each handshake. One woman presented him with a small shillelagh. Mrs Clinton stood in the background, in conversation with the Lord Lieutenant. The President spied one child a row back and parted the crowd to reach over and gently ruffle his hair before pausing with a group of uniformed air stewardesses, then entered the airport building.

Devine by now had broken from the greeting line and rushed on ahead, after a White House staffer told him that in a change of plan Clinton was to go to the upstairs lounge to use the bathroom. "I ran in to find one of his aides hanging up a shirt," remembered Devine. "As I came dashing back out after cleaning the sinks I met the President head on in the doorway. He stepped back and I stepped back, neither of us knowing who was going to give way. Finally he beckoned me out of the road and took off his jacket and asked me to hold it." Clinton took the eight inch shillelagh out of his pocket and told his aide: "This is going on my desk when I return to the White House." As the President changed his shirt, the First Lady made a telephone call from the business lounge. On his way out Clinton stopped on the stairs to gaze at pictures of Amelia Earhart, the first woman to fly solo across the Atlantic. Devine told him she'd landed not far from the airport, at a place called Ballyarnett. Before leaving young Mark Sheridan gave Clinton a lapel badge bearing the RUC crest. "He looked at it straightaway and shoved it into his pocket," said his father Peter. "Normally Secret Service agents take everything off him but they were saying to me afterwards that he actually collects pin badges and that's why he put it into his pocket." Clinton's motorcade then left for the Guildhall, the President unprepared for the outpouring of joy which awaited him in a city that bore some of the deepest scars from two-and-a-half decades of conflict.

It was a civil rights demonstration in Duke Street in 1968 which sparked the violent confrontation between police and marchers that first brought Northern Ireland to worldwide attention. A year later rioting on the edge of the Catholic Bogside estate led to British soldiers being put on the streets. Some killings too had far-reaching consequences. The shooting dead of 13 civilians by members of the British Army's Parachute Regiment on Bloody Sunday in 1972 – a fourteenth died later – hastened the demise of the Stormont Parliament and the introduction of direct rule from Westminster.

During these turbulent decades, John Hume emerged as Derry's most eminent political figure. Born in 1937, he was the eldest of seven children born into a working-class Bogside family. "My first political lesson was when I was ten years old," Hume enjoyed telling people. "I was at a Nationalist meeting at the top of the street. They were whipping up emotions and waving flags. My father, who was unemployed, was with me and he said, 'Don't be getting into that stuff, son.' I said, 'Why not da?' He said, 'Because you can't eat a flag.' In other words, no matter what country you belong to, if you can't earn a living it isn't much use to you. So my central issue in politics has always been to get jobs and houses for people." His two heroes were John F. Kennedy and Martin Luther King, both of whom he liked to quote often. One of Hume's first forays into the political arena, agitating for decent housing for Catholics, addressed the practical consequences of Unionist control of the city. Electoral boundaries had previously been mapped out to ensure that, while Protestants only numbered a third of Derry's inhabitants, their political representatives were in a council majority. The reforms which followed the civil rights agitation ended that cosy arrangement and since then Londonderry's Protestant population has steadily shrunk.

Protestants shared in Derry's economic good fortune but that didn't check a growing sense of alienation. The Derry that Clinton came to is exemplified by a city-centre sculpture of two figures with their arms outreached to each other, but just failing to touch. He too, through an ill-judged decision by staff, would unwittingly contribute to the feeling of Protestant disenchantment.

John Hume's links to Washington stretched back to 1972. "When I first got elected I made my first contacts in America very early on," he told the authors. "I could see from the beginning there was a very strong Irish-American interest and involvement in what was happening here. There'd always been a strong support for the IRA, largely in terms of finance, but in the political arena there was always a simplistic approach to our problems." Hume set about changing that.

In late 1972, Hume received a telephone call at his Derry home from Ted Kennedy. The seeds of a long friendship were about to be sown. Kennedy, who was attending a conference in Germany, suggested the two meet in Bonn. "I was not all that well known but he said he'd been advised that I was the person to talk to," said Hume. This was the SDLP leader's entrée to the Democratic Party. "When I started going to places like Boston and New York to speak to Irish Catholics I realised it was a waste of time," he recalled. "You would speak to them one night and then they would bring in somebody the next week who was pro-IRA and the emotionalism would take over. So I decided to concentrate on the politicians of real influence in the Senate and Congress and got them totally anti-violence."

Through Kennedy, Hume established links with the other most influential Irish-Americans in the Democratic Party – Speaker of the House Thomas 'Tip' O'Neill, Governor Hugh Carey of New York and Senator Daniel Patrick Moynihan. Hume encouraged them to speak out against violence and in 1977 the 'Four Horsemen' – named after a group of quarter-backs at Notre Dame University – issued a landmark statement to that effect. Hume later summed up the two-fold objective of his American mission. "One, stop support for violence, which was very considerable in the sense that a lot of people with a simple Brits-out mentality paid money to support violence. Two, the best way to help is economically, because if we provide hope and jobs for our young people there's less of a chance they'll be sucked into violence."

O'Neill started the tradition of St Patrick's Day lunches, putting Hume at the top table with the President of the day. (The Derry politician has dined with each occupant of the Oval Office since Carter.) Hume was making powerful allies. "After the Anglo-Irish Agreement Tip O'Neill asked how they could help," remembered Hume. "I said, 'Economics, Tip, economics.' He then set up the International Fund for Ireland. I tell the party we've not been claiming enough credit for that." Reagan and Bush would politely listen to Hume every 17 March but it wasn't until a Democrat entered the White House that the Irish issue had priority. Said Hume: "Every President up until Clinton was totally advised by the State Department, who said, 'Don't interfere.' What changed it was here was a Democratic President strongly dependant on his own support in the Congress and Senate."

Through Kennedy and Senator Chris Dodd, the Democratic Party boss, Hume exerted a meaningful influence. "They were very, very strong in the peace process, supporting me strongly and getting the President involved," said the SDLP leader. "Given their very senior standing in the Democratic Party they'd a very strong influence on Clinton. The Adams visa was all done through me, Ted and Chris Dodd. They and others I'd worked with down the years were all saying to him, 'Right, help.'" Commented Dodd: "John Hume has been for many of us a sort of a rudder through all of this. Our great disappointment, frankly, is that there hasn't been the emergence of a John Hume on the Unionist side, someone who would represent a more moderate voice on that side. It's been a great disappointment that Mr Trimble hasn't emerged to lead his constituency in that direction." Another Hume ally is the former Speaker of the House, Tom Foley. "He is one of the great, great heroes in this whole effort to bring about peace, reconciliation and justice in Ireland," mused Foley. "There's been no-one who has taken greater risks personally or committed more energy and spirit to the cause. He's had enormous influence in this country because of that."

Hume's influence determined that a Presidential excursion to the Maiden City was always on the agenda. However, the British had reservations. "There was resistance to the President going to Derry but we had to go because of Hume," said a senior source at the White House. "Derry was always definitely on the agenda from our standpoint but it had to be negotiated with London and Northern

Ireland Office officials." The Irish Government, through diplomatic channels in Washington, sought to counterbalance the British position. "That was one of the areas where we would have had an input and where we would have felt that the visit should include Derry as well as Belfast," said an insider at the Irish Embassy.

Hume's friends in high places were also pressing for the city's inclusion on the trip itinerary, Senator Kennedy among them. "I encouraged the President to go to Derry but it didn't take much lobbying. John Hume is widely respected in America for his efforts to bring about a peaceful solution that is fair to both communities. A visit to Derry was likely from the start," Kennedy maintained. Hume's lieutenant, Mark Durkan, went to the White House in the summer of 1995 and picked up positive indications. He met old friend Nancy Soderberg, whom he had worked under during an internship in Kennedy's office in 1985. "Nancy was very committed to Derry. She visited it herself and she felt it was part of balancing the visit all round. It wasn't a gilt-edged guarantee but a commitment you knew in good faith terms was as good as a promise." Realism soon prevailed at the Northern Ireland Office. "We knew it was going to happen. It would've been very surprising if there wasn't some sort of event there. We always said the President would have to go west of the River Bann but we didn't want him to be so focused on Derry that it would be interpreted as the President being solely a captive of Nationalism, embodied if you like in John Hume. That would've immediately unbalanced the programme and we weren't going to have that."

The weekend before the President's arrival, members of the US advance team made tracks to see Hume in County Donegal to tell him, for security and political reasons, not to cling to Clinton's coattails during the Derry segment of the visit. Most senior among the Americans were Emerson and Hall, whose task it had become to marry the halves of the Northern Ireland visit. (There was a competitiveness between staff in the two cities, each wanting their events to be better than the other's.) The SDLP chief took them to a favourite haunt, a seafood restaurant in Greencastle, a short distance from his second home. Said one of the American diners: "Hume invited eight but about 15 of us showed up. We sat down and did a lot of talking to John about what we wanted to accomplish. What we wanted at the end of the day was to have people look at the totality of the schedule and say, yes, it was balanced. But what would've thrown that off was if John Hume's involvement with the programme in Derry was seen to be so overwhelming. We didn't want to see him ride in the President's limo and then escort him. Wherever the President went we didn't want John Hume at his shoulder." Added another source: "They tried to brief John on etiquette. They knew John would've wanted to stick close to the President for all the right reasons, unaware of the difficulties he would have been causing. They had to get him off-side as subtly as possible." The Secret Service was aware of a recent visit to Derry by Irish Prime Minister John Bruton during which Hume had prompted an unscheduled stop in the Bogside. They wanted no repeat performance with Clinton.

As the wine flowed freely, Hume crooned two of his legendary party pieces, 'Danny Boy' and 'The Town I Loved So Well.' Emerson said: "We had the most riotous dinner and sang Irish songs. My God, what a night." In return for Hume's hospitality, the Americans sent him a case of Californian Chardonnay.

For Nashville-born Emerson, working in Derry was a labour of love, a first homecoming. "It was a pretty intense process to get on the trip but Paige Reefe was good enough to recognise my Irish roots," he said. He described himself as one hundred per cent Irish, with his ancestry on his father's side originating in Belfast. He was an avid reader of local history. "I was going to go to Belfast originally but when Derry was added they asked if I wanted to be in charge of that piece. I had read about Derry all my life and wanted to go there. Its whole history is the ground zero of the conflict. I'd never been before but I'd seen pictures of the barricades and the walls. I almost cried when I arrived, it was amazing."

Emerson worked on Clinton's 1992 White House campaign and after the election took up a post in the Vice President's office under Jack Quinn. The 38-year-old called himself the 'Kid from Kankakee', an Indian village in Illinois where he'd lived for 20 years from age five. "I liked the idea of having my own fiefdom. It was only three or four hours in the middle of a very long European trip but it was all mine. I could hang out, visit the pubs," said Emerson. "His energy was incredible," said Town Clerk Keanie. "He thought we were kindred spirits. We were both absolutely determined to make it work. We'd a couple of good battles but at the end of the whole thing he nearly strangled me in a hug, he was so delighted." There was, however, concern in some American quarters that Emerson's emotional attachment threatened to impair his objectivity. For that reason Hall was used as a counterweight to ensure that what happened in Derry fitted in with the bigger political picture.

To begin with, the Americans were uncertain about what the President would do in Northern Ireland's second city. Said a top White House aide: "Very early on we decided we would do Derry, partly because of John Hume, partly because we wanted to go somewhere other than Belfast. The logistics of it were a nightmare. There was a lot of discussion about what we should do while the President was there, but frankly it came down to a matter of time." The initial indecision emanating from Washington caused problems for the trip co-ordinators on the other side of the Atlantic. One said: "We weren't quite sure what some people in the White House had in mind for the Derry part of the schedule which, for a time, was the least focused." Strong economic ties between the region and the US made a factory visit an obvious option. Fruit of the Loom, Du Pont and Seagate were each cased during the site survey. A briefing document circulating in Washington stated: "We were reminded by our hosts of the number of American businesses located in the area and the number of Londonderry immigrants who left from the port for new lives in the US in the nineteenth century, but we heard no compelling reason for the President to visit."

Reconnaissance missions to community centres and schools in Nationalist Creggan and predominately Loyalist Waterside were also undertaken, but it soon became evident that the constraints on time would limit Derry to one set-piece event. "It was a time thing," recalled Emerson. "It was very unfortunate." Keanie, who had assembled a City Council team to work hand-in-glove with the Americans, was downcast, especially as he had rather optimistically set his sights on Clinton spending the night in Derry instead of Belfast. "It wasn't too long until it became clear that that was not going to happen. I remember having pangs of disappointment at that stage. It was going to be an in-and-out visit. I was worried that if it was all frenetic stuff there would be no message. I felt a certain amount of time would be required to get our message across to the world."

Keanie sought and believed he'd received a mandate to handle the arrangements for the visit from the leaders of the council's major parties, after chairing a round-table meeting with Pat Devine of the SDLP, the DUP's Gregory Campbell, Mitchel McLaughlin from Sinn Féin, and Ulster Unionist John Adams. "It wasn't a particularly sensitive thing to do," said Keanie. "I have a method of working and, if there is an issue to be dealt with which could have political repercussions, I tend to bring in the Mayor and party leaders, discuss the issue, openly tell them of my fears and say, 'this is how I'm going to deal with it.' The whole reason for that meeting was to explain how we had come up with a focus for the visit with the Americans and how there were certain things I couldn't do, and they would have to take their own action in that respect."

The Town Clerk warned the city's elected politicians, who had ideas of their own for the Americans, that any unseemly display of in-fighting over the President's schedule could place the visit in jeopardy: "From time to time the Americans would quietly remind us that anything can be cancelled, anything could be changed," remembered Keanie. "I wouldn't quite call it a veiled threat but there'd always be the possibility that you could blot your copy book very handy on this. I told the councillors that I saw real evidence of the Americans' understanding of the political sensitivities. I did not have to be overt with the message about working together. They knew that was what the visit was all about and I got their unanimous support."

Keanie's words held sway with DUP Alderman Campbell, who had mixed feelings about the trip. "I was delighted to see a President of the United States coming to Northern Ireland. Unionists as a whole felt it could be a 'green' approach and I felt it could be a 'mega-green' approach in Londonderry but as it got nearer to the visit the Americans were emphasising that it would be equal, fifty-fifty, and that everybody was going to get a slice of the action. I think that's what attracted Unionist acquiescence rather than saying we didn't want him to come." The SDLP grouping had no such reservations however. Councillor Durkan said: "Derry Council has worked and developed over the years in a spirit of partnership. If the President was coming to set some examples and make appeals for people to take risks and to take positive initiatives then it would have been crazy for him to come and preach that message and not come to Derry."

The President's team inevitably looked at the Guildhall, the imposing home of the City Council, and immediately fell in love with its Gothic splendour. Here was a photogenic backdrop to showcase the President. Colin Sharp, the council superintendent responsible for the Guildhall's upkeep, said: "The Americans were most impressed. Buildings in America are generally new and they would have had nothing of the character of the Guildhall. Once they saw it I don't there was any doubt they were going to go anywhere else."

The Guildhall had withstood a major fire in 1908 before being damaged by two IRA bomb attacks within a week in 1972, one of which blew the head and an arm off a marble statue of Queen Victoria. It was forced to close for five years, and not long after its re-opening was blasted again though the damage wasn't so extreme.

Its locale in the city centre, in the shadow of Derry's Walls, was also important to the Americans. "This is where we started to use the idea of parity of dissatisfaction," said a key member of the advance party. "One thing we were told was that the Waterside was Protestant and the Bogside was Nationalist, but city centre in Derry is still neutral territory. So while there might be a sort of Nationalist cast to Derry in general we couldn't go too far wrong if we stayed around that particular patch of ground. It was exactly the right thing to do." One of the White House's most senior officials added: "We were definitely nervous about the implication that this was going to be, quote, a Nationalist stop. There was a lot of discussion about what we should do and in the end it came down to doing one event involving the two communities."

RUC superintendent Peter Sheridan, who as force liaison officer was well-placed to see the American operation unfold, said: "They felt there wasn't much to be achieved by moving the President anywhere else in the city when they could do everything around the Guildhall. It was nothing to do with us though it suited our purposes for him not to be moving about. If they'd wanted him out at Seagate we would have taken him out to Seagate, but in doing that it would have split the crowds, whereas the impression I got was that they wanted to create that big crowd atmosphere." At one point in the planning stages consideration was given to the President strolling around a section of the seventeenth-century walls, but the idea was dropped for security reasons. Said Emerson: "The security guys had to win a couple of battles and that was one of them."

173

Initially, planners envisaged Clinton delivering his address from Shipquay Gate in the corner of Guildhall Square and then walking up the steep incline of Shipquay Street and calling at a craft village. "We were going to do the whole event under the Gate and build the crowd straight up Shipquay Street with the overflow crowd in Guildhall Square," recalled Emerson. "But it was a question of securing all those buildings all the way up that hill and I ultimately lost that fight. In any case, I couldn't figure out a way of pushing him through the crowds." Consideration was also given to a walkabout in the Fountain, the Protestant enclave on the west bank, though logistics made that impossible. "It was just too complicated to try to do something like that," explained a member of the American party. "We just wanted to get the President down to the Guildhall area and not move too much."

The Secret Service relied heavily on the anti-terrorist expertise of the RUC when considering the options for Clinton's movements in Derry. The bond formed between agent McGettigan and superintendent Sheridan was indicative of the professional relationship which developed between their two organisations. White House and British officials stood aside and let the Secret Service and RUC deal amongst themselves. Said one of the US trip team: "Cops are the same all around the world. They talk the same language. We just closed the door, let them scream and shout or arm wrestle and they ended up working it out. We didn't get involved. As far as I could see they developed a healthy, mutual respect." The visit became educational for both. Said Sheridan: "They are very good at crowd control whereas we are much more sophisticated in clearing an area of explosives. It was only after the Oklahoma bomb that they began to worry more about bombs. Up to then they had only concentrated on close-quarter shootings, like the assassination attempt on President Reagan. So it worked very well in that here was a good balance. They were good at close quarters and we were able to teach them things on the explosives front."

McGettigan and Sheridan's superiors had first got together at the White Gables Hotel in Hillsborough, County Down. Assistant Chief Constable Lewis led the RUC team and across the table were the European Director of the Secret Service and the head of the President's personal security detail. Lewis recalled: "This was where the game plan was laid out. The Secret Service agreed with it. They were well briefed, knew who we were and what we were about. My main concern was to ensure the understanding was clear that once the President arrived in Northern Ireland we would be responsible for his safety while he was moving about in public. That understanding was clearly received. Relations were good from the outset."

Meetings between the two sides culminated in a session at the RUC's Garnerville base in east Belfast on 15 November. It was the only time all security personnel involved in the Clinton trip assembled under the one roof. After it, agents and officers paired off at all ranks and specialities. RUC officers used it as a charm offensive, aiming to counter the force's bad press in Irish-American circles. "We did a presentation on what arrangements we'd already made for the visit, what we knew about it, and gave them a picture of ourselves and Northern Ireland in general," said Sheridan, who gave the Londonderry debrief. "The inaugural meeting made all the difference. There'd been friction between them and the Metropolitan Police, and because they'd looked upon us as a UK force they expected to find more of the same. They didn't expect us to be so helpful, but the personalities helped to break down the barriers." By agreement, the American agents were made to apply for temporary firearm certificates so they could be legally armed while protecting the President in Northern Ireland.

It was at Garnerville that Sheridan and McGettigan teamed up and travelled together to Derry. McGettigan, a keen golfer who spent spare time on courses in the north-west, based himself at a command post in the Broomhill Hotel where he and the other members of the US team stayed. Relations were put on an even better footing after RUC detectives recovered two White House passes, stolen during a break-in at the hotel. The two security men linked up each morning and were all-powerful, maintaining a right of veto on the President's movements. "I have to be fair to the Secret Service," Sheridan said. "Anywhere along the line, if we had said we'd difficulty with a particular aspect of the visit they would have pulled the plug on it right away. But virtually anything they wanted we were happy to go along with. We recognised how important this was for Derry and for history, and we weren't going to be the ones to spoil the occasion."

The RUC's nerve centre was a room at its Maydown Barracks which had been equipped with the latest computer technology.

Unlike the force's operation in Belfast, officers in Londonderry used the HOLMES computer network which up until them had only been used to collate data in serious crime and terrorist investigations. "It didn't matter what it was," explained Sheridan. "Every manhole was listed and every time someone did a house inquiry it was listed. The idea was that if something went wrong it would simply be a matter of checking the information already in the system."

A major challenge for Sheridan was securing a mainly rural, nine-mile route between the airport at Eglinton village and the Guild-hall. The RUC invoked the fury of Nationalist residents with house-to-house calls along the route Clinton's cavalcade was to fol-low, with Sinn Féin accusing it of using the pretext of the visit to gather intelligence and conduct searches. Home-owners questioned in streets not on the route into the city didn't realise that a path to Altnagelvin Hospital also had to be secured in case of a Presiden-tial medical emergency. All the information gleaned was fed into the computer banks at Maydown. Sheridan defended the exercise. "It was a propaganda thing by Sinn Féin. Houses were never searched. All we wanted to know was that when the President was driving past a specific house on Clooney Road on that morning there should be a red car outside and that the number of people in the house should be four, five or whatever. We needed that informa-tion so that if we got a call to say there was a bomb on the route all we had to do was go to the computer. It was all done in consultation with the Americans."

Keeping thousands of spectators off the roads caused another headache. It would have taken up to 8,000 officers – half the force – to line the route to keep the crowds at bay. The cost in manpower would have been £500,000. With the stockpile of crash barriers in the province already depleted, Sheridan discovered a supplier in London. At a cost of £65,000, eight-foot-long barriers were shipped in to line both sides of a seven-mile stretch of road between the airport and Caw roundabout, on the eastern edge of the city. They arrived in sixteen lorries and 32 men set them in place on the night before Clinton's arrival.

Every inch of barrier was needed to restrain the excited masses that turned out for the President when, just after 1.00pm, he em-barked on the drive from City of Derry Airport. Hillary Clinton was in the back of the Cadillac with the President, who had requested that they be unaccompanied by officials on the journey into the city. The size and enthusiasm of the crowds lining the route would linger in the memory of many senior staff travelling with the Clintons. Said Presidential aide Susan Brophy: "I'd never seen anything like it. We were weaving through the streets and the further you got into the city the bigger the crowds. There were people as far as the eye could see. The President loves to be warmly received and he was absolutely overwhelmed. He was elated. It was impossible for him to be happier than he was."

Hume and Mayor Kerr were sharing a lift in the motorcade. Hume, a front-seat passenger, had his window rolled down and was waving to the crowds. Some were holding aloft banners proclaiming a welcome for Clinton. "The people were actually waving to the President but it didn't matter to John," joked Mayoress Carita Kerr. "I was absolutely amazed at the number of people lining the route. It started thinnish near the airport but by the time you got into the city the streets were crammed." That Mrs Kerr had even a part in the Clinton visit was remarkable. She had been diagnosed as having breast cancer ten days before the trip, had emergency surgery the following Monday and been discharged on the Wednesday so she could be at her husband's side. "Staff at Altnagelvin Hospital told me later that they were watching me on television and every time I shook hands with somebody they'd say, 'Oh, I can feel the pain.' But I felt nothing. I was totally high on adrenalin and the joyousness of the day." Both the President and First Lady, informed of her bravery by Emerson, had hugged Mrs Kerr at the airport. "I thought they would ignore it and think, well, it's nothing to do with us, but they didn't. They were absolutely wonderful, very human and very kind," she said. Added the Mayor: "It had been hard to get a great sense of moment about the whole visit because Carita's situation totally transcended it. But it did come on the day and it helped me get a perspective on what life was about."

The momentous sense of occasion wasn't lost on Congressman Jim Walsh, who was leading the delegation of American politicians. He recalled: "The closer we got the more and more people there were, to the point where the police had to literally separate the crowds from the buses so we could get through. I never saw anything like it in all my days in politics. I've never seen such passion and warmth. It was palpable." Trip-planner Ed Emerson was in another car in the Clinton convoy. "I'm sure the President had a temptation to stop, but on a deal like that we tell him before he gets into the car he'd have all these people waiting downtown. I had people coming over the radio from Guildhall saying, 'There's twenty-five thousand people down here. It's going to be great.'"

Emerson breathed a mighty sigh of relief for, incredible as it now seemed, he and his planning team had been sweating over the possibility of a poor showing for the President. Said Town Clerk Keanie: "The Americans were very nervous about whether there would be a crowd. We never doubted that there would be a huge crowd. We kept telling them that the Derry people would come out." Derry's citizens had been packing the city's historic centre from mid-morning and now every inch of space in front of a stage beside the Guildhall was claimed by young and old, their faces reddened by a chill wind coming off the Foyle. Despite the advice, the Americans hadn't left their attendance to chance. Advertisements had been placed in local newspapers and leaflets dropped through letter-boxes. Emerson even recruited a one-hundred-strong pool of student volunteers from the University of Ulster's Magee campus. "The Americans' big worry, ironically, was that they might not get a crowd in Derry," said the university's John McCaffrey. "For two days in a row myself and Ed Emerson went round lectures and gathered the students into a room. Ed gave them a real pep-talk. 'Go out there and get them,' he said. 'We want all your friends and family to come to this. The President wants them all there.' The Americans covered every angle."

For their trouble and for security reasons, the willing students were alone given a privileged grandstand view of proceedings from the top of the city walls. They looked down upon crowds sectioned into four areas: two lampposts and a tourist information kiosk had been removed, helping to pack them in. Surrounding shops had been told not to pull down their security shutters down as this would give a bad impression. Claire Lundy, who'd been part of the City Council's Clinton planning team, said: "Ticketing was such that in three of the four areas there was a controlled balance of old and young, Catholic and Protestant, which would be the focus of the television cameras. The fourth area, which was the largest, was open to anyone who turned up on the day." Consideration had been given to placing huge video screens in Waterloo Place but at a cost of £20,000 each the council deemed they were unnecessary. Up until the Clinton's arrival the crowds were entertained by the city's favourite daughter, Dana. The singer, who at 17 brought a ray of sunshine to the city during some of its bleakest days by winning the Eurovision Song Contest, cheered the masses with a rendition of her winning song, 'All Kinds of Everything'. One person in the crowd, nurse Josephine Hegarty, said: "It was like street theatre. We were all being carried along on the high of the day." Tip O'Neill's daughter Rosemary, who was in the crowd, added: "John Hume pointed out to us that it hadn't been one hundred paces away where Bloody Sunday had happened, and yet here we were with this fabulous, joyous occasion."

Not all the warm-up acts however were so pleasing to everyone. Some Unionist councillors in the VIP enclosure, who already felt they were being sidelined, took exception to a folk band called Calgath, led by local musician Roy Arbuckle. "There was concern about a lot of things that were going on," said Deputy Mayor Richard Dallas of the Ulster Unionist Party. "The diddly-dee music certainly wasn't part of the Protestant culture." (The band was in fact invited along at the request of the DUP's Gregory Campbell because it featured Scots-Irish music in its repertoire.)

A hush fell over Guildhall Square as Clinton's motorcade crawled into view. Two identical limousines broke from the convoy; the decoy car going left, and the one carrying the Clintons turning right. It made for a back door of the Guildhall and rolled under a canopy, which had been built on security advice to block a potential gunman's line of sight from across the Foyle. Patrol boats buzzed up and down the river to guard against any eventuality. "Anybody could have left Libya and come round the coast of Ireland and down Lough Foyle," superintendent Sheridan of the RUC commented. "You could've easily had a Middle East crackpot who could see this as an opportunity to launch an attack. It was a big concern to them. We had a Royal Navy destroyer off the coast monitoring shipping in the lough for days in advance." Security concerns didn't stop there. The First Couple were entering a building which, in the paranoid world of the Secret Service, had been practically taken to pieces and reassembled in the preceding 48 hours. Guildhall superintendent Colin Sharp revealed: "The police and army moved in and virtually pulled the building apart on five occasions for different checks. They even took the boiler in the basement apart. The first big check was for Semtex. They gave each of the staff a pair of cotton gloves to rub themselves down from head to toe. You took the gloves off and they were analysed by a computer for traces of explosives."

The Guildhall's labyrinthine, six-level interior was broken down into one-metre-square zones and bomb disposal experts donned gloves to painstakingly dust every centimetre. Hi-tech scanners were also deployed to sweep behind antique oak-panelling, a feature of the building. The square around the Guildhall was also combed. A US source said: "On the morning of the visit a truck drove around, blasting out radio frequencies to trigger any bombs that had been set. We had to turn off all the bank machines and pay phones. It was a very intense and unpleasant part of the trip."

Inside the Guildhall, Clinton dashed to the toilet and then went to the Mayor's parlour where he and Mrs Clinton spent five minutes with the Kerrs. The President munched on one of the apples he'd bought on the Shankill Road and declined an offer of a shot of Irish whiskey. "They were extremely exhausted," said Kerr. "At one stage the President put his head down on Hillary's shoulder. He was very tired." Emerson knocked on the door and told Clinton: "Mr President, the crowd's ready for you." The retinue left the parlour and was directed down a darkened corridor. Clinton's friend Jim Lyons said: "We were walking towards the front door and you could hear the people's cheers grow louder. When we got to the steps the daylight hit us and we saw there were thousands of people in that tiny square. It was an overpowering experience. He was touching people's lives here. I talked about it later with the President and told him he wouldn't be as well regarded in some places in Arkansas. He said ,'Yeah, you're probably right.'"

Keanie was sent as advance man to the stage, which had been built only a few metres from the door. It was surrounded by red, white and blue carnations intended for inside the Guildhall until staff were told Clinton was allergic to them. "Emerson gave me a shove and said, 'Go for it, buddy,'" Keanie said. Emerson then began briefing Clinton on what was to follow. "Clinton was totally focused, trying to get himself fired up," the advance man remembered. "I had my hand on his chest literally trying to keep him back from going out too soon. The crowd was so out of its mind he was charged up to get out there."

Keanie had barely uttered his first welcoming words when Clinton could wait no longer and started marching to the stage ahead of schedule. Once he went they all went. The crowd was in raptures. Recalled the Town Clerk: "When I hit the platform there was a surge of noise. We had twenty-five thousand watts of a personal address system that day but I had to roar at the top of my voice to be heard. It worked like an absolute dream." Said Emerson: "The second John Keanie spoke the President started walking. I couldn't hold him back he was so excited. Clinton was actually coming up on stage before John had finished the introduction. It wasn't exactly as we'd planned it, but John was great. He just nailed that introduction." Amidst the cheers could be heard the distinct rustle of thousands of tiny Stars and Stripes which the crowd waved almost in rhythmic unison. Derry City Council staff had scoured Britain and Ireland, snapping up every available flag. "We phoned everywhere looking for flags," said Clare Lundy. "It was like buying shares on Wall Street. Somebody would discover a company in England had so many to sell and we would all shout, 'Buy, buy.' We bought every Stars and Stripes available. We ended up with five thousand of them, costing two thousand pounds." Hundreds of them had pointed tips and that morning American security ordered they be broken off. A source joked: "It would've been quite poignant if the President had been stabbed with a plastic Stars and Stripes."

Clinton gazed in wonderment at the adoring crowds, as one by one, Keanie bellowed out the names of the platform party, which included John Hume and his wife Pat. The President later revealed to the authors: "I was honoured to share a dais with John Hume and I know that added to the warm greeting we received. Derry was wonderful. Every part of the steps, the square and the street was filled with the songs and the spirit of the moment." Clinton's regard for Hume was such that he was the only politician invited to share a stage with the President in his own right. Kerr, in mayoral chain, took to the podium. To his right stood a large Christmas tree and, above him on the Guildhall's façade, a light display depicted Santa's sledge being pulled by reindeers. At a pause in Kerr's speech, spectators began chanting: "We want Bill, we want Bill." Clinton leaned nearer to Hume, who was seated beside him, and asked: "Why are they saying, 'We want bull?'" The Derry accent was clearly troubling him. Kerr reassured the restless onlookers: "You'll get

181

Bill in a minute, no problem." His closing words caused controversy, as they were spoken in Irish. Punching the air with a clenched left fist he proclaimed: "*Ceád míle faílte romhaibh go Doire Colmcille*," which translates as, a hundred thousand welcomes my friends to Derry. Hume interpreted for Clinton. The DUP's Gregory Campbell, watching from a Council enclosure, remarked: "In a different context I don't think it would have been a problem, but on the day it was almost the icing on the cake for a whole series of things of a Catholic culture. John Kerr must have got caught up in the emotion, but I'd people ringing me later saying how appalled they were. It didn't go down too well." Kerr would defend his actions, saying he wanted to stamp his personal identity on what was a speech written in consultation with the Americans.

It was then Hume's turn to mount the Presidential rostrum. The clamour of approval matched that which greeted the first glimpse of Clinton. Hume motioned with raised hands for quiet. It was almost a papal gesture from a man whom many in the city regarded a saint. There was reverent silence. Hume was quick to point out that this was Clinton's day. "The reason we're all gathered in our streets today to say thank you to President Clinton is because peace in our land has been central to the President's policy from the day he was elected," Hume told the crowd. Sir Patrick Mayhew, seated beside the First Lady, launched into eager applause. Only yards away, standing under the Christmas tree, was the leading Sinn Féin strategist Martin McGuinness. "It was a very, very important occasion for Derry," he said. "The fact that so many people came to Guildhall Square clearly showed the amount of warmth there was for Bill Clinton and his role in bringing about the ceasefire. The size of numbers was undoubtedly related to the fact people saw him as an American President who had put his shoulder to the wheel in the search for peace in this country." Gregory Campbell surveyed McGuinness and others in the crowd around him. "I felt the November chill bite into my bones as I stood in the Square looking out over the thousands of faces," he said. "Hardly any were from the Protestant Waterside. Instead they had come from the Creggan, Bogside, Shantallow and Rosemount, some to hurl abuse at the small band of Unionist councillors where I stood."

Fatigue now long forgotten, Clinton flipped open a leather-bound folder embossed with his seal of office and began his second major speech of the day. "There have been many Presidents of the United States who had their roots in this soil. I can see today how lucky I am to be the first President of the United States to come back to this city to say thank you very much," said Clinton. The clock above him on the Guildhall had been stopped from chiming on the full, half and quarter hour so that the President's speech wouldn't be interrupted. There was none of the political substance of the Mackie speech in what followed; the President delivered an address more personal and historical in perspective. Hume was singled out for special praise: "I'm proud to be here in the home of Ireland's most tireless champion of civil rights and its most eloquent voice of non-violence, John Hume." Also mentioned was Paddy 'Bogside' Doherty, a man who'd spent a third of his 70 years trying to bring jobs and hope to teenagers in a city ravaged by violence. "It was quite unexpected when he mentioned my name," remembered Doherty who was down in the crowd. "It was one of those days when you felt good and everybody around you felt good. It was a good day to be alive." (Doherty was probably one of the few, if not the only person in Guildhall Square, who could lay claim to having seen the first Presidential visit to the island of Ireland. In 1963 he and his wife Eileen had gone to Galway to catch a glimpse John Kennedy.)

Clinton's speech was also littered with references to some of the city's famous literary figures, playwright Brian Friel and poet Seamus Heaney. It was a line by Heaney, the Nobel Laureate, which Clinton said encapsulated the mood perfectly. "History says, don't hope on this side of the grave, but then, once in a lifetime the longed-for tidal wave of justice can rise up. And hope and history rhyme." (Clinton later used Heaney's words in a book title.)

Dusk was falling as Clinton came off stage and into the vast crowd where he had an unexpected encounter with a face from his past. Newtownbutler-born Sheila McLoughlin, a nurse who'd worked in Little Rock, Arkansas, had first met then-Governor Clinton in 1982 at a shopping mall. She'd fled the Troubles with her family but had returned to Northern Ireland and was now working at Altnagelvin. "He was reaching out shaking hands over my head, but looking at me all the time," she said. "All of a sudden he re-membered me and asked was I on vacation. I said, 'No, I'm working at the local hospital', and he said, 'Thanks for coming down to see me.' It was so exciting to see a man I'd met years ago in Arkansas now in my home town as President of the United States. He is a very special man to me." Clinton afterwards expressed his surprise at the one-in-a-million chance meeting. "I've just met a woman I knew years ago in Arkansas," he told Kerr. (Susan Brophy was one of several Clinton staff to testify to his powers of recall. "He has an incredible memory for people he's met," she told the authors.)

Hume hovered close to the President throughout his walkabout, at times encroaching on the sacred security bubble. Said an American source: "We had to point out to John a couple of times, 'O.K. John, let go of the President, let go of the President.'" Added Mayor Kerr: "I looked down from the steps of the Guildhall and saw Hume shaking hands alongside the President. The politician came out in me and I wandered down as well. I heard one of the security guys say, 'Just the President', as he pulled Hume back. But it was Hume's patch and it didn't matter who it was. God himself wouldn't have stopped Hume in his own town." Emerson was ahead of the President, helping deal with crowd control. "I got right to Shipquay Gate and there were three women standing up on a ledge," he said. "One of them had half her body over the railings and I told her she'd have to get down and she said, 'No, I'm going to fall right into the President's arms.' The President was getting closer and then, sure as hell, she pitched forward and into his arms. The Secret Service just grabbed her and pulled her to the side, but what a great moment for her." Clinton rewarded the overflow of people outside Guildhall Square. Ducking into Shipquay Street he grabbed a microphone to express an impromptu thanks at the turn-out.

Clinton reflected on the crowd's ebullience as he chatted over a late lunch back inside the Guildhall some minutes later. "You know they tried to pull my wedding ring off," said Clinton to his wife. She replied, "Yeah, yeah, I'm sure." The view from the Green Room, whose refurbishment for the President even stretched to a new toilet and bathroom fittings, was panoramic. Its leaded windows framed the Waterside, with the Donegal Hills in the background. Food laid out on a table loaned by a furniture store had been prepared in a basement kitchen by a Derry chef, under the watchful eyes of the President's catering staff. His slices of beef and pork were sampled before being taken to Clinton on one of four sets of china brought in for the occasion. "The strangest part of the job I do is that I have

Star performer... Clinton after turning on the Christmas tree lights at Belfast City Hall. He spoke from behind a bullet-proof shield. The Secret Service ordered it used "because they couldn't look at every window facing Donegall Square." *(John Harrison Photography)*

Above, flag-waving spectators among an 80,000 crowd at Belfast City hall listen to Clinton's address. "What he did was give a bit of hope and vision for Northern Ireland," said Mo Mowlam. *(John Harrison Photography)*. Below, preacher-cum-Belfast Lord Mayor Eric Smyth, Bible in hand, with Clinton at City Hall. "I took no offence at the scriptural reference," said the President after Smyth's address was jeered by some sections of the crowd. *(John Harrison Photography)*

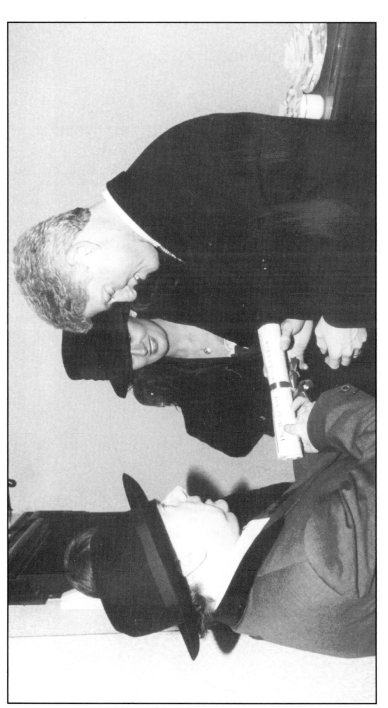

Belfast-born rock star Van Morrison gives Clinton a memento during a private meeting at City Hall after playing to vast crowds outside. The White House press "discovered Van Morrison that night and it's one of the legacies of the trip," remarked a Clinton spokesman. Looking on is Morrison's fiancée, Michelle Rocca. (*White House*)

Twelve hours after touchdown... Clinton's still on his feet addressing guests at a reception at Queens University. "I have known many people with high levels of energy but President Clinton is in a league of his own," said Senator George Mitchell. In the audience can be seen SDLP MP Eddie McGrady and former Belfast Lord Mayor, Hugh Smyth. (*White House*)

Above, DUP leader Ian Paisley before fiery private talks backstage at Queen's. "It wasn't very easy telling the world's strongest man to his face that you'd like to put your boot in his backside," said Paisley. Seated to the President's left is US Ambassador to London, Admiral William Crowe. *(Crispin Rodwell)*. Below, in the firing line... the two 'Presidents' snapped before their meeting at Queen's. "It was a fairly good day politically for Sinn Féin in terms of acknowledgement by the President," said Adams' Press Officer, Richard McAuley. *(White House)*

Taking a back seat... First Lady Hillary Clinton at Queen's University wearing a brooch presented to her in Derry made by a local silversmith, Tony Langan. Someone like Nancy Reagan would have wanted to be "the belle of the ball," said a White House official. *(White House)*

Above, Ulster Unionist leader David Trimble shared a limousine ride with Clinton to the Europa Hotel for the day's last engagement. The President went to bed at midnight. "I looked in his eyes and saw he was beat," said an onlooker. *(Crispin Rodwell).* Left, two wise men... Senator George Mitchell (left) and National Security Advisor Tony Lake relax at the end of a long day. "Lake's the one who believed we could pull it off," said a White House staffer. *(John Harrison Photography)*

Looking back on a triumphant trip... the Clintons walk away from Queen's University. "I will remember this day for as long as I live," said the President. *(John Harrison Photography)*

Bye, bye Bill... Secretary of State Sir Patrick Mayhew and his wife Jean bid Air Force One farewell. "My impressions were of somebody prepared to go the extra mile and then another mile in terms of personal effort," said Mayhew of Clinton's peace efforts. *(John Harrison Photography)*

Billy and the kid in the Oval Office... days after Clinton came to Belfast, Catherine Hamill went to Washington. "It's been a long time since kids relaxed in this room," remarked one of Clinton's assistants. (*White House*)

opportunities to sit down and talk with the President of the United States," said Emerson, who was alone with the Clintons. Emerson had come off his motorbike in June 1994 just after returning from France where he'd worked on the D-Day commemoration visit. He suffered multiple injuries and was on a life support machine for some time, taking several months to recover. At the time of the accident he was working as a scheduler in Al Gore's office, and both the Gores and the Clintons took great interest in his recovery. "The three of us had all this food. The President was eating short-bread and saying, 'These are really good', but Mrs Clinton warned him, 'But they're one hundred per cent butter and that's all fat.' I felt a bit uncomfortable but Mrs Clinton had asked me to sit down with them. It was a nice moment because no-one was asking him for anything and he could truly relax." During the 20-minute break, the three read letters sent to the US Consul General's office in Belfast in the run-up to the trip. "The President was talking about meeting Catherine Hamill in Belfast and we began reading some letters," remembered Emerson. "They were just beautiful, so touching and tender. One said, 'I'm glad you've come to Northern Ireland. I hope you don't get killed.' It was like, my God, this was a seven-year-old kid writing this. It was one of my favourite moments of his Presidency."

While the President wasn't able to address the subject of his ancestry during the visit, one senior member of his White House staff was. As the Clintons lunched, Presidential Press Secretary Mike McCurry came face to face with his Irish roots. Earlier in 1995, Wallace McCurry from Limavady had written to Washington after seeing the Clinton aide giving a press conference on television. "I noticed Mike had a McCurry nose," laughed the Du Pont factory worker. "I thought he must be a direct descendant of the McCurrys from the Isle of Islay and therefore a member of the clan. I sat down one night and penned a letter to him." As well as a family tree, Wallace McCurry told his most famous cousin of the clan's attempt to gain recognition for its role in bringing the song 'Danny Boy' to the world. He said: "We've proved beyond doubt that it was our ancestor Jimmy McCurry, a blind fiddler, who played the 'Londonderry Air' on Limavady's Main Street in 1851. Today that haunting melody is famous the world over as the unofficial anthem of the Irish people."

It stuck a chord with Mike McCurry whose reply, on White House notepaper, arrived the month of the President's visit. "You cannot imagine how much your research on 'Danny Boy' meant for my reputation at the White House," stated the Clinton spokesman. "Ms Glynn, Ms Brophy, Mr Gearan, Ms Higgins, Mr [Mack] McLarity [White House advisor] and a good many of our other prominent Irish-Americans have finally ceded some ground to the Scots-Irish caucus! And forever will I sing that sad song with pride." McCurry ended his letter expressing a hope that their two paths might cross during Clinton's trip. And sure enough they met at the Guildhall.

University of Ulster employee John McCaffrey, who was recruited to Emerson's Derry planning team, had arranged for Wallace McCurry, a friend of a friend, to be at the Guildhall. Recalled McCaffrey: "I said to Mike, 'You never guess what. I've your cousin Wallace upstairs', and he said, 'That's so great. I can't believe it.'" After the Press Secretary made some phone calls, there was a mini-gathering of the McCurry clan in the building's main hall, which was filled with dignitaries awaiting Clinton. Said Wallace: "We shook hands and he put his arms around me. Mike said, 'I knew you were here because as soon as we arrived in Guildhall Square '-Danny Boy' was playing.' I said it was a special request just for him. The meeting was very nostalgic." The White House McCurry, from the Scots-Irish Bible Belt of South Carolina, recalled: "We'd a great time. For a lot of us on the trip there was a great deal of personal meaning because of our own ancestry. It was just a very moving experience."

The get-together ended as President Clinton came into the hall for his next engagement, the establishment of a peace studies chair in honour of the late Tip O'Neill, the former Speaker of the House of Representatives, at the University of Ulster. The event, Washington's brainchild, caused a degree of unease in the run-up to the visit. It certainly came out of the blue to Derry City Council. "The Tip O'Neill thing sneaked up on us," said a source. "It just emerged out of the ether." Some American planners were concerned, not least because O'Neill had been so synonymous with Hume and Irish Nationalism. "We had heard a lot about the O'Neill family thing but because it was all coming out of the political side of the White House we couldn't find out what was going on," a source disclosed. "We were worried the whole thing could turn into the singing of

Irish songs." A university source disclosed: "Without being too cynical, there had to be a pay-back for the Boston community. The Irish-American lobby, with its very strong contacts and friends in the White House like Nancy Soderberg, were pushing heavily for something to happen." Derry's Unionists had their concerns. "The O'Neill chair was within the gift of Clinton but I was worried about the whole ambience of the thing," said Gregory Campbell, who had in his pocket two letters for Clinton written by women whose husbands had been murdered in acts of IRA terrorism. "In the end it was warmer inside the Guildhall, but no more comforting to a Protestant."

The American Ireland Fund was the chair's financial backers and it was its President, Loretta Brennan Glucksman, who performed the honours in front of Clinton and his audience. Turning from the rostrum towards the President, she said: "I am so proud to be an American today, Mr President. I am personally grateful for all your work towards peace." Clinton nodded in thanks. To recognise the establishment of the chair – which would finance the study of conflict resolution – a decorative stone tobacco leaf from the original Capitol building was handed over to the university from the O'Neill family, forty of whom had come from Boston especially.

The stone leaf which Clinton stepped forward to admire had almost been lost on its travels across the Atlantic. Tip O'Neill's daughter, Rosemary, who worked at the State Department, had decided to post it to her good friend Paddy Doherty. "A week before the visit we still hadn't received it," said Doherty. "We were phoning all over the country and we couldn't get a handle on it. We were beginning to panic and, what's more, we didn't know exactly what we were looking for. At one stage an MP in England was involved and I was threatening hauliers I'd get the FBI on them." Suddenly, on the Tuesday evening before the visit, a car pulled up at Doherty's house at Westland Street and the elusive stone was taken out of the boot. Almost misdirected to Rome, it had been sent to London and passed through the hands of several haulage companies before finally arriving in the Bogside. "When I got it I kept it under lock and key in the front room. Every time the kids walked past it they saluted it," said the Derryman. (While the stone wasn't lost, one of the O'Neill's other gifts was. A gold-plated putter belonging to Tip, which was later presented to Clinton, never found its way back to Washington.)

After this ceremony, Clinton was presented with an honorary doctorate from the University of Ulster. The presentation was stripped of all its customary pomp and ceremony and was probably the quickest in the university's history. (Clinton's university robes were delivered to the White House in 1996.) It was something the university had been pushing for since the announcement of Clinton's visit, although its approval only came at the last minute. "We'd been in the White House and faxed them every week, but the point came where we thought we weren't going to get the honorary degree," said McCaffrey. "It became clear they were going to do the Tip O'Neill chair and we thought the degree wasn't going to happen. It was really only in the last week, when the US advance team was on the ground in Derry and the relationship we built up was very solid. Ed Emerson turned around and said, 'What can I do for you?' I said, 'the degree'." Vice-Chancellor Trevor Smith handed Clinton his scroll. The President examined it and muttered to himself: "I'll have to frame that." In remarks that followed, Clinton joked: "You know, I wonder how far it is from a degree to a professorship? I have this job without a lot of tenure and I'm looking for one with more tenure."

The Guildhall event concluded with a sing-song. Kerr introduced musician Phil Coulter, whom Clinton immediately recognised as having entertained him before. The President's eyes lit up. Kerr teased him about joining Hume and Coulter in a late-night rendition of 'When Irish Eyes Are Smiling' at the White House. The President was also familiar with many of his songs, having relaxed to Coulter tapes on the campaign trail in 1992. "I had to cancel things to be there, but when you get that kind of call you drop everything," said Coulter, a good friend of Mark Gearan. Coulter, in yellow waistcoat and tweed jacket, pointed at Clinton in a gun-style fashion and winked as he sat down at a piano. "Mark told me beforehand to play 'The Town I Loved So Well' and said that the President then might actually sing 'Danny Boy' afterwards," recalled Coulter. "But word came back that he couldn't because his throat was a bit raw." (Clinton had learned the second verse of 'Danny Boy' especially.)

Coulter pulled over a microphone and made himself comfortable. He had attended the same school as Hume, Heaney and Friel, and penned 'The Town I Loved So Well' after returning to Derry from a spell abroad. It tells of a city brought to it knees by the Troubles. "During some pretty dark hours in this part of the world I wrote a song in which I prayed for a bright, brand new day," Coulter said to an expectant hall. "Little did I dream that I would ever perform that song in this Guildhall for a President of the United States who's done so much to bring that bright, brand new day ever closer to us, and we're eternally grateful to you."

Clinton was already teary-eyed as the first notes tinkled from the piano. As Coulter sang of bombed-out bars and armoured cars the lyrics seemed ever more poignant. He later recalled: "The words took on a whole new vividness. I saw those streets again that are enumerated in the song. All those ghosts were around me and I was thinking, God, if only my mother and father were alive to see me here. Professionally it was a high, but it was far more important personally. I was numb for hours afterwards."

As the President swayed in his seat, mouthing the words to the chorus, his figure contrasted sharply with that of Sir Patrick Mayhew to his left. Congressman Peter King observed: "You could see the anguish on Mayhew's face when Coulter sang about the army tanks and the guns. He was staring straight ahead and moving uncomfortably in his chair. It obviously wasn't what he'd anticipated. I think he was looking forward to a nice rendition of 'When Irish Eyes are Smiling' or something." Unionists weren't joining in either. Gregory Campbell of the DUP claimed it contained "twisted words which almost blame the army for ruining the city." Deputy Mayor Dallas agreed. "The song wasn't too suitable," he added.

Indeed, Unionist discontent surfaced as Clinton circled the hall on leaving. Recalled Dallas: "I wasn't even introduced to the President and I was the Deputy Mayor. I was standing talking to Edward Daly [the former Catholic Bishop] and councillors were waving, not for me to come over to be introduced, but him. I actually held the rope down for him to get over. The whole thing was nothing but a Nationalist jamboree." Dallas cursed his treatment within earshot of Church of Ireland Bishop James Mehaffey, who had every sympathy for him. "I felt Richard Dallas was overlooked," he said later. "My feelings of the day were mixed. I was delighted the President came to Derry. It was a short visit I know, but there was a lack of thought put into how the Unionist-Protestant tradition would be recognised. I blame the city fathers. There was an emphasis on one tradition at the loss of the other. There was not so much anger among Protestants as disappointment."

Worse was to follow. As Clinton said his goodbyes, the Protestant Waterside was getting ready to receive him. They had turned out to cheer him on his way into Derry and now he was scheduled to stop on his way back to the airport. Indeed many hadn't gone to Guildhall Square for that reason. Oakgrove Integrated Primary School was the chosen spot for Clinton to pause and say hello; Secret Service agents had already scanned the crowds with hand-held metal detectors.

The President's convoy sped over Craigavon Bridge. Ed Emerson, Secret Service agent James McGettigan and RUC superintendent Peter Sheridan were in the forward car. Word came over the radio that Clinton was running late for Belfast. The Waterside stop was to be abandoned. Said Emerson: "I'd people call me from Belfast shouting, 'There's a hundred thousand people down here all waiting. Don't do anything.' The whole time we'd an off-the-record in the Waterside built into his schedule but it was dependent on whether he got to us on time and whether our event ran to time." Added Sheridan: "He'd to switch on the Christmas tree lights in Belfast and time beat him. Nothing more than that. Right up to the point we crossed the bridge he was stopping at Du Pont and Oakgrove."

The decision, however innocent, added to the bitterness felt by the city's minority community at the Clinton visit. "Not calling on the Waterside was unforgivable and the worst thing was the Americans just didn't know what they'd done," said Campbell. "For them it had already been a wonderful day full of music, colour and spectacle. But they didn't realise they closed out the Protestants. There was just no balance." The US planners in Derry weren't politically sensitive enough to argue against the advice to press on to the airport. "It wouldn't have happened in Belfast," contended one American source. "Brady, Kathy and Blair wouldn't have let it."

IX

Days like this

*What he did, which the rest of us as politicians of
any colour had failed to do, was give a bit of hope
and vision for Northern Ireland. In a sense he
reached out to the public across the heads of the
politicians. The crowd was mostly young. They were
a generation that wanted to believe there was hope
for the future and he gave them that.*

Dr Mo Mowlam, Shadow Northern Ireland Secretary

Belfast had not seen a street carnival anything like the night the
Clintons topped the bill at the home of Northern Ireland's very
own political vaudeville. The City Hall attracted in the region of
eighty thousand Protestants and Catholics, galvanised by their spell-
binding ode to hope. It was a magical evening. But the brightly
coloured fairy lights that twinkled from the Christmas tree in the
season of goodwill contributed to an optical illusion, though few at
the time hesitated to rub their eyes. As O'Dowd and Morrison hid
their firsthand knowledge of the fragile state of the peace process,
the IRA set in train a ceasefire-breaking bomb plot. "I certainly
wasn't spreading doom and gloom," recalled O'Dowd as he sat in a
grandstand staring out at a sea of happy faces, "but I had it in my
mind we were in deep trouble." The contradiction jarred with

Morrison too. "It was pretty distant from the political reality," the Irish-American later stated.

The City Hall and the switching on of the Christmas tree lights was the visual centrepiece of the Clinton trip to Northern Ireland. Said a member of the British Government planning team: "The tree was the symbol of the visit. This was Hollywood to the Americans. They saw the imagery straight away and it was good because it got City Hall into the itinerary. Two things always stayed on right from the start – Mackie and the Christmas tree."

The huge turnout at the City Hall was proof that Clinton had succeeded in capturing the hearts and minds of the people. Cynics who had spent the week ringing radio talk shows, claiming they were in a majority which resented the President's peace mission, were forced to eat their words. Indeed, some were probably now among the teeming masses. "There was a magic in the air which ended up drawing people like magnets," said a Washington official. "There was something special going on and people wanted to be part of this slice of history. In a perfect world that's the way things are supposed to happen but it's not something you can plan for. You hope the stars line up right and that's what happened."

Ten days before the President's arrival, the US trip planners had tapped into the consciousness of the country. "It has now dawned on just about everyone, politicians and public alike, that the visit is the biggest thing to happen in a generation or more," an American document written during the preparation for the visit stated. "It symbolises the world coming to Northern Ireland and Northern Ireland to the world on a scale never seen before. The President's visit is recognised as a huge peace dividend. Civic pride, business hopes and political ambitions have combined to create the conviction that no-one can afford to be seen as a spoiler." The City Hall reaped the reward of the cumulative effect of the earlier events. Mark Gearan, who had left the White House in September and was now accompanying the President as Director of the Peace Corps, thought the Christmas spirit contributed to the great sense of occasion. "I had always thought if the President could get to Northern Ireland he would be wonderfully received, because of his personality as much as his achievement in terms of the peace process." A source at the White House added: "To see all those people, who not that long ago would've been afraid to go out at night, come out together was incredible, just absolutely incredible."

The British suggested the tree-lighting ceremony during the trip's early planning stages and it was one of the few things the two sides saw eye-to-eye on instantaneously. Explained a London government official: "The planning process was one where we came up with ideas and bounced them off the Americans and the Americans came up with ideas and bounced them off us. Sometimes we agreed an idea was brilliant, like the Christmas tree." Its genesis apparently lay in a flippant remark by a civil servant. The Northern Ireland Office had minuted its various departments on suggestions for events, prompting an employee within the Department of the Environment to observe: "It's a terrible time of year for the President to be coming. Sure all he could do is switch on the lights on the Christmas tree." The Americans latched on to the concept after it was first floated at a meeting in Belfast in mid-September, called to sift through a list of locations to be visited on the forthcoming site survey. A British memorandum written on 19 September recorded the Americans' positive response. Said a White House official who travelled on the site survey: "The minute I heard about it I knew we were going to light a Christmas tree, because it was too good an event. It was exactly the right kind of event to send out the message that the President was coming to Northern Ireland to do." Added another American source: "We saw it as the nightly news event. We saw it in terms of the photo."

The Christmas tree event was doubly perfect in that it got the City Hall onto the schedule but, importantly, with none of its political baggage. Some American planners perceived the British to be initially lukewarm about it as a venue, though they warmed to it in the course of a few weeks. "In the early stages they were very much Hillsborough, Stormont," recalled a US source. "City Hall was not somewhere they could control, but this all moved over the course of several weeks."

The City Hall was a citadel of Unionist rule, despite the creeping electoral advances of Sinn Féin, the second largest party on the Council by November 1995. (There was a period of time when Unionist councillors upped and exited the chamber when a member of Sinn Féin rose to speak.) Following the Anglo-Irish Agreement, it operated an adjourned policy in protest and introduced a ban on British Government ministers which lasted for six years. Irish President Mary Robinson was barred too, for shaking Gerry Adams' hand.

As Unionism fought a rearguard action, Belfast City Council became a cockpit of tribal backbiting. While many other local authorities in Northern Ireland embraced the concept of power sharing, its Unionist majority, living on borrowed time which finally expired in May 1997, hung on to the levers of power by the fingertips. Certainly the Americans were only too well aware of the City Hall's reputation. Sinn Féin had informed Nancy Soderberg that Belfast City Council was synonymous "with Unionist discrimination against Catholics at a number of levels – political, social and economic."

The City Hall's notoriety was a major reason why it was not selected as the venue for a political reception. Furthermore, the Americans didn't want to rub the potentially volatile city fathers up the wrong way. "The reception wouldn't work there because of sensitivities in the City Council about who might come from the outside," said a one of the US trip planners. In this the Americans found themselves at one with the Council's top administrators who worked to the elected representatives. "It became quickly very clear the Americans didn't want the City Hall bit of the trip political," said Chief Executive Brian Hanna. "They wanted it to be civic and festive and that fitted in quite well with ourselves because we certainly didn't want to get involved in any political difficulties or differences. The switching on of the lights wasn't to be a political event. It was to be a celebratory event of the circumstances of the time." One of Belfast's councillors added: "Brian is very, very competent and handled this thing bureaucratically, took it out of the political arena when there was a risk of some political chicanery by some of our more lunatic brethren."

The City Hall provided a splendidly elegant backdrop to the Clinton extravaganza. It had taken eight years to build and, on completion in 1906, it dominated downtown Belfast, covering an acre and a half in Donegall Square, where shopping and business districts later came to merge. Constructed of Portland stone in the classical renaissance style, its most distinctive feature is a copper-covered dome, 173 feet tall, topped with a stone lantern. Stained-glass windows commemorate events in its history, including its bombing during World War II. Its open-plan gardens are dominated by statues, including one of Queen Victoria, who granted Belfast the status of city in 1888. The City Hall was built in response to this and it symbolises Belfast's development from seventeenth-century village to twentieth-century city.

During the Troubles, the City Hall became a rallying point for Belfast's more politically active citizens, most notably attracting over one hundred thousand for a Unionist protest against the Anglo-Irish Agreement. In the wake of terrorist atrocities it became the focus of peace vigils and, in the 1990s, Sinn Féin took its street politics from the ghetto to the City Hall to symbolise its demand for parity of esteem. It was at a peace-time gathering at the City Hall in the run up to the Clinton visit that Adams told supporters, the IRA "haven't gone away, you know." The President's open-air performance was unique in City Hall's history, however, in that this was a celebration, not a demonstration.

The Americans offered to provide a Christmas tree as a symbol of their historical ties with Northern Ireland. Hanna said: "When Kathy Stephens told me I was rather taken aback. I thought, how on earth were they going to get a tree that size to Northern Ireland? But she said, 'Don't worry. We'll deal with that.'" However, what no-one knew at the time was that the innocent suggestion would end up going all the way to the British Government's Cabinet Office amid fear of censure from the European Union. It almost throttled NIO trip planners in red tape became the bane of Northern Ireland Secretary Mayhew. "It did make me extremely angry. That made me very cross indeed," he later recalled. Said an American official: "One British official described it as the lost episode of *Yes, Minister*. He said, 'By the end the notes on it were half a foot thick, with every agency having to have a say.'"

The 49-foot-tall, 4,000lb white pine was felled on 17 November, on a golf course in Belfast's sister city of Nashville in Al Gore's home state of Tennessee. Before the 30-year-old tree left on its eight-day journey to Belfast it was checked by the US Agriculture Department's Animal and Plant Health Inspection Service for a bug that destroys forestation. The test, though, did not impress UK officials for, as one Whitehall specialist pointed out: "We're going to have to import something that under European law we are not allowed to."

Forestry products were the subject of a trade dispute between the European Union and North America because of concern that the import of American timber would threaten domestic industries.

Said a British official: "I thought this was a joke for a Monday morning and then realised it wasn't. The UK Permanent Representation to the European Union were saying, on the one hand let's not get crazy about this, but on the other we don't want to end up at the European Court or be accused by our partners of causing a serious breach in forestry product policy." Mayhew, who had enough on his plate with the peace process and Clinton's visit, became extremely irked by the issue. "I said, 'Their bloody Christmas tree is going up and I don't care. Any trouble and you can blame me. Now get it up.' And it went up." A British official reported: "What seemed like a good idea at the time had turned into a nightmare. It seemed a joke, but by the end nobody was laughing." One of the US side added: "They weren't going to keep President Clinton's tree out. You could see the headline: Gesture of Goodwill from Belfast Sister City held up by EU Inspectors. The Euro-sceptics in Major's Government would've gone crazy." Britain's Ambassador to Washington, Sir John Kerr, was drawn into the tree saga too. He recalled: "I remember the diplomacy of that bloody Christmas tree. I sent quite a lot of signals from here saying, come on, grow up. I probably spent more time on that than on the contact they planned with Adams actually." David Watkins at the NIO wanted to avoid a fuss and, even though no signs of disease were found in it, an undertaking was given that the tree would be incinerated when done with. (Someone had suggested it be auctioned for charity.) In the meantime Belfast City Council had a local tree selected for the chop in case the American one didn't arrive.

The Nashville pine was shrouded in plastic and flown in alongside Cadillacs on a US Air Force Galaxy transport plane. Kathy Stephens and Lord Mayor Eric Smyth watched it being hoisted into place at the front of City Hall on 25 November. But it had suffered in its long journey, and one council official commented: "It was the worst tree we'd ever had. We had to wire all the branches to give it back its shape." In a postscript, the council planted 20 white pines in 1996 in different parts of the city to commemorate the visit.

The Christmas tree saga was only one half of the quirky sideshow at the City Hall before the President's arrival. Before definitive plans had been laid for Clinton to throw the switch on the peace party, Mayor Smyth had booked the children's television characters, the Power Rangers, to perform the task. Traditionally the occasion was one for the city's youngsters and drew crowds of several thousand. Hence in the run-up to the trip the press, fed by mischief-making Unionist councillors only too willing to oblige with a quote or two, pitched Clinton head-to-head with Rocky Red Ranger and Tommy White Ranger, two of the karate-chopping, kung-fu kicking band of American action heroes. At one point a majority of respondents in an telephone poll conducted by a local television station favoured the Power Rangers over Clinton. The episode wasn't altogether surprising to those familiar with the antics at the City Hall, which one scribe once christened the 'Dome of Delight'. "There was never an issue with the Council, never," insisted Hanna. "It was a wonderful story for the media. It was put across as some sort of great debate between the President of the United States and the Power Rangers but it was never that kind of situation."

However, some councillors attempted to put a more serious spin on the story, stating that a £4,000 booking fee could be forfeited if the Power Rangers lost the first fight in their history. They also pointed out that traders wanted the switch-on, which usually signalled the onset of a shopping frenzy, earlier than 30 November. Frank Caddy, Chief Executive of the Belfast Chamber of Trade and Commerce, said: "We don't rely on the lights switch-on that much, but the day Clinton was here was the worst day's trading in living memory because of the disruption caused. Retailers were happy to put up with it though. They treated it as an investment in their future." Deputy Lord Mayor Dr Alisdair McDonnell of the SDLP accused Unionists of playing party politics with the biggest night in the city's history. "That some sectors of Unionism felt the Power Rangers were a more suitable alternative was more a reflection on their mentality than anything else. They made fools of themselves and embarrassed the rest of us with their stupidity." One of the US trip team recalled being stunned into silence when the issue was first mooted at a planning session with the Council's administrative executives. "I don't think anybody on our side said anything. It was bemused silence. Basically, you know, you've got to be kidding. It was never anything more than a kind of standing joke among ourselves. I expect between Brian Hanna and some members of the Council it may not have been so much fun though." Hanna most certainly wasn't laughing. He could see Belfast's great chance to alter its negative international image being jeopardised. "There was to be massive television coverage throughout the world and this was a huge opportunity to promote Belfast as a place to visit and invest in at that time of the ceasefires."

At the end of October, the Council's powerful Policy and Resources Committee declared the 'contest' a draw and reached a compromise. The Power Rangers duo would guest at a family fun night on 16 November, Clinton at the Christmas tree ceremony two weeks later. One of those who dealt with the Power Rangers said: "The whole Clinton versus the Power Rangers thing was nonsense. The Power Rangers ended up in the middle of something they shouldn't have been in the middle of. The whole thing was very badly handled by City Hall." To finally lay the matter to rest, Mayor Smyth issued a statement saying that there had "never been any intention to snub the President." And to dispel any persisting notion that he objected to Clinton's visit on political grounds, the DUP man went on: "I will do everything in my power to make President Clinton welcome and look forward to treating the President with courtesy and showing him some true Northern Ireland hospitality."

The chasm between the political parties at the City Hall meant that the President wasn't considered for its highest recognition and rarely bestowed honour, the freedom of Belfast. The privilege instead was left to Dublin. "The thing about a freedom is that you need a two-thirds majority in the Council," explained Hanna. "It would not have been a good idea to get into a political debate about whether or not the President should have received the freedom. If you're going to do it you have to be certain you're going to get agreement otherwise it would be very embarrassing." The Deputy Mayor was left ruing a missed opportunity. "It was never under consideration but it should have been," said McDonnell. "Dublin did it but we failed to grab the chance. We're not good at these things, not good at PR. Sometimes in our petty politics we get bogged down in too much trivia."

So Clinton wouldn't follow in the footsteps of former President Dwight D. Eisenhower, who was made an Honorary Burgess when he visited Belfast as a US army general in August 1945, seven years before his election to the White House. Thousands gave Ike a rousing ticker-tape welcome. The City Hall citation read: "Few Ulstermen, and no-one from another land, have established a stronger hold upon the admiration of the people of Northern Ireland than you, and the victories achieved by the Allied armies in Europe are in themselves eloquent testimony to your gifts as a great commander." Eisenhower in fact returned to Belfast in 1962, having served the maximum two terms in the Oval Office, and showed his wife, Mamie, where he'd signed the visitors' book 17 years earlier. While the Americans were staggered by the bizarre goings-on at the City Hall, those who worked for the Council on the Christmas festivities were left awestruck by the scale of event Washington had in mind. "Think big and don't worry about the cost," one of the American team kept telling them. "Clearly, if you bring the President of the United States to your premises you bring with him the whole rigmarole of security and all the rest of it," said Hanna. "You have to accept that, but it was worth it." The Council assembled a co-ordinating group drawn from various departments and took over an office dubbed the Clinton room. Initially, communication was unsatisfactorily effected via a facsimile machine. The White House sent over sketches in which the City Hall bore a striking resemblance to Capitol Hill, with signs reading 'peace' hanging from its grand façade. (They never appeared on the night.) "The difficulty with an event like this was you have nothing to work back on, you have no other UK city to refer to," said Brian Morrison, the senior man on the City Hall team. "I remember saying to the chief, 'It's getting bigger and bigger every day.' All I could do was manage the chaos." Not only had his team to construct a stage and VIP galleries, but take care of sound and vision. The Americans insisted on two advanced sound systems – one a back-up – to relay the President's address to the crowd, with no time delay between podium and the furthest spectator. The equipment had to be hired in England from a company more accustomed to dealing with the promoters of outdoor opera performances. "The electrical supply for all this was unbelievable," said Chris Waring who oversaw the mechanics of the colossal operation outside the City Hall, all performed daily under the gaze of a mesmerised public. "We had to take over a guy's office in the City Hall and his floor was a mass of switch gear. They were pulling cables up through the floor from the basement and drilling holes in cupboards to link the gear to the generator."

With one eye always on the ledger, sponsorship was sought for the huge video screens that would project the President's image down Donegall Place, the city centre's main thoroughfare leading from the City Hall. "We could only guess how much all this was going to cost and at one point our councillors were getting very concerned," said Morrison. One City Hall source added: "They'll never know exactly how much it all cost." US telecommunications firm CableTel forked out more than £40,000 for the screens. The British Government also chipped in towards spiralling costs. "I look at it from the point of view that you spend money in order to get benefits," said Hanna. "I think the benefits we got were enormous. We had been doing tremendous lobbying in the States to bring investment here and then there was the whole issue of tourism." Washington too saw the potential to use the event, and indeed the entire visit, as a commercial for attracting visitors to Northern Ireland. "You don't go to promote tourism, obviously, but when Air Force One touches down in a place and the President moves around Americans see things with an open mind," said Mark Gearan. "When the daily diet they're getting on the news is bunker footage that's a rather skewed view."

The exterior of the City Hall was coincidentally undergoing a multi-million-pound facelift by the Department of the Environment in the months prior to the Clinton visit, which contributed to the woes of those planning the spectacular. "It wasn't a smooth ride," commented one of the City Hall team. One small bonus though was that large, sandstone pillars and iron gates hadn't as yet been set in place at the front of the City Hall so at least the stage dimensions could be met without having to demolish masonry. The stage size seemed to be constantly changing and had to be widened a couple of extra feet the morning of Clinton's arrival, under protest from exhausted workmen. An army of them were seen through nights of preparation, and vouchers issued to them for free food from a nearby hamburger chain, which remained open especially.

In the run-up to the event it began to generate its own momentum, and the question of entertainment arose. "It became fairly obvious if he was going to arrive at seven o'clock at night the people coming down would have to stand and wait for a long while, so we wanted to put on some entertainment," said Hanna. A 'big band' orchestral was pencilled in, then word filtered back that the city's most famous rock son, Van Morrison, was willing and available. A Clinton-Morrison dream ticket was sure to pull the crowds. At the outset, particularly before it was generally appreciated that the

Clinton visit was striving to be balanced and well intentioned, the Americans were concerned at just how well attended the City Hall event would be. Added Hanna: "The 'x' factor was how many people would appear, would the people of Belfast come down to it. There were all kinds of uncertainties about the numbers, which was a major difficulty. But I think we benefited from the build up. The President was covered live on television and people could see things went smoothly at Mackie, in Derry and so on." The Americans ran a poster competition to publicise the Christmas tree event and 60 art students from the University of Ulster submitted entries. A Stars and Stripes candle design by Paula McElroy was picked and she got to meet Clinton at the City Hall.

Security troubled the Secret Service. They were, according to one American diplomat, "professional paranoids" who more than met their match in the RUC. The anxiety of the President's protection unit increases at outdoor events and for the Christmas-tree lighting ceremony there were literally hundreds of potential vantage points for a gunman. The City Hall is surrounded by dozens of shops and office blocks, each with windows overlooking the spot where the President was to speak. (On the night the lights of office blocks were left on so anyone at a window was immediately seen.) "They were particularly concerned because they couldn't necessarily look at every window facing Donegall Square," said a US Government official. "The Secret Service wasn't going to let him out without the three-inch thick bullet-proof glass which the press didn't want because it didn't give a good shot. We didn't want the message to be, Clinton in Belfast stands behind shield. We wanted a seasonal message, but at the same time we didn't want to expose the President to danger. There's always that kind of tension inherent."

In the event the deployment of the shot-stopping glass – the only time it was used during the Clinton visit to Northern Ireland – posed more problems for Chris Waring, not least ensuring that the stage could take the weight of the five large panes. "I was at a meeting and this typically American guy came up to me at the end and said, 'Buddy, you've been looking for me and I've been looking for you,'" Waring said. "His job was the bullet proof glass. The glass was flown in and arrived in this American wagon with chrome wheels and flashing lights. It was something else, brilliant when you saw it arriving." A crane carefully lowered the glass into position in a precisely choreographed two-hour operation. One schoolboy walking by was heard to say: "What do they need that for? Sure there's a ceasefire." A screened walkway also had to be built covering the fifty or so metres between the front door of the City Hall and the stage. The potential for a flare up among spectators attending the event also preoccupied some of the Americans. "We were concerned about the possibility of things occurring in the crowd. You know, rowdy groups out in Donegall Square and you have a clash between Celtic and Rangers fans."

Spectators started assembling at the crash barriers lining the front of the City Hall around 10.00am, eight hours before the warm-up entertainment began and just after Clinton had walked the Shankill Road. "I had to get the police to move them at lunchtime," said Waring. "Everybody had to move out of that area and come back in through the metal detectors. I was standing behind the crowd barrier at one o'clock as the people rushed up to the front. The atmosphere was great." Many were carrying American flags and the good-natured revelry heated the spirits in the biting chill. Inside City Hall the councillors began arriving by 4.00pm. They were held on the ground floor, the Secret Service having swept and sealed the first floor. Some councillors were restless and agitated. Used to having the run of the place, a few took umbrage at the restrictions on movement during the wait. "Initially the councillors were a bit cool," recalled McDonnell. "But I must say, as the evening wore on they became as excited as I was. Some individual councillors were very conscious of the weightiness of the occasion. You don't just get the President of the United States coming along any day."

The councillors were permitted to bring guests and one person's appearance caused a flap among Unionists. Veteran Republican Joe Cahill had travelled up from Dundalk that afternoon with the intention of expressing gratitude to Clinton for approving his 1994 visa. "I wanted to personally thank him," said Cahill. "The chance of meeting him was a big plus. His visit was of great importance, a great fillip for the peace process, but obviously it didn't create the necessary momentum." Though a guest of Sinn Féin councillor Bobby Lavery, he'd managed to slip into the City Hall without his invitation. "The councillor responsible for co-ordinating the passes, Sean McKnight, didn't turn up at the Sinn Féin offices on the Falls Road so I headed on down. There was a group of six of us," recalled

Cahill. "They showed their passes when they got to the City Hall but nobody asked me. I just walked on through. I was amazed it was so simple." It was just like old times, creeping by the American sentries.

As Cahill tucked into the food on offer, one Sinn Féin councillor delighted in highlighting his presence. Even visiting Irish-Americans were taken aback. "There was real panic stations among Unionists when they saw me," said Cahill. "A lot of heads were coming together in wee groups. One of our councillors said, 'Joe, you're creating some havoc.' The DUP would've had me put out if they could." Out, however, Cahill went because Clinton was running late, thus forcing a change of plan. He and other guests who had hoped to rub shoulders with the President beforehand were asked to take their seats beside the Christmas tree, for on arrival the President would more or less be whisked straight out for the lighting ceremony. McDonnell felt Cahill's appearance was significant. "The most exciting thing for me on the day was that Joe Cahill was there. That for me said more about the commitment to peace by the Provos than anything. It was no longer total war and this was his endorsement of Clinton."

Outside, television presenter Eamonn Holmes compèred the pre-Clinton cabaret, introducing American singer and saxophonist Curtis Stigers, who was performing a concert later that night in Belfast, and Van Morrison, backed by another local pop star Brian Kennedy. When Belfast-born Holmes, who had previously been to a few, poorly-attended peace rallies at the City Hall, was contacted in London by the White House and asked to participate he thought at first he was the victim of a practical joke. He'd no hesitation in accepting though. "In my professional career I've been part of some special events," he said, "but this was the most memorable night of my life. For the first time we all dared to believe it was all over, that this must be the end of violence for good. It was almost surreal. Here was a place known for large demonstrations and suddenly in the middle of it was Clinton." The melancholic Morrison, in ill-fitting long coat, black hat and sunglasses, belted out a trio of his best-known hits in a 15-minute set which was greeted with wild applause and approving cheers.

His girlfriend, former Miss Ireland Michelle Rocca, slow danced in time with the rhythm and mouthed the lyrics at the back of the stage. Morrison's song, 'Days Like This', which was being used as a backing track to a British Government television advertisement promoting the peace process, captured the mood perfectly. The travelling White House press corps were immediate converts to Morrison. Mike McCurry's deputy, Mary Ellen Glynn, another member of the White House's Irish-American clan, said: "Our guys are not the most enlightened crew culturally and when we told them who was going to be playing right before the President some of them replied, 'Van who?' Now there's a bunch of people who talk about him all the time. They say they discovered Van Morrison that night and now have all his albums. It's one of the funny lasting legacies of the trip for the press corps." Morrison's trio of hits included a love song, which he said was "a special request from Bill to Hillary," and his song called 'No Religion'. Down in the thick of the crowd, reporter Ivan Little was broadcasting live for Ulster Television. "We're still waiting for President Clinton to arrive but what a reward, listening to Van Morrison and Brian Kennedy," he told viewers. "A sign of hope even in that. Brian Kennedy, a Catholic from west Belfast, and Van Morrison, a Protestant from east Belfast, and they've just been signing a song called 'No Religion'. I'm sure there's a message in there."

Kennedy found himself having come full circle. "Here I was in front of the City Hall, where I used to meet with my old band in an old van, performing for the President," he recalled. Kennedy, as much as anyone in the crowd, knew what peace meant to Northern Ireland. "I grew up in Beechmount in the centre of a war, basically. The Troubles is an inadequate phrase because my experience is one in which you had to take care of your life every day. You had to negotiate a path to school and encounter soldiers who literally had you sighted down the barrel of a gun." Kennedy was overcome with emotion as he sang his heart out on backing vocals for Morrison. "The buzz I felt from the audience defies words. People were hugging and crying and there was such a sense of celebration in the air. Having somebody like Van sing 'Days Like This' suddenly had such significance lyrically, never mind emotionally. The impact was astounding."

Leader of the Alliance Party, Dr John Alderdice, who was also a city councillor, sat transfixed in a reserved enclosure. "There was very much a carnival atmosphere. The one regret I have is that there wasn't a jam session between the President and Van Morrison on their saxophones." There had been speculation all day long that Clinton might play the instrument – it had become something of a party piece on the 1992 campaign trial. No provision was made for it in Belfast though. Said a member of the US advance team: "That was never on the agenda. It's a hackneyed image the White House doesn't want to see. It's too frivolous for such a serious visit. We wanted the picture to be the President and the Christmas tree, not the President goofing around with a saxophone."

Some of the Washington delegation arrived at City Hall 30-40 minutes ahead of Clinton. Deputy Mayor McDonnell teamed up with Commerce Secretary Brown and dipped into the crowd. "Brown must have shaken 150 hands up and down the front of the throng and he says to me, 'I can't go on.' There were tears rolling down his cheeks. I think it got to him. He was from Harlem and a white crowd in the United States would never have given a black guy, no matter how prominent, that kind of euphoric welcome. That's how emotional it all was." McDonnell also chatted briefly to Soderberg about the success of the visit.

As joyful music filled the night air, Mayor Smyth sought refuge in an office deep within the marbled bowels of the City Hall. He needed quiet to prepare for the introduction he was shortly to make to President Clinton. A devout Christian from age 14, the former security man who had once checked buses for bombs, sank to his knees and prayed. "I knelt beside a chair with the Bible open and asked for wisdom and help with what I was about to say," said Smyth. The fundamentalist was more used to preaching before 60 people at his tiny Jesus Saves Mission on the city's Limestone Road, not a huge crowd coupled with a worldwide television audience. "I was very nervous," he later remembered. He carried the Bible for inspiration. "The one thing I was worrying about was my dyslexia. I thought I might freeze while reading, which sometimes happens." Emerging into a larger outer office, he encountered his wife, Frances, Chief Executive Hanna and several of the President's team. "They said to me, 'We have to go now', but I said, 'Hold on another minute.' There must have been 30 people and I asked them all to close their eyes. You could have heard a pin drop. I prayed for the President, his wife, his staff and the security forces."

Clinton arrived from the airport through the rear gate of the City

Hall, its high-sided courtyard providing better cover for the Presidential entourage than the east wing entrance, which was the more likely option early on in the trip's planning. He was greeted at the door by Smyth, in black Mayoral cloak edged with intricate gold brocade, and Hanna, himself in ceremonial robes. The Clintons asked after the Lord Mayor's two handicapped children. Said the Chief Executive: "Clinton looked a little tired I thought. He is a very personable man, tall and striking. He was very informal in a way perhaps that our royal visitors wouldn't be." A room had been set aside for the President and First Lady to compose themselves after the trip from Derry, and before going on stage they were introduced to two schoolchildren, one Protestant, the other Catholic, who had won a letter-writing competition organised by the *Belfast Telegraph,* supported by the US Consul's office.

Extracts from the best of the 4,000 letters which poured in from around the country were sent to Washington for consideration by speechwriters, where they had a profound impact. An internal American memo stated: "The letters thoughtfully and movingly tell the President what peace has meant in their lives and what they hope for the future. The sophistication and diversity of responses has surprised both the newspaper and the Consulate. Together the letters are telling calls from children to their elders not to let intransigence, arrogance or complacency get in the way of forging a permanent peace and a lasting accommodation." Part of the two children's prizes was to share the stage with the Clintons. "He congratulated me and asked me how I was," said 12-year-old Cathy Harte, who attended St Dominics, a Catholic girls' school on Falls Road. "He was very friendly. I liked him. When I was in the house getting ready to go to the City Hall I was watching Catherine Hamill on the television. She was excellent and I thought, I hope I don't fall on my face." Beside her was Mark Lennox, aged 15. "The men from the Secret Service took us through a plan of what we had to do and where we had to stand. When President Clinton came in he congratulated us," said the Glengormley High School pupil. "He was late and it was like, well done, let's go."

Offstage, Clinton was introduced to his warm-up man as he peeped over a security screen and waved at a crowd so adoring it matched any campaign rally. "Mr President, this is your host for the evening, Eamonn Holmes," said one of his aides. "You're doing a great job," said Clinton. Holmes responded: "No, you're the one doing a great job by being here." Told that the President was waiting in the wings, the John Anderson Big Band abruptly cut short its rendition of the wartime Glenn Miller hit 'Don't Kiss Under the Apple Tree'. The crowd began chanting: "We want Bill, we want Bill." An exhausted Holmes, out of view, then fluffed his introduction line, stumbling over Clinton's middle name, which came out as "Jessup" before he quickly corrected himself.

The President was led up the steps onto the brightly-lit podium by Smyth. He let others take their places as he stood waving in all directions at the thousands whose pent up anticipation was released in a crescendo of cheering. The two schoolchildren were dazed by flashbulbs as a bank of press photographers loosed off dozens of shots. Mark Lennox said: "I'd seen the film *In the Line of Fire* just before the visit, which was about someone planning to assassinate the President. I just kept thinking of that because of all the cameras and security." Added Cathy Harte: "When I saw all those people I thought I was going to faint. I was overwhelmed."

Cheers echoed around the packed streets as Smyth welcomed the President and First Lady. As he'd stepped to the podium seconds earlier he made up his mind that his speech would conclude on a biblical theme. Following a prepared introduction typed out by his secretary, he ad-libbed, reciting Matthew 1:22,23. "I kept thinking of the issue of Christmas and what it was all about," he explained afterwards. "I decided to centre it on Christmas and the message of the gospel. I felt the occasion gave me the opportunity to speak to the people and I couldn't miss it." The catcalls grew more boisterous as his Mayoral welcome to the President transformed itself into a sermon, and the Presidential podium became a pulpit. Smyth glared down at his hecklers and battled through the boos with his message: "Let us remind ourselves of one who is the man of peace and that is the Lord Jesus Christ." A young girl's voice carried above his. "Get down, get down," she screamed.

Clinton's eyes remained focused on Smyth. A politician proud of his Baptist roots, the President had an affinity with Smyth's sermon, if not the manner in which it was received. Clinton later said: "I took no offence at the scriptural reference. After all, Christmas is a religious holiday." The Lady Mayoress, seated to Clinton's right, had pride in her eyes as she gazed at her husband. As the barracking persisted, she glanced at the President to gauge his reaction and to her satisfaction found him locked in concentration on Smyth's speech. "I wasn't worried about the crowd," Smyth remembered, "because I had made up my mind what I was going to do and went for it. They showed their ignorance and let themselves down, but that's the way people are." Smyth's performance, which had some officials and councillors cringing with embarrassment, was the subject of much public debate afterwards. The Lord Mayor received hundreds of letters, those critical of him in the minority. "He got as many compliments as brickbats," said Hanna. "It was his prerogative, and as a man of very deep religious convictions he felt he wanted to make the point that this was a Christian festival." One of the American trip strategists said Smyth's performance didn't detract from the event. "He said what he had to say and it obviously didn't bother the President. We had said to the Lord Mayor that we would expect him to speak for three to five minutes. We told him the President would speak about family and Christmas values and that it wouldn't be political. But we didn't ask to approve the Lord Mayor's speech."

The jeers turned to cheers when Smyth introduced Mrs Clinton, her coat buttoned up to the chin. "Tonight is a night filled with hope and peace," she began. The speech, conveyed with grace and poise, concentrated on the children who'd grown up in the conflict. Young people's issues, after all, were a strong feature of her legal and public life. She quoted from the winning girl's letter first. "My name is Cathy Harte. I am a 12-year-old Catholic girl. I live in Belfast, Northern Ireland, and I love it here. It's green, it's beautiful and well, it's Ireland." The First Lady's perfect delivery enlivened the line. She flashed a broad smile and pointedly turned towards the schoolgirl as the crowd roared its approval of her plain, but effective penmanship. The President too appreciated the line and clapped as Cathy Harte's cheeks glowed. Even the chisel-faced expression of Agent Alto, who was as ever just one step behind the President, relaxed into a grin, though just for a second. "I thought somebody else must have written that letter," said Cathy, the second Cathy to make an impact upon the First Couple in just eight hours. "I couldn't believe it was mine. I'll never forget it as long as I live. My sister videotaped it and my father cried as he watched it over and over again."

As Mrs Clinton went on to read of the girl's simple hopes for the future, it was evident from the delight of the crowd that her words rivalled anything that could have been put to paper in the White House. The First Lady's passion brought the youngster's feelings to life and struck a chord with the tens of thousands gathered around the City Hall and the millions watching on television sets the length and breadth of Ireland. Her thoughts were their thoughts on an exceptional night in which Northern Ireland rejoiced in peace. "My dreams for the future? Well, I have a lot of them. Hopefully the peace will be permanent, that one day Protestants and Catholics will be able to walk hand in hand and will be able to live in the same areas."

Moved by the innocence of the children she'd encountered in the eleven hours since arriving, Mrs Clinton's thoughts wandered to her daughter at home when she introduced Mark Lennox as being the same age as 15-year-old Chelsea Clinton. The schoolboy closed his eyes and grimaced as the First Lady spoke his words: "I am very pleased about the chance of permanent peace in Northern Ireland and the chances of living in a secure atmosphere. Some people want to destroy the peace and the peace process in Northern Ireland. We must not allow this to happen." Mark said afterwards: "I'm very shy and I don't like people looking at me. I was proud but embarrassed when Hillary Clinton spoke about my letter because I knew some of my friends were in the crowd." Mrs Clinton then rounded off with a few words of her own: "Let us remember that we seek peace most of all for our children."

The President, under the awkward stage direction of Smyth, got to his feet to switch on the Christmas tree lights. He stood with each arm around the shoulders of the two children behind a box marked 'peace on earth' as the crowd's countdown quickened from ten down to one. Clinton then threw a dummy lever for the cameras as a worker in a hut behind the tree flicked the real switch. Their timing wasn't perfect, but close enough. "We deceived thousands," said Waring. "Clinton didn't switch the lights on. It was our electrician Alec McAllister." The President turned around and pointed up at the illuminated tree. "It's beautiful," said Cathy Harte. "Yeah, you're right. It's beautiful," responded Clinton. He patted Mark Lennox on the back before presenting his third major address of the day. Said a member of the American advance team: "The big speech was Mackie. That's the one we got the text out for and wanted to work. Derry we had to say something, but without overshadowing the message because the event we wanted to see on American television that night was the Christmas tree lighting. This was one of the tensions between the people who were concerned about Derry. At the Christmas tree we wanted to say some things about peace and hopefulness, kind of a more spiritual message."

Clinton noisily kicked the platform behind the podium on which Smyth had been standing out of the way and told the audience he was honoured to perform the lighting ceremony, given the opposition. "Now, to become President of the United States you have to undertake some considerable competition." Laughter spread through the crowd. They knew what was coming. "But I have never confronted challengers with the name recognition, the understanding of the media and the ability in the martial arts of the Mighty Morphin Power Rangers." It set the speech's light-hearted tone. The red-cheeked President beamed his way through most of it. He too drew from material provided by young letter-writers whom he said clearly hadn't lost their sense of humour in the adversity of violence. "I got a letter from 13-year-old Ryan from Belfast. Now Ryan, if you're out in the crowd tonight here's the answer to your question. No, as far as I know an alien spacecraft did not crash in Roswell, New Mexico, in 1947. And Ryan, if the United States Air Force did recover alien bodies they didn't tell me about it either, and I want to know." The jovial moment lasted long after. At the end of the night at the Europa, McCurry faced the White House press corps a final time. "Mike, this will probably end the briefing," said one reporter. "Did the President actually inquire of the Air Force in gathering the information for the answer he provided 13-year-old Ryan from Belfast if they were holding extraterrestrials?" Clinton's Press Secretary replied to chuckling: "You're right, that ended the briefing."

In the midst of a City Hall crowd hanging on Clinton's every word was the British Labour Party's Northern Ireland spokeswoman, Mo Mowlam, who'd found herself separated from the official party accompanying the President. She'd spent the build up wandering the streets, experiencing the party mood. "What he did, which the rest of us as politicians of any colour had failed to do, was give a bit of hope and vision for Northern Ireland," the future Northern Ireland Secretary of State later recalled. "In a sense he reached out to the public across the heads of the politicians. The crowd was mostly young. They were a generation that wanted to believe there was hope for the future and he gave them that." Jim Lyons was also down amidst the masses, having slipped out of an enclosure to the annoyance of the Secret Service. He said: "I had the opportunity to sit with everybody else but where it was happening was down on the streets. It was astounding. The look on people's faces was just incredible. I told the President about it later. I said, 'Too bad you couldn't have come with me.' The night just blew me away. I can't say how many people from the White House came up to me and said, 'This is unbelievable. Did you have any idea?' I couldn't say I did have. It was just so overpowering." Ambassador Crowe, who hadn't forsaken his privileged seat, added: "I didn't anticipate those crowds, just plain didn't. I was quite stunned. The euphoria was hard to describe. When the President left I think we all had a feeling that this had been a tremendous contribution." Sir Patrick Mayhew offered another perspective. "Seventy thousand people on the streets was a massive evocation of longing and demand for peace, true peace, and I thought all of that would make it much harder for the IRA to go back, or if they did go back to violence to carry people with them," he said. "It was a most remarkable single occasion in terms of involvement of the public without any doubt at all. It was very moving."

The President concluded his speech at the City Hall on a high. "Ladies and gentlemen, this day that Hillary and I have had here in Belfast and in Derry and in Londonderry County will long be with us as one of the most remarkable days of our lives." Mrs Clinton appeared to be reflecting on her husband's words as the crowd cheered. Tony Lake, senior National Security Council advisor, re-called: "Nobody could forget the faces of all those people gathered in front of the Christmas tree. When you work on issues you tend to do it in meetings with political leaders or through memos and phone calls. But when you see in such tangible terms the impact peace could have it was very moving. Those faces would always remind us to concentrate." Added his assistant Nancy Soderberg: "Usually historical moments aren't clear until later. This one was clear as it was happening. It's the only time I've not seen the press cynical either. Even they were just awed. It was all because the President of the United States had the guts two years earlier to stick his neck out for this process and to see the impact of the Presidency on a popu-lation was just amazing. This had happened because we sat around one Sunday morning and decided to give Adams a visa."

Niall O'Dowd noticed the effect on many Americans around him. "The reaction on their faces was extraordinary. Some of these guys were businessmen that hadn't really been focused on what Clinton had done in Ireland. Suddenly they realised he'd done something special. My abiding memory is the reaction of the Americans. Their culture is incredibly hard on politicians and it took this to show the good that an American president could do." Added Bruce Morrison: " It was really the most emotional of the events in my view because it was tapping into people wanting to be able to live normal lives. It was a joyous occasion."

Clinton's closing remarks weren't scripted. He urged people to remember the words of the Lord Mayor and then misquoted from the Bible for his trouble: "Blessed are the peacemakers for they shall inherit the earth. Merry Christmas and God bless you all." Smyth appreciated the President's sincere show of unity. "That was nice at the end," the Lord Mayor told him as they shook hands after the speech. "It just goes to show that Presidents can make mistakes too," he afterwards said of Clinton's slip-up. (The meek inherit the earth, the peacemakers are the children of God.) The watching Alderdice reflected: "Others commented on the Lord Mayor not being well received by the crowd but the very sensitive way which the President dealt with that, and turned it around in a positive way, said a lot about him to me."

Clinton led Hillary off the stage by the hand and then dived into the loving embrace of the crowd. Behind him a Secret Service agent held a powerful torchlight above his head, ensuring a clear view of all close encounters with the President. To Clinton's right was the wide-eyed Alto, to his left the impassive RUC man, Ervine. More agents guarded the President's back, keeping him inside what they termed the 'bubble'. One held open Clinton's bullet-proof coat. Said Lyons: "He was clearly energised, that's his style. Bill Clinton's idea of relaxation is to go work a crowd. These were people he cared about, continues to care about, and who were responding to him." Suddenly the air was filled with the distinctive sound of pan pipes playing a haunting Irish melody. Mrs Clinton followed some way behind the President, keeping a dignified distance from well-wishers. Joe Cahill, determined to have his moment with Clinton, battled his way through the crowd towards the front with the wife of a Sinn Féin councillor. "When Clinton was considering my visa he said to Albert Reynolds, 'Have you seen this man's CV?' Reynolds replied, 'What did you expect, a parish priest?' So I had it in my mind to introduce myself as the non-parish priest, but I got within five or six feet of him and then he was away," said the Republican stalwart. Instead he had to make do with shaking the hand of Ron Brown, whom he was introduced to by Niall O'Dowd. "The only one who could've pulled that crowd was Clinton," reminisced Cahill. "The feel good factor will stick in my mind as long as I live. I thought the bullet-proof screen was an insult to the people of Belfast though."

One person who did get to shake Clinton's hand was a Religious Education schoolteacher, Gary Trew. Little did the 41-year-old realise that 18 months later he'd be standing in the Oval Office as a winner of a prize for those promoting peace at grassroots level, which the President had just announced in his speech. "I was able to get away from school in Antrim early that day and get right up to the front. I don't recall ever being as excited as that before – the hairs on the back of my neck were standing up. It was a wonderful experience being in that crowd, being there with all the hopes for peace." Dozens of pocket cameras flashed in the crowd as Clinton patiently worked his way along. Even Andy Wood, the Northern Ireland Office Information Director, couldn't resist taking snaps. As an encore for those who found it impossible to get near him, Clinton bounded back up onto the stage to bid them farewell. He waved, saluted and applauded. His eyes moistened. He paused to gulp. The night had got to him. He later disclosed to the authors: "It was then that I realised how much the people want peace. It was an unforgettable evening. What I remember most was standing before a sea of people, literally as far as I could see, who were there to support the cause of peace."

Clinton had two more tasks to perform. He rededicated a memorial commemorating the landing of US forces in the city in January 1942. General Eisenhower had inspected a naval guard of honour beside it when he visited in 1945. The stone column had been dismantled during building work in the grounds of the City Hall and reassembled at a new location for the Clinton visit. It was a simple ceremony. Said Hanna: "We had a new plaque put on the ground and he uncovered it. Not many people saw it happening because it

223

was behind the stage and the nature of the arrangements outside didn't allow for it to be visible to many people." Clinton impressed the few who were present by reeling off facts about the American servicemen's wartime sojourn in Northern Ireland, gleaned from the book David Trimble had presented to him in Washington. "He told me he was very pleased he'd read the book on the American GIs when I saw him later, as he was able to make some comments to the Lord Mayor," said Trimble.

As the Clinton entourage snaked around the path back towards the City Hall, Eamonn Holmes was grappling with four Secret Service agents on the lawn within ten yards of the President. "Identify yourself, identify yourself," they screamed. Two of the security personnel had his arms twisted behind his back. "What do you mean? I'm the man who's just introduced the President on stage," replied the bemused Holmes. He was released after a top RUC officer came to investigate the altercation. "He's fine. I can vouch for him," said the policeman.

Inside the City Hall Clinton craned his neck to admire the elaborate plasterwork of the domed ceiling. The councillors were lined up in party affiliation around a Christmas tree, the Sinn Féin grouping standing out as the only members not in official gowns, as he signed a visitors' book and was presented with gifts. The one absentee was DUP councillor Sammy Wilson, whose Clinton-bashing had gone down well at his party's annual conference. Wilson defended his stay-away policy: "I felt the man was abusing this place for his own domestic reasons. His motives weren't pure. His job was to give credibility to Adams and Sinn Féin. I thought the party should have nothing to do with him."

Across Belfast, Ian Paisley was considering a boycott of his own.

X

Toasting triumph

*The President decided he should break open a really
great bottle of Irish whiskey someone had presented
him. We all sat and had a couple of sips and felt very,
very good about the day. We had a fine time in the
Clinton suite. We left him and the First Lady sipping
whiskey probably about two in the morning. He was
so full of energy that night he wanted to bounce off
the walls.*

Mike McCurry, Press Secretary to the President

The occupants of number 256 Ravenhill Road were watching
Clinton milk the crowd at the City Hall on a television set in an
upstairs room. Democratic Unionist Party leader Ian Paisley had
been in the large terraced house, which was his office, for much of
day. Now decision time was fast approaching. He was scheduled to
leave shortly for his first ever meeting with the President at Queen's
University. But the man with a penchant for protest – he'd once
been ejected from the European Parliament for heckling Pope John
Paul II – was thinking about giving Clinton the brush off. With him
in the room were Peter Robinson, the Revd William McCrea, MP
for Mid-Ulster and minister in Paisley's Free Presbyterian Church,
and two of the leader's lieutenants, Nigel Dodds and Ian Paisley Jr.
A debate was in progress across the table. Said one of the

participants: "By this stage we were all aware of what was seen as the deliberate slight, with no reference to the party leader in the Mackie speech and the fact that Clinton went out of his way to accidentally bump into Adams on the Falls Road. It was against that backcloth that the reservations were there."

There was certainly no love lost between Paisley and the Clinton Administration. Of all the local parties his Democratic Unionists were unashamedly the most antagonistic towards the close attention being given to Northern Irish affairs in Washington. They weren't behind the door about displaying their hostility either. "This party prides itself in saying in public what we think in private," boasted one senior member. The 1995 party document submitted to the Administration admitted: "Contacts between the DUP and the US Administration have been less than friendly and at times strained." The party claimed attempts to sideline them were evident when Tony Lake pulled out of a 1994 meeting. McCrea in particular took great insult when stand-in officials told the visiting delegation they believed Paisley would fair badly in the forthcoming European elections. "I related to them very forcefully that, whether they liked it or not, you'll never get a resolution in Ulster without Ian Paisley. He's the voice of the authentic Loyalist-Unionist person. They didn't like the message but they got it loud and clear." Added Paisley: "We just had a good go at them, then left."

The DUP concluded that US Government policy, based on "an unrelenting acceptance of the views, demands and position of Irish Nationalists", ran contrary to the constitutional position of Northern Ireland and furthermore was at variance with the wishes of most of those who lived in the region. To back their case they cited a 1993 Congressional Research Service Report by Karen E. Donfried which stated: "Northern Ireland is an integral part of the United Kingdom in domestic and international law, a relationship supported by the majority of the inhabitants of Northern Ireland."

American dollars were a different matter. For the DUP it was a case of, yea for investment, nay for political nose-poking. A suggested concentration on matters economic formed the basis of a 12-paragraph letter Paisley sent to the President on 22 January 1993, not long after his inauguration. "What I wish to stress is the importance of what can be done under the circumstances," Paisley wrote on House of Commons notepaper. "I realise that during the

Presidential campaign you suggested the possibility of sending a peace envoy to Northern Ireland. This action if pursued, I fear, would not achieve the end result which I understand you have in mind. I must also point out that the title itself is a misnomer. Who do you wish to make peace with? The law-abiding people of Northern Ireland want an end to terrorism. They do not want the IRA to be recognised as legitimate and brought into some sort of peace negotiations."

Paisley hadn't been averse to personally carrying the Unionist message to America down the years, though he usually didn't publicise his travels and many of his low-profile trips were more concerned with church work. At the prompting of Irish-Americans such as Senator Kennedy, he had once had a visa revoked by the State Department on the grounds of the "divisiveness" of his statements and actions. It prevented him playing a full part in Operation USA, a joint DUP/UUP publicity tour of America in early 1982, though he did succeed in getting onto American network television from Toronto and his wife Eileen delivered his speeches in the States. Ulster Unionist deputy leader John Taylor was his party's representative on the visit. He said: "It wasn't done with the blessing of the Ulster Unionist Party, I'm sorry to say. I was very strong in my opinion that we should be developing a Unionist presence in America even in those days when the rest of my party were very much against it." A book, *Ulster, the Facts*, was produced for the US audience. To shock them it contained some grotesque pictures of victims of IRA violence. Said Dodds: "Overall DUP policy is that America has no role to play in Northern Ireland and we don't or didn't want to be encouraging them down that road. John Hume was there to try and get America interested and involved. Our view was, let's keep them informed, but we discouraged any idea that they somehow had a right to come over and interfere politically. We tried to feed in the Unionist perspective so people were aware there just wasn't one side to all this."

Prior to Clinton's Presidency, the party founded by Paisley in 1971 had little or no real cause for panic – Republican Presidents Reagan and Bush had no compulsion to become involved and were anyhow guided by America's valued relationship with Britain. Irish-America was a scourge whose principal function, in the DUP's view, was to financially support the IRA's murder campaign and agitate politically for a British withdrawal. Through this period Paisley's most significant contacts on Capitol Hill were two Republican Senators from the conservative south, Jesse Helms of North Carolina and Strom Thurmond of South Carolina, neither of whom had a track record on Northern Ireland. "When I go to the States I go principally to see the Senators and Congressmen I've gotten to know personally," said Paisley. "I find my contacts with the two Senators are very good. I've known Strom Thurmond for 25 years." (A photograph of Paisley with Helms hangs in the DUP leader's office. It's inscribed: "To my remarkable friend honourable Ian Paisley with very best wishes. I enjoyed your visit and hope you will come again soon.") Added Paisley Jr: "They're both top drawer contacts, very influential people on Capitol Hill. They have always been very accessible to the party. Their interest would be general as opposed to specialist, but that interest is one Northern Ireland politicians can use to their advantage." The younger Paisley had been spreading the DUP gospel in America himself and in some unusual places at that. On one trip he was flown by helicopter by Ted Kennedy's son Patrick to his family compound at Hyannis Port on Cape Cod.

After Clinton's election, the DUP, like their Ulster Unionist cousins, had to adopt a more aggressive lobbying position in an attempt to correct what they perceived as his dangerous Nationalist sympathies. "My father's initial view was that he was treated very badly by the Administration," said Paisley Jr. "He was excluded quite deliberately. For a period he was the only party leader not invited to the White House. Now, he never sought to be invited but the protocol was there – he has the largest vote in Northern Ireland in European elections." The coolness in the relationship was reflected on the ground in Belfast, with one senior party official pointing an accusing finger at US Consul General Stephens. "We'd a very good relationship with both Doug Archard and Val Martinez. Val had fortnightly and sometimes weekly meetings with us on a regular basis. There's been no serious effort by Kathy to keep that contact alive, which is very disappointing." It was a view shared by prominent members of the Ulster Unionist Party. Claimed one: "Her two predecessors definitely did show a greater interest in the Unionist political position." Paisley was able to bypass Stephens by establishing a rapport with her immediate boss, Ambassador Crowe in London, who one American source said had "a blindspot for

Paisley." Nancy Soderberg, the White House's chief strategist on Northern Ireland policy, fared even worse than Stephens in the DUP's estimation. (Paisley disparagingly referred to her at his regular news conferences as Nancy Sodabread.) "She came from Ted Kennedy's staff and it was well known where her political sympathies lay," contended Dodds. "She was always very courteous and said she wanted to understand but we were always aware she was coming from a particular viewpoint, especially in the early days."

As the Clinton Administration's commitment to the peace process grew and the Presidential visit loomed on the horizon, political necessity forced Washington and the DUP towards *détente*. However, the gentle thawing of relations threatened to freeze back over with the Adams handshake on the Falls Road, the main topic of conversation as the party hierarchy, unknown to the Americans, deliberated standing up Clinton at Queen's. "The handshake with Adams was an appalling act," Dodds said. "They fell into the Sinn Féin trap there and the fact that they deliberately snubbed Ian in the speech was a provocation to him." Added a party source: "It wasn't that Ian was dead set against going, it was more up for discussion. Believe me I've seen him in the frame of mind that if he didn't want to do something then nothing will make him." McCrea was the chief persuader. One of those in the room revealed: "He had to be convinced to do it and the strongest in convincing him was William McCrea. The argument that eventually won him over was that if you're given an opportunity to meet this man and put him right on things, then you've got to take it. People won't forgive you if you don't." McCrea later recalled: "I think Ian made a very courageous decision. It proved the size of the man that he would not return Clinton's insult. It was Ian's decision to go and see the President and in doing so he disproved the impression others would have liked to have seen – here comes the leader of the western world to Ulster and Ian Paisley snubs him."

So Paisley departed for Queen's University and a meeting which was to be the first act in a political finale to Clinton's heady Northern Ireland experience. No matter what happened now the trip was already a roaring success, not least for Clinton personally. "The trip ranks as the moment that has been most important and most thrilling to him because of the response he got," said White House Press Secretary Mike McCurry. "It came at a very good time because we were preparing for the showdown battle with the Republican Congress over budget priorities. It might be too much to say it was like kryptonite to Superman, you know, gave him a source of strength, but it certainly helped. I think there's merit in the argument that he was somehow strengthened as a leader in the eyes of the American people because they saw the response he got in Northern Ireland."

Throughout the day the President had touched and been touched by a people invigorated by peace; it was time now to rub shoulders with politicians who had thus far been reluctant to embrace its potential in full negotiations. "The day had gone so well that even had the political reception at Queen's University not gone well it would not have characterised the visit," said a leading American organiser of the Clinton trip. "The day had already built to a crescendo and then it dipped just because a reception is a reception." Added a Washington colleague: "The success of the reception was due in large part to what had transpired leading up to it for the whole day. Events served different purposes. The reception from the standpoint of the politics of the trip was probably the most important event. From a perspective of how it played on television you could say it was anti-climactic."

An event, or events, conceived specifically to give Clinton time with Northern Ireland's political representatives was a fixed item on the American agenda from the beginning. Washington quickly discovered, however, that it was easier said than done, given the limitations on time and the reluctance by the Unionists to participate in functions alongside Sinn Féin. A document written during US preparatory work on the visit referred to meetings with political leaders as being "probably the most meddlesome of all the issues surrounding the Presidential visit." (The Mackie/Adams quandary was at that juncture still some way off.) Almost straight away the idea for a series of individual meetings with leaders with most if not all of the major parties was discounted. "You couldn't have had six or eight 20-minute meetings with a press conference after each," an American source explained. "That didn't make any sense." The Americans were equally anxious that Clinton avoid being drawn into the minutiae of local political debate in questions from Northern Ireland's media – the President gave no press conference during his visit. A classified trip memorandum penned on 20 November disclosed that the visit was an opportunity for Clinton to portray the ceasefires as a watershed in history that there could be no turning back on. "This galvanising message will be the lasting legacy of the trip. The power of this message should not be diluted by the President getting into the specifics of the immediate debate over decommissioning and all-party talks," it read.

Combined meetings with parties created predicaments of their own. "It is fairly well understood that the UUP and DUP are extremely reticent about attending functions in common with Sinn Féin," an internal US document stated. "Many people overlook that the UUP and DUP are not terribly comfortable with the Loyalist parties either. Even between the UUP and DUP there can be considerable tension. Therefore splitting up meetings into Unionist and Nationalists does not make the problems go away. It also raises the question of where to put the Alliance Party."

The Americans debated a number of possible solutions, such as separate meetings along sectarian lines. "Conceivably we could have one function in Derry principally for Nationalists and one in Belfast principally for Unionists," an American discussion paper on the issue outlined. It was envisaged that Alderdice could go to Londonderry. The British Government was dead against the idea. For a start this would give the erroneous impression that the cities were exclusively of one political colouring. It could also have led to one event being compared with the other. "The Americans put certain proposals to us initially about how they would hold the talks with parties and we were not at all happy with those," explained a British source. "It seemed to us they would be dividing parties into camps in a way that was not going to play helpfully into Northern Ireland politics." Outside Washington, those Americans more sensitive to the situation in the field were in full agreement with the Northern Ireland Office. "Two meetings, one with Unionists and one with Nationalists, wouldn't have been the right image," said one. "We didn't want to reinforce division. We wanted to do something to break it down." A more imaginative, though equally unworkable approach would be to have a series of meetings based on offices as opposed to parties – separate gatherings of MPs, MEPs and mayors – which would cut across party lines. But the idea was impractical and Gerry Adams did not fit into any of the classifications. Nor for that matter did representatives of the Loyalist parties.

One common reception, despite the inherent problems, seemed

the best and only option from relatively early on. Brady Williamson and Blair Hall had dealt with a similar puzzle before on the President's Tokyo trip. Explained Hall: "The Japanese Prime Minister was facing an election that wouldn't take place until after President Clinton left. He was a lame duck so we had to get the President to meet the other political leaders but we couldn't have meetings with all of them because time was so short. Brady and I and another colleague came up with the idea of a reception that the American Ambassador would host, which gave us the opportunity to invite leaders of parties, businessmen and the great and the good. We had the cameras in for some shots and them moved them out so the President could go off in a corner and have some chats. It turned out that we had the next three Prime Ministers in the room and the President got to meet every one of them. So we had this model in mind."

In tandem with discussions about the format of the reception, the selection process was underway for a venue. This wasn't such a problematic procedure. To a large extent Queen's University picked itself. Hillsborough Castle, Belfast City Hall and Stormont Castle, the conventional reception venues, had too many Unionist or British Government connotations. The US Consul General's residence was also considered. The Americans came to Queen's on both the site survey and the pre-advance visit. "We have traditionally been a place where visits take place," said Denis Wilson, the university official who gave the guests a guided tour of the Whitla Hall, the building chosen for the reception. He added: "The university is not a venue involved with party politics and I think a number of factors came together. It was our one-hundred-and-fiftieth anniversary, we had the facilities and the university was acceptable as neutral ground, a place which both communities could give allegiance to."

The Ulster Unionist Party was also lobbying at high levels in the White House for a Presidential halt at Queen's, on the basis that it was located in the south Belfast constituency of one of its MPs the Revd Martin Smyth. Party leader David Trimble later claimed: "We actually suggested two things to do in south Belfast, one which involved local industry, the other the university. The university has totally ignored the fact that were it not for Martin Smyth the President would never have visited Queen's. He got that for them."

The British Government, meanwhile, was trying to wrest control of the reception from the Americans as a point of principle.

Said a senior official: "We felt it would have been a bit undignified actually if the President had come to Northern Ireland and at no point had had any hospitality from the Secretary of State for Northern Ireland who, after all, was the representative of the government hosting the visit. We were also anxious from a protocol point of view that we should do it." Hosting it also meant the British Government would collect the £30,000 tab. (Sir Patrick Mayhew joked with officials that Queen's should order in a good wine "because it's not coming out of my budget, it's coming out of London's.")

Washington's misgivings were in part based on whether Mayhew's guest list would include the name of Adams and other top Sinn Féin representatives. (There had been a rumpus over Sinn Féin invitations to an economic conference organised by the British and attended by John Major in Belfast a year earlier. It had been resolved when Adams' party lobbied the White House, which was sending Commerce Secretary Ron Brown as guest of honour.) A member of the American team explained: "It took a while for us to get a meeting of minds with Her Majesty's Government, because when they heard the word reception it was a way to show hospitality for a state visitor. We didn't care about the hospitality. It was simply a way to put the President together with the political leaders. Then there was the question of who hosts the reception. If the Secretary of State's the host could we have the kind of neutrality we wanted. If we were going to have Gerry Adams in there we didn't want to be rude to the Secretary of State. And these sorts of things." Countered a British Government official: "I think they were concerned that we would have this reception and we wouldn't have Sinn Féin there. We made it plain very early on that this thing was to be balanced and by balance that meant we were going to have Sinn Féin. We had no difficulty with that and whenever we assured the Americans they had no difficulty." The British Ambassador to Washington, Sir John Kerr, was also relaying the same message to the White House. "The idea that Adams should be there at the party at the university was fine," he said. "I can't remember anybody at the NIO telling me or London telling me I should try to get the Americans to keep Adams out of that part."

Mayhew himself was eager to host the event, not least because it would strike the right note politically. "The Unionists might have thought this was something of a sort of takeover, or the British

Government were content that the head of another state, however friendly, could come in and make a big political pitch with the British Government rather on the sidelines," he explained. "I think that would have happened supposing the reception had not been hosted by the British Government. These things are symbolic but all of us know that symbols are very important in Northern Ireland." The issue had arisen at the Stormont dinner during the October pre-advance. "I guess the biggest headache, the issue I had most difficulty with, was the reception," said a leading member of the US travelling party. "We parried and we thrusted with the British. At that dinner if we had said to the British we're going to co-host this reception and we're going to put out invitations together they would have been happy. In the end they did better." Finally the Americans conceded. "In the end we realised we could live with the Secretary of State being the host and had no problem with it," said a trip planner. "But we held onto it. We didn't agree to let them do it until the last minute. We traded that off in a negotiating session. We wanted a smaller group at the reception, the Northern Ireland Office always wanted a bigger group. I think in the end they told us they agreed on a smaller group and invited the bigger group anyway."

Although the President's team had given way, they still exercised a considerable degree of influence over the event. But not now enough to call the shots. The British vetoed the idea of a two-tiered reception, where political leaders would be downstairs in the ring, as it were, and representatives of the wider community, clergymen and businessmen and the like, upstairs. "We were thinking of a lot of different ideas including the two-tiered event," said a US source. "You would have had say blue tickets for one area, green for the other. The Secretary of State was completely against the two-tier. He didn't want to have anything to do with it." The prototype the Northern Ireland Office had in mind was that used for the Hillsborough garden parties frequently held for visiting members of the Royal Family. "That's the British idea where people are spread out and the Secretary of State or Queen or whomever comes through and says a few words," said an American official. "That's when we came up with this modified idea of the rope line, which the Secretary of State didn't like because he thought it was too impersonal, but we said the President always does that. If he's going to work through the room it's too hard to have this crush of people around him."

If there was any hope of getting all parties under the Whitla Hall's roof then the event had to be cleverly manipulated. "Washington's a political town so we have some experience of people not wanting to be in the same room," said a US planner. "We sat down with the NIO and worked out how we would place people along this rope line. It turns out if you do it in alphabetical order, using the DUP's full official name, the Ulster Democratic Unionist Party, they happen to be all the way down here and Sinn Féin all the way up there. We then put civic people, groups of religious leaders, trade union leaders, in between to separate the parties out even more." Pods, as the Americans christened these groups, would contain around six to eight people who would greet the President and First Lady as they progressed through the hall. Intricate floor plans were drawn up showing which political party was standing where and who would act as buffers between each. Each pod would have a British or American minder – Blair Hall for instance looked after Sinn Féin – and Mayhew, as host, would handle initial introductions. As in Tokyo, press photographers and television cameras would be allowed only brief access and were corralled so that delegations uncomfortable with one another couldn't be squeezed into the same shot from ingenious angles.

From day one the DUP's alarms bells were ringing. A letter from a Paisley aide to Kathleen Stephens on 6 September explained the party's position. "I think you must be made aware that in no way will the DUP leader attend any function which is to be addressed by the President if Gerry Adams or his associates are present. If the President is genuine about listening to the views of the people then it is only right that he should meet with Dr Paisley but in no way will Dr Paisley be bounced into a situation where he is with, or associated in any obscure way with, the leader of IRA/SF." Paisley then began playing some hardball with Clinton's staff, who in time appreciated that if the trip was to be the accomplishment it was it had to be all-embracing. Recalled Paisley: "I told his aides, 'I'm not queuing up to see him. I want a separate slot. If it's not done like that I'll not be visiting.' They told me it would be arranged but then the pressures came on. They said, 'No, we can't do it like that now. Gerry Adams is coming up to Queen's and you'll have to come, line up and just take your turn.' I said, 'I'll not be there. I'll go to the press instead. It might do me a lot of good with people by refusing to see him.' Then they came back and said, 'It's all arranged. You'll have your separate room. You'll not see Adams.'"

By the time Clinton's cavalcade was snaking its way from the City Hall to Queen's through streets crammed with well-wishers, Ian Paisley was waiting for the President in an ante-room at the Whitla Hall. Adams and the other guests were already gathering out front. The university had closed for the day at 3.00pm. The room in which Paisley was offered tea and soft drinks was a rarely used private dining-chamber which had been kitted out especially for the night by a local house furnisher. Tables, chairs, settees, fireplace and pictures all contributed to the cosy atmosphere. Nigel Dodds was with Paisley as his notetaker. (He had been introduced to Clinton as the youngest Lord Mayor in the Commonwealth.) Said Paisley: "They'd a very nice room for me, complete with fire and all. They'd two seats together and they said, 'You sit here, the President sits there.'" The 69-year-old DUP man's customary charm and affability disguised from the American entourage the harshness of the message he was about to communicate to their President. "He's a very gracious person. Very much the gentleman," said one of the senior White House team. Paisley, who'd been outraged that Clinton's Westminster speech the day before had made no mention of the suffering inflicted by the IRA, mulled things over in his mind as he waited. He'd brought with him a letter penned that morning for the President and some political literature.

Clinton and Paisley hadn't met before, indeed it was one of the reasons why the talks had been convened in the first place. Stills photographers allowed in to snap the opening exchanges captured a jovial President and a stern-looking Paisley. Crowe was reclining on a sofa to Clinton's left. Other American officials present included Lake, Soderberg and Stephens. The two men exchanged greetings, the President telling Paisley that while a student at Oxford he'd watched his entry into politics on British television. Remembered Paisley: "I said, 'That's very nice but, Mr President, you're a busy man and so am I, so we'll cut out the pleasantries and get down to business.'" By all accounts what followed was vintage Paisley. An Administration member present throughout the meeting said: "He was his lively, powerful, strong-viewed self. He gave a very strong rendition of the situation. He basically laid out his view of the world for 16 minutes." DUP sources characterised Paisley's performance as "polite but forceful," adding that there seemed "a good rapport" between the two men.

The President said very little after inviting him to speak. Clinton Press Secretary Mike McCurry said afterwards that the President had "listened very carefully and very respectfully." Paisley drew parallels between the Oklahoma bombing and the IRA's Shankill Road explosion and lambasted Clinton for "contriving" a meeting with Adams on the Falls. Paisley recalled: "I said, 'I feel like kicking you out after your actions today. Ulster people are saying, mind your own business or you'll get a bloody nose.' He was visibly shaken. He went as pale as snow when I pointed to his hand that had shaken Adams'. I felt he'd been licked up to, that nobody had told him the truth. So I looked upon it as my duty to do so." An American source said of Paisley's diatribe: "It was absolutely incredible." In an interview with the authors, Ambassador Crowe commented: "I thought it was a pretty good meeting. I may not agree with what Paisley says but, by God, he says it. He's straightforward and you don't come away with any question about where he stands. It gave the President a good feel for how deep in the soul all this goes." Once through, Paisley made a crack about having gone on for too long, that it was the preacher in him. Clinton laughed. He hadn't heard a sermon like it. For all the serious talk, the meeting ended on a relaxed note. Paisley later said: "I've a lot of experience in tight situations but it wasn't very easy walking into a room filled with people and telling the world's strongest man to his face that you'd like to put your boot in his backside. He's a clever man and a clever performer. He performed well in Northern Ireland. I liked his style and his oratory."

Paisley left the Whitla Hall and briefed the waiting news media on the one-sided encounter. He also made public the letter he'd handed over to Clinton. "Now that I've finished I have all this in writing for you," Paisley had informed the President. The letter's language was as uncompromising as had been the DUP leader's performance. It said: "Under the smokescreen of taking risks for peace you insist we sit down with terrorists. The fact that you granted IRA/Sinn Féin leader Adams a visa and welcomed him to the White House with a hand of friendship revealed as never before to the law-abiding citizens of Northern Ireland just where your loyalty lies." Commented Paisley: "It was a very strong letter. I never got a reply but then it was done for a propaganda thing." While the DUP leader made his well-publicised leave, party associates remained behind to attend the reception he himself had wanted nothing to do with. He saw no inconsistency in the decision. "My DUP colleagues attended the function because they'd the opportunity to put the same views I was putting to the President to all his aides who were there," he said. "It also gave us the leverage that if things didn't go right we could have pulled them all out. We could have said, none of our boys are attending, and that would have left a terrible gap." Said a US Government source: "In the end Paisley decided he couldn't come into the room but I think even he and his party recognised that we'd made a good faith effort. We weren't trying to do anything to embarrass anybody. We'd built in all these protections – how the press was going to be treated and how the room was going to be arranged."

So remain DUP members did, but they were selective in the company they kept. Deputy leader Peter Robinson said: "I instructed our delegation to put their hands in their pockets and shake hands with no-one unless they knew who that person was. Certainly we didn't go near Sinn Féin." Added William McCrea: "The atmosphere among some folks was tense. I certainly did not want to be next or near any Sinn Féiner. To be in the same room is too much for me." The group barely budged from its spot at the opposite end of the room from Sinn Féin.

A jazz band in white tuxedos did its best to relax the mood, making the Whitla Hall sound more like a rhythm and blues club. Some guests milled around on the polished wooden floor while others zealously guarded their places along the rope line. Nonetheless a few interesting huddles were forming. Roy Bradford, a former Unionist MP in the old Stormont Parliament, placed a hand on the shoulder of Martin McGuinness of Sinn Féin as they debated a political point. "Bradford was really bending Martin's ear," said Gerry Adams' aide Richard McAuley who was among the party's delegation in the Whitla. (He very nearly wasn't allowed entry. Blair Hall had to get him and Adams' driver in personally when they showed up at the door.) Niall O'Dowd, broker of the IRA ceasefire, shared a joke with Loyalists Gary McMichael, Billy Hutchinson and John White, whose pale green suit made him immediately distinguishable in the soberly-dressed crowd. O'Dowd and Morrison had been informed of the state of play among the Loyalist paramilitaries a short time earlier. "We met them in an ante-room for about 20 minutes while we were waiting for Clinton," McMichael disclosed. "The PUP and UDP went in together. They wanted a briefing about how things were sitting concerning the Loyalist ceasefire." Added Hutchinson: "They were very keen to hear our analysis." However, the Americans revealed nothing of what they'd been told of the precarious nature of the IRA ceasefire sooner in the day.

Elsewhere in the hall Gerry Adams fingered his beard as he held court with a succession of American politicians, including Senator Chris Dodd. "I was telling politicians it's a pity Clinton couldn't stay for a month," Adams remembered. The Sinn Féin President wasn't alone in having come a long way. Congressman Peter King unexpectedly bumped into a community worker who he'd first encountered when she was a waitress in the Felons' Club in west Belfast 13 years earlier. "The night still strikes me," King recalled some time later. "One thing was seeing Gerry Adams and Peter Robinson in the same room. The other is introducing a woman who used to be a waitress in a Republican club to the President of the United States in Belfast."

The mood of expectancy in the hall was increasing. Said one guest: "The anticipation was building about Clinton coming into the room, which was reasonably small given the number of people there. It was a great atmosphere. It was interesting to watch all the different personalities under the one roof." One American official observed: "I was standing near Adams looking round at everyone else who counts in a political sense in Northern Ireland. I thought, 'wow, nobody else could do this, nobody else could bring these people here together.' It's an image that will always stay with me."

Like the opening night of an amateur dramatic production, heads kept poking out from behind curtains that sectioned off half the hall. One false alarm preceded another until the band ended a jaunty tune with a pronounced drum roll, which cut the conversation. The clapping grew steadily louder after an announcer introduced the President and Mrs Clinton, who emerged smiling through a gap in the curtains. Sir Patrick and Lady Jean Mayhew followed them onto the stage. The Clintons sat as the Northern Ireland Secretary addressed his guests from a podium between two Queen's University banners. Mayhew could barely contain his delight. "You give us all tremendous pleasure, Mr President and Mrs Clinton, by being with us here tonight and we would like to thank you at the end of a gruelling day for you," he said in his introductory remarks. Clinton, the bags under his eyes seeming even more pronounced than usual, leaned across, clasped his wife's hand and laughed. Senator George Mitchell, who was in the audience, lauded the President's staying power. "I have known many people with high levels of energy and powers of concentration but President Clinton is in a league of his own," he later observed. "Having been in politics myself, you know a person can be buoyed up by the reaction of the crowds and he clearly was." Added one of the American planning team: "I was exhausted but the President was elated. Clinton was incredible. He was on such a high." Some of his zest looked like it had rubbed off on Mayhew, who stumbled over the occasional word in apparent excitement.

Clinton rose to speak but before he could do so someone called out, "Four more years." Cheers grew. Unlike at Mackie, this was the kind of outburst he appreciated. The President responded: "The plane for America leaves tomorrow. I want you to be on it." Clinton began his remarks proper by announcing a scholarship programme at the university, the Fulbright Fellowship in Conflict Resolution, named after the Arkansas Senator under whose tutelage he had started his political education. He went on: "I will take away from this visit a lot of enduring memories, a lot of lasting impressions of peace. I will remember this day for as long as I live." Clinton cast his eyes about the room that contained key figures in the political negotiations that would lie ahead. In an unscripted conclusion he said: "The question of whether you will go forward is all up to you, but if you do we will be proud to walk with you." Mayhew got to his feet and shook his hand. "Very, very well done," he said. Mayhew had been stirred by Clinton. "My impressions were of somebody prepared to go the extra mile and then another extra mile in terms of personal effort," was how he later summed him up. Added one of Mayhew's entourage: "Sir Patrick was really very struck and very favourably impressed by the President. It seemed to me that they got onto a wavelength. In my opinion there was a chemistry between them." As they stood receiving the applause, the microphones picked up Clinton enquiring of Mayhew what to do next. "Now are we supposed to go down the line and shake hands?" he asked the

Northern Ireland Secretary. "Yes, we've got them in groups," responded Mayhew as they strode off the stage.

First in line was the university's hierarchy, given place of honour as facilitators of the event. Among those greeting Clinton was the future President of Ireland, Mary McAleese, a Pro-Vice Chancellor at Queen's. The cameras were still rolling to record their encounter. If the Americans had had their way the exchange wouldn't have happened at all. At the last minute they had wanted Clinton and Mayhew to start further up the line, leaving the university group to their spouses. It caused a row between the British and American planning teams. One of those on the British side revealed: "We said, 'No, sorry, it's been set. It's in the Secretary of State's programme, and why should the education sector be the ones who take the fall?'" Mayhew, who was behind Clinton, had the names of guests written on cards in his pocket. They'd been prepared by one of his officials, David Watkins, but it seemed to be Stephens who was making most of the introductions. Watkins himself was up ahead trying to ensure things were in order, and was very nearly prevented from accompanying the Presidential entourage. "We just simply had to say to them, 'Tell your Secret Service to get stuffed,'" recalled a British official. Ambassador Sir John Kerr had no such problems, being at Clinton's shoulder, and was enjoying at close quarters a glimpse of a supreme politician at work. "I do think he's the best stump politician I've ever seen," commented Kerr afterwards. "Working a crowd he's absolutely brilliant. He has this knack of persuading somebody in a 45-second conversation on a rope line that he's got their point, agrees with it and is going to try to do something about it. He's a brilliant, professional performer." By the time President Clinton reached John Alderdice and his Alliance Party delegation the plug had been pulled on television pictures from inside the hall.

Further up a rope line sprinkled with the great and the good, Clinton met Northern Ireland's church leaders. Earlier in the day they had hosted an event in Armagh city for American clergymen, who were part of the larger touring party. Church of Ireland Primate Dr Robin Eames told him how thrilled he was to see him. He recalled: "I then said to the First Lady that I was delighted, as Anglican Primate of Ireland, to meet her. She said, 'I'm a Methodist', and I replied, 'Well, I began life as a Methodist so therefore we've something in common.' It was general chat. Their time was relatively short. How they could be expected to take on more than just genialities I don't know." Washington's UK-based representatives had consulted with Eames during the planning of the visit and he'd stressed it was crucial the President was seen to reach out to the Protestant community. "I don't think he put a foot wrong," said Eames. "A lot of homework had been done. The visit helped the ordinary people of Northern Ireland feel there was an even-handed approach coming from the White House. It would have been very divisive and probably put us back a good many years had it been otherwise."

When it came to Sinn Féin's turn, Mayhew got off-side after "fairly quickly" shaking Adams' and McGuinness' hands. "We had spent a lot of time on planning this because the Americans didn't want us to interpose ourselves between Sinn Féin and the President," a member of Mayhew's team explained. "Equally, we didn't want an introduction misinterpreted as some sort of exchange. So the protocol was met. The Secretary of State did the introductions – there was no difficulty in shaking hands – and then moved on to the next pod." Clinton's tone with the Sinn Féin representatives was light-hearted – the serious politics were left to a private meeting which would follow. McGuinness had been sceptical when Adams told him the President had mentioned reading one of his books when they met on the Falls earlier. Said the Sinn Féin President pointing at McGuinness: "He doesn't believe that you've read *The Street.*" Clinton answered: "Of course I read *The Street.*"

There was nothing blithesome about the President's encounter with Democratic Unionist Party members, William McCrea leading the verbal charge. He seized his opportunity. "Everybody seemed to have this notion that the IRA's terrorisation of the community should be swept under the carpet," said McCrea, a successful gospel singer who's been recording in the United States for 14 years. "Americans have this romantic idea that we're a wee green island with thatched cottages and hens sitting on a half-door. But there's nothing romantic about seeing a young girl of 21 blown to bits. I was at Queen's to draw Clinton's attention to this, not as William McCrea but as an elected representative for an area that has suffered." McCrea preached from the heart. His home in Magherafelt had been riddled by bullets a month before the IRA ceasefire and relatives had been murdered in other attacks. "I told him the peace was a farce and it hurt my constituents to see Adams paraded in the White House. I said it because I'd been there, my family had suffered. He was taken aback. It struck home."

As Clinton left the hall for talks with Adams, guests were left to reflect on the significance of what they'd been part of. "We were milling around and I found myself next to Martin McGuinness," commented an American diplomat. "I asked him what he thought of the day and he said, 'Ah, it was brilliant.' Then I saw Peter Robinson and I congratulated him on his speech over in east Belfast and said, 'How do you think the day went?' He said, 'Brilliant.' Now if you have two characters like that using the same word you can't hit it any better."

The President of Sinn Féin occupied the same seat as Paisley had for his talks, almost knee-to-knee with Clinton. It was their third encounter of the day. No other local politician had seen so much of the President. As photographers clicked away the Sinn Féin leader came across more as being more convivial than his DUP counterpart. He even stretched out and shook the hand one of the local press photographers. Adams' press officer Richard McAuley, who'd a ringside seat, said: "We've a good rapport with the US people, whether they're from the White House or the State Department, and they were going out of their way to be nice to everyone, which probably helped." McAuley was so mesmerised by the occasion that he forgot to take notes on the discussion which followed. Unlike the Paisley meeting, there was a greater exchange of views between Clinton and Adams. "Adams is a more personable person," claimed a US source. "I wouldn't say that the meeting was warm and fuzzy but it was a conversation." Added a senior White House official who attended both sets of talks: "The Paisley meeting was very substantive. It was more of just Paisley talking to the President about his view. The Adams meeting was more of a discussion. Traditionally meetings with Adams are that they go through their list of goals and concerns about what's happening."

Clinton spoke of his hope that the twin-track initiative would move the peace process forward and, while imploring Adams to back it, he didn't seek a commitment there and then. McCurry explained in a briefing to White House correspondents at the Europa Hotel later on in the evening: "While not getting into a specific endorsement of the Bruton-Major proposal, which the President

didn't seek, it was clear Mr Adams has a very continuing and positive attitude towards the peace process itself." Adams thanked the
President for the risks he'd taken, adding that he deserved some of
the credit for its progress thus far. McAuley said: "It wasn't the sort
of meeting where both sides were going to sit down and have a long
hard discussion. It was a very friendly, very relaxed discussion which
went in very quickly. It was a good day politically for Sinn Féin in
terms of acknowledgement by the President of our role." Adams
had about 20 minutes with Clinton – the same as Paisley – before
Tony Lake brought the meeting to a close.

Meanwhile, David Trimble had slipped out of the Whitla Hall to
a pre-arranged meeting point at a side exit. He was about to be
recognised, as the leader of Northern Ireland's largest party, with a
ride in the President's car, a rarely bestowed honour. The idea had
been floated during the planning stages of the visit when the Ulster
Unionist chief had been pressing for a private meeting with Clinton.
"I was told, you'll not be disappointed. You'll get your quality time,"
he recalled. "We did want to have some sort of visual or public
acknowledgement of Trimble," explained an American involved in
shaping Clinton's schedule. "We'd a meeting with the Unionists
who roared at us about the balance of the programme. We were
trying to think of what we could give Trimble. They seemed quite
happy with the idea of the limo ride. I mean, it's a pretty big deal.
The Secret Service does not like it very much in general." Indeed,
when Trimble first walked up to the President's heavily-guarded
limousine, a seemingly-uninformed agent had enquired what on earth
he thought he was doing.

The symbolism of a short car journey to the Europa hotel wasn't
lost on Trimble or for that matter his party colleagues. "I think the
fact they drove down in the car together was a very significant gesture by the President," said John Taylor. "It showed Clinton
recognised there wasn't just an Irish Nationalist position on this
island, that there was more to the Irish story, and the other side was
the Trimble side, the Unionist side."

Taylor had been amongst a minority of Ulster Unionists to fore-
see the albeit-slender advantages of engaging Washington in the
Northern Ireland problem years before the Clinton Presidency made
it a prerequisite of political life. It had in fact been Taylor, under the
aegis of Operation USA, who had asked the then party recruit and

Queen's University law lecturer David Trimble to become involved in the American debate by contributing to the *Ulster, the Facts* publication. "John Hume did excellent work from his point of view," argued Taylor. "I don't agree with what he did but as a politician he was very successful in milking support. Unionists have caught on belatedly but it's better to catch on late than not to catch on at all. What we're trying to achieve there now is very important and I know the British Government appreciates it because up until recently they were seen to be the English defending the situation in Northern Ireland, which played into the hands of the Irish."

Others, like Martin Smyth, the late Harold McCusker and Ken Maginnis, were also Unionist trail-blazers on the new political frontier. Smyth's networking began more than a decade before he was elected to the Commons in 1982, his visits on Orange Order and church business bringing him into early contact with the likes of Ted Kennedy. He first met the Senator from Massachusetts in the mid-seventies. "It was an interesting meeting in many ways," he recollected. "He recognised my argument that he was being absolutely one-sided as he'd forgotten about the contribution of the Scots-Irish, the legacy of the Irish Protestants to the United States." In Feburary 1994, when Gerry Adams was in New York, Smyth coincidentally led a UK delegation at a 'prayer breakfast' in Washington and came face-to-face with Clinton. "I asked him to make sure he was taking a clear stand against terrorism," said the Presbyterian clergyman. Trimble later acknowledged the contribution of Smyth and others. "There were leading members of the party doing a lot of this, but in an unstructured way," he said. "They'd been one-offs, but the message came back that you cannot have influence on a one-off basis. The significant decision was taken by Jim Molyneaux who decided we should do it officially as a party and in a more structured way."

It was the first Adams visa in 1994 which brought about a change in policy. Until then America had been well down the list of priorities. With Unionists (then under Molyneaux's leadership) refusing to attend Bill Flynn's conference on Northern Ireland, Adams' argument went unchallenged. Party official Jeffrey Donaldson, who later became Molyneaux's successor as MP for Lagan Valley, said: "The resulting publicity blitz Adams gained was a chastening experience for Unionists. I think it brought the party collectively to a realisation that they had to get out there. We could no longer afford to ignore the American interest." Donaldson's personal fascination with the US political scene pre-dated Clinton's election to the White House. At the turn of the decade, he had inherited the mantle of the Smyths and the McCuskers. With Hume as something of a role model, the party discreetly encouraged his travels and contact with the foreign policy staffers of Congressmen and Senators on the Hill. However, he didn't have the whole-hearted backing of colleagues. "You will always get within any political party different views on various issues," he said. "There would have been some people who took a view that it's too late, you needn't bother, you're wasting your time in America, but it never manifested itself in the form of opposition."

Seventy-five-year-old Molyneaux put little store by the United States until the twilight of his 26-year leadership of the Ulster Unionist Party. Before then he'd happily entrusted the British Government to lobby in Washington for the maintenance of the *status quo* in Northern Ireland. "There was a school of thought that said it was not our job to go out and change American attitudes, it was up to the Foreign Office," one MP asserted. Molyneaux saw no need to rock the Reagan-Thatcher relationship, for example, was which impregnable. "Any attempt by me during Reagan's time to do anything about making contact would have tended to play me off against the British Government of the day," he explained. "Given Margaret Thatcher's way of doing things it would have been behind her back. That was why I never encouraged any thoughts of doing that sort of thing. I only became convinced that it was worthwhile to work hand in glove with our own Government in John Major's time."

Molyneaux's first trip to the White House came in April 1994. It said something of Northern Ireland's newly-found status that the leader of a party with just nine MPs in Westminster followed the Prime Minister of Greece through the door of Vice President Al Gore's office. But the mild-mannered Molyneaux's standing was enhanced at a stroke when he presented Gore with a personal letter for Clinton from John Major. Gore and Molyneaux hit it off. Recalled Molyneaux: "He said to me, 'Are you going to make any speeches when you're over? It's a good chance to project yourself back home." I said, 'No, they wouldn't be interested. I'm the droll dog of Irish politics.' And he said, 'Yeah, well I'm your opposite number in America.' It was one of those chemistry things." The relationship grew – Gore once rang him from Air Force Two on his way home from Cairo and later insisted he accompany him during an engagement on a visit to Britain. Even after Molyneaux stepped down as leader a line of communication remained open between the two. "If there's something boiling up or if there's anything I think he ought to know I send it over to him," said Molyneaux. "He drops notes and things like that." Added Donaldson: "I think of all the players in Washington the one that we've developed the strongest relationship with would be Vice President Gore. He's taken the time to lift the phone and ring Jim Molyneaux. On a personal level he's the one we've most struck a chord with."

In 1995, Molyneaux sanctioned the opening of a Washington office, concrete evidence of Unionism's presence in America. Based in business premises at Dulles Airport, about 20 miles from Capitol Hill, it was donated by Derry-born entrepreneur Tony Culley-Foster and is operated by Anne Smith, a Scot. Trimble, who took over at the helm shortly afterwards, admitted its limitations mirrored that of his party's. "We're never going to be a major player there in terms of trying to exercise influence and we're not trying to. Our operation is just a 'me too' sort of thing, pointing out to people when you think of this issue think of us as well."

On that basis the Ulster Unionist Party's efforts paid dividends in securing Trimble a seat beside Clinton on the President's car ride out of Queen's University. The one-mile journey in the cavalcade to the Europa didn't allow much scope for a conversation. Clinton though found time to thank Trimble for some books he'd given him on his October visit to the White House which provided information that had come in useful at Belfast City Hall. "He was quite struck by the reaction of the people on the streets," remembered Trimble. "They were shouting and waving and he was comparing them to rallies in the States. For some reason, I'm not sure what the connection was, he kept comparing it to Seattle."

Donaldson met up with his party leader at the hotel where they were scheduled to have talks with Clinton. An informal chat over a drink in the famous Crown Bar across Great Victoria Street had been mooted at one stage. Secret Service agents were staking out the bar on the off-chance, as were eager photographers who had reserved their spots much earlier in the day. (One eager brewery had its cheque book open for the best photograph of Clinton supping one of his pints.) An American trip planner said: "One of the ideas we kept open was to maybe have the President and Trimble pop over to the Crown, go in the back and have a pint. But by that time of night we didn't want to do it."

It was 10.30pm when the President's car rolled into the sheltered garage parking zone at the side of the Europa Hotel, just opposite Trimble's party headquarters. Clinton took a service lift to his tenth floor suite, room number 1011, to freshen up before coming down to a second-floor meeting room where Trimble had been left to kick his heels. He was tired, having had to return to Belfast following a crucial morning meeting at Westminster. The Ulster Unionist leader was impressed by the President during their talks, although by that stage he was already won over. "I think what really impressed people about the Clinton visit was that first speech at Mackie," reflected Trimble. "That Mackie's speech transformed the Clinton visit because of the things he said, particularly with regard to saying to terrorists that their day is over. There would not have been anything like the crowds there were at City Hall that night but for those statements."

The twin-track agreement again loomed large in the President's third and final private talks session. "It was a general discussion on how the day had gone," recalled Donaldson. "The President was very, very pleased. We also discussed some of the wider issues like arms decommissioning. He appeared tired." Exhausted Clinton may have been, but his mind was alert. "I was quite impressed by how clued-up he was. He's no dozer," said Trimble. "Not only was he up to speed but he was putting in a couple of questions, not very many, but they were just right on the spot. I came away thinking it was a good serious discussion not just about twin-track. It went beyond that, right down to hard policy issues. We looked to the future, where we would be at the end of the talks process." Tony Lake later characterised the Trimble, Adams and Paisley meetings as being "essentially just a continuation of the consultative process."

While President Clinton talked about an historic peace settlement in Northern Ireland, the First Lady shopped on the twelfth floor. Local giftware suppliers had been summonsed especially. "Her aides told us she wanted to look at crystal and sweaters," said the

Europa's deputy general manager Doug Heady. "Companies brought in boxes of the stuff and laid everything out on tables. The First Lady and some of her staff then went through and said, give me three of those, four of those, bang, bang, bang. Probably gifts for people back in the States. I don't know what the total was but she had her share," added the colourful American, who'd arrived in Belfast via New York, San Francisco and Palm Beach.

He had watched as his hotel quite literally became a White House overseas in the course of the preceding eight weeks. It was the kind of organised chaos he'd been pushing for ever since he got word of the visit in the second week of July. Robin Greer, a press officer at the US Consulate in Belfast, had called to enquire about using the Europa as an international media centre but Heady had bigger ideas. When Chuck Meissner brought a trade delegation the fast-talking Heady got permission to address them with his wife by his side and the youngest of his three children cradled in his arms. "I said, 'President Clinton needs to come here to re-affirm there's peace in Northern Ireland. If he stays outside town he's doing what every business person's done for the last 25 years because they're worried about bombs and trouble.' My message was he needs to be here," Heady remembered. The psychology graduate needn't have worried; those who counted were already on the same wavelength.

Normally a President stays in American-owned property when abroad but on this occasion Clinton had decreed otherwise. He and his trip planners felt the Administration's faith in the peace process would be underscored by overnighting in a hotel which had been rocked by twenty or more bombs down the years. It was owned by the local Hastings Group. Said a senior member of the White House advance party: "The minute I walked into the Europa I just knew he'd be staying there because of its history. Not because I said so, but because for Bill Clinton it sent out the right message."

One hundred and fifteen of the Europa's 184 rooms were occupied by what was only a fraction of the Clinton entourage. The bill was £211,000, paid by the American Government in a series of cheques. (A final £11,000 had been held up over an unsigned receipt for six salmon lunches. "I rang and asked them who ordered them and they said 'room 1011,'" laughed Heady. "I said, room 1011 was the President's room and he had the food rushed to the City Airport under RUC escort in time for his flight to Derry.") An embassy detachment of Marine Corps guards was billeted on the second floor, as were the Secret Service, and coded security passes were required to move through a checkpoint to anywhere above. Guest lifts were modified to prevent access to the President's and other sensitive floors. White House communications took over the ninth floor and had around two hundred telephones installed. "They're military and are the ones who provide all the communications," explained a Washington official. "They set up their own switchboard and command post. They can operate the full White House. You pick up a phone and you've got direct satellite. In the lead up to the visit when you called the Europa they'd say 'Belfast signal.' Signal is what they call the White House operation. When the President's in residence then the operators answer 'Belfast White House.' Wherever the President is that's home."

The Clintons retired for bed just before midnight. "I looked in his eyes and saw he was beat," said Heady. It wasn't your normal suite, with two large bullet-proof shields in front of both windows and call buttons by the double bed, television and toilet, and a dining table groaning under a platter of cold cuts of meat and Irish cheeses. At the push of a button a valet could have been summonsed from an adjoining room or a world leader contacted by phone. "They literally moved the American Government with him," Heady said. "He had a console there where he could have called anyone in a finger push. You know, bang Russia, bang Jerusalem. I mean they talk about the red phone but the red phone's really about half the size of a desk." The White House had requested foam pillows and a large handled mug for the President. "They told me no chocolates, absolutely no chocolates," revealed Heady. "And they said when he drank he would prefer a beer as he's not a hard liquor guy."

Clinton couldn't unwind. He wanted to toast the accomplishment of the day in the Crown Bar where some of his staff were whooping it up. Jim Lyons was one of the last people to see the President on the night of 30 November. "He was pretty emotionally charged at the end of the day. He was physically shot, but in some ways he's like your oldest child," said the observer to the International Fund for Ireland who, in October 1997, replaced Senator Mitchell as Clinton's economic envoy. "We had to say to him, 'You have to go to bed.' He said, 'But you guys are going across the street', and it was like, 'yeah, we're going across the street, you're going to bed.' Well, I tried to be more respectful than that."

As Lyons left the suite a call came through from Washington about budget discussions and a defence bill. Said Mike McCurry: "We got a report of some favourable development in our Congress and the President decided that he should break open a really great bottle of Irish whiskey someone had presented to him that day. The President isn't much of a drinker. He'll take a beer now and again, but more than one or two and his face takes an allergic reaction." Also in the room were Tony Lake and the President's Chief of Staff, Leon Panetta. "The First Lady was also there," went on McCurry. "She usually goes her own way and doesn't fraternise with the staff, but we all sat and had a couple of sips of that Irish whiskey and felt very, very good about the day. We had a fine time in the Clinton suite. We left him and the First Lady sipping whiskey, probably about two in the morning."

Next day on leaving for Dublin the President confessed he'd had a little too much of the whiskey. "I was stunned because a hangover is something Bill Clinton's maybe only had two or three times in his whole life," McCurry said. "He was so full of energy that night he wanted to bounce off the walls."

Postscript

Seventy days after the triumph of the visit came despair. National Security Advisor Tony Lake was in his first floor office in the west wing of the White House when a call came from Belfast. It was 9 February, a day in the life of Irish policy every bit as memorable as the previous 30 November, but for all the wrong reasons.

Gerry Adams was on the line. "He sounded quite disturbed," Lake remembered of their brief conversation. The Sinn Féin President told him the 17-month IRA ceasefire was over. Official word came in a statement issued in Dublin. Publisher Niall O'Dowd, who like many other Irish-Americans had sweated for the truce, tried to raise Adams from New York. The line was busy. "I hoped some eejit had just got hold of the IRA's codeword," said O'Dowd.

One hour later, at 7.00pm GMT, Canary Wharf in London was rocked by an explosion. Two people were killed, millions of pounds worth of destruction caused and incalculable damage done to the peace process. The emotions at the epicentre of the superpower could not have contrasted more sharply with those that warmed the soul in Belfast and Derry but a fond memory ago. "We all felt sick," recalled Nancy Soderberg. "It was one of the lowest days in my life."

Blair Hall, one of the visit's key planners, had just arrived back in London from a holiday on the night of the bombing. The news came like a kick to the stomach. He, like others swept along by the events of 30 November, took it personally. Jim Lyons, a Clinton confidante who had shared in all his triumphs, was in Dublin for a board meeting of the International Fund for Ireland. He cancelled dinner, took a walk and cried. Across the city, Ireland's Foreign Minister Dick Spring spoke for them all: "It was hard to believe the ceasefire could break down after the endorsement of the peace process shown on the streets of Belfast."

When the feelings that clouded cool judgement lifted, the truth was that the writing had been on the wall for some time. Nonetheless, it shocked many in the White House when it became known that the planning of Canary Wharf had been taking place in south Armagh at the time of the Clinton's visit. Prime Minister John Major's dismissal of the Mitchell Report on arms decommissioning and the calling of elections in Northern Ireland – one more hurdle to all-party talks – was but the final straw.

Clinton was annoyed at the ceasefire's collapse. Ulster Unionist leader David Trimble saw him at the White House soon after. "He could not conceal his anger," said Trimble. "I was doing an introductory comment and he just burst in saying, 'They were damn fools, damn fools.' Oh he was angry." Adams found himself, once again, *persona non grata.* The White House was off limits to him on St Patrick's Day in 1996 and again in 1997.

The President's rage, however, didn't prompt the jettisoning of the peace process and emotional attachment was part of the reason. After his visit, Ireland had claimed him as one of their own. "The Irish have the same affinity for President Clinton that they did for my brother," Ambassador Jean Kennedy Smith said. There were those in Washington who said that Clinton should disengage but, just like the first Adams visa, he choose not to heed them. "He didn't panic when a lot of his political strategists wanted him to forget Ireland," said Congressman Peter King. Like King, others on Capitol Hill kept faith with Adams, despite his being officially cold-shouldered. The view that the Sinn Féin President was committed to peace but having trouble bringing his entire movement with him found receptive ears at the White House.

While Clinton never diluted his denunciation of terrorist acts, it was clear he was in for the long haul. "He's like one of those pilots you see in the movies," said Lyons. "The plane begins to go wrong but he keeps trying everything until it lands on the ground." But his was not the job to create the conditions necessary for a restoration of the IRA ceasefire and he neither could or would claim any credit when it came on 19 July 1997.

The all-inclusive peace talks Clinton wanted finally got under way two months later. By then he found himself, in a strange way, the grand old man of the Northern Ireland peace process. Gone were John Major and John Bruton, replaced by Tony Blair and Bertie

Ahern respectively. "He has made a tremendous contribution to the peace process," Blair told the authors. "His visit to Belfast was a great long-term boost to peace efforts. I have no doubt the view the President expressed so clearly during his visit, that the men of violence were the past, was right then and will be fully vindicated in the future."

Appendix I

President Clinton's address at Mackie International, Belfast

This is one of those occasions where I really feel that all that needs to be said has already been said. I thank Catherine and David for introducing me, for all the schoolchildren of Northern Ireland who are here today, and for all whom they represent. A big part of peace is children growing up safely, learning together and growing together.

I thank Patrick Dougan and Ronnie Lewis for their remarks, for their work here, for all the members of the Mackie team who are with us today in welcoming us to this factory. I was hoping we could have an event like this in Northern Ireland at a place where people work and reach out to the rest of the world in a positive way, because a big part of peace is working together for family and community and for the welfare of the common enterprise.

It is good to be among the people of Northern Ireland who have given so much to America and the world, and good to be here with such a large delegation of my fellow Americans, including, of course, my wife, and I see the Secretary of Commerce here and the Ambassador to Great Britain, and a number of others. But we have quite a large delegation from both parties in the United States Congress, so we've sort of got a truce of our own going on here today.

And I'd like to ask the members of Congress who have come all the way from Washington, D.C. to stand up and be recognised. Would you all stand?

Many of you perhaps know that one in four of America's Presidents trace their roots to Ireland's shores, beginning with Andrew Jackson, the son of immigrants from Carrickfergus, to John Fitzgerald Kennedy whose forebears came from County Wexford. I know I am only the latest in this time-honored tradition, but I'm proud to be the first sitting American President to make it back to Belfast.

At this holiday season all around the world, the promise of peace is in the air. The barriers of the Cold War are giving way to a global village where communication and cooperation are the order of the day. From South Africa to the Middle East, and now to troubled Bosnia, conflicts long thought impossible to solve are moving along the road to resolution. Once-bitter foes are clasping hands and changing history. And long-suffering people are moving closer to normal lives.

Here in Northern Ireland, you are making a miracle – a miracle symbolized by those two children who held hands and told us what this whole thing is all about. In the land of the harp and the fiddle, the fife and the lambeg drum, two proud traditions are coming together in the harmonies of peace. The ceasefire and negotiations have sparked a powerful transformation.

Mackie's Plant is a symbol of Northern Ireland's rebirth. It has long been a symbol of world class engineering. The textile machines you make permit people to weave disparate threads into remarkable fabrics. That is now what you must do here with the people of Northern Ireland.

Here we lie along the peace line, the wall of steel and stone separating Protestant from Catholic. But today, under the leadership of Pat Dougan, you are bridging the divide, overcoming a legacy of discrimination where fair employment and integration are the watchwords of the future. On this shop floor men and women of both traditions are working together to achieve common goals.

Peace, once a distant dream, is now making a difference in everyday life in this land. Soldiers have left the streets of Belfast; many have gone home. People can go to the pub or the store without the burden of the search or the threat of a bomb. As barriers disappear along the border, families and communities divided for decades are becoming whole once more.

This year in Armagh on St. Patrick's Day, Protestant and Catholic children led the parade together for the first time since The Troubles began. A bystander's words marked the wonder of the occasion when he said, "Even the normal is beginning to seem normal."

The economic rewards of peace are evident as well. Unemployment has fallen here to its lowest level in 14 years, while retail sales and investment are surging. From the gleaming city centre, to the new shop fronts of West Belfast, to the Enterprise Centre in East Belfast, business is thriving and opportunities are expanding. With every extra day that the guns are still, business confidence grows stronger and the promise of prosperity grows as well.

As the shroud of terror melts away, Northern Ireland's beauty has been revealed again to all the world – the castles and coasts, the Giant's Causeway, the lush green hills, the high white cliffs – a magical backdrop to your greatest asset which I saw all along the way from the airport here today, the warmth and good feeling of your people. Visitors are now coming in record numbers. Indeed, today, the air route between Belfast and London is the second busiest in all of Europe.

I want to honour those whose courage and vision have brought us to this point: Prime Minister Major, Prime Minister Bruton, and before him, Prime Minister Reynolds, laid the background and the basis for this era of reconciliation. From the Downing Street Declaration to the joint framework document, they altered the course of history. Now, just in the last few days, by launching the twin track initiative, they have opened a promising new gateway to a just and lasting peace. Foreign Minister Spring, Sir Patrick Mayhew, David Trimble and John Hume all have laboured to realise the promise of peace. And Gerry Adams, along with Loyalist leaders such as David Ervine and Gary McMichael, helped to silence the guns on the streets and to bring about the first peace in a generation.

But most of all, America salutes all the people of Northern Ireland who have shown the world in concrete ways that here the will for peace is now stronger than the weapons of war. With mixed sporting events encouraging competition on the playing field, not the battlefield; with women's support groups, literacy programs, job training centres that serve both communities – these and countless other initiatives bolster the foundations of peace as well.

Last year's ceasefire of the Irish Republican Army, joined by the Combined Loyalist Military Command, marked a turning point in the history of Northern Ireland. Now is the time to sustain that momentum and lock in the gains of peace. Neither community wants to go back to the violence of the past. The children told of that today. Both parties must do their part to move this process forward now.

Let me begin by saying that the search for common ground demands the courage of an open mind. This twin-track initiative gives the parties a chance to begin preliminary talks in ways in which all views will be represented and all voices will be heard. It also establishes an international body to address the issue of arms decommissioning. I hope the parties will seize this opportunity. Engaging in honest dialogue is not an act of surrender, it is an act of common strength and common sense.

Moving from ceasefire to peace requires dialogue. For 25 years now the history of Northern Ireland has been written in the blood of its children and their parents. The ceasefire turned the page on that history; it must not be allowed to turn back.

There must also be progress away from the negotiating table. Violence has lessened, but it has not disappeared. The leaders of the four main churches recently condemned the so-called punishment beatings and called for an end to such attacks. I add my voice to theirs. As the church leaders said, this is a time when the utmost efforts on all sides are needed to build a peaceful and confident community in the future.

But true peace requires more than a treaty, even more than the absence of violence. Those who have suffered most in the fighting must share fairly in the fruits of renewal. The frustration that gave rise to violence must give way to faith in the future.

The United States will help to secure the tangible benefits of peace. Ours is the first American administration ever to support in the Congress the International Fund For Ireland, which has become an engine for economic development and for reconciliation. We will continue to encourage trade and investment and to help end the cycle of unemployment.

We are proud to support Northern Ireland. You have given America a very great deal. Irish Protestant and Irish Catholic together have added to America's strength. From our battle for independence down to the present day, the Irish have not only fought in our wars, they have built our nation, and we owe you a very great debt.

Let me say that of all the gifts we can offer in return, perhaps the most enduring and most precious is the example of what is possible when people find unity and strength in their diversity. We know from our own experience even today how hard that is to do. After all, we fought a great Civil War over the issue of race and slavery in which hundreds of thousands of our people were killed.

Today, in one of our counties alone, in Los Angeles, there are over 150 different ethnic and racial groups represented. We know we can become stronger if we bridge our differences. But we learned in our own Civil War that that has to begin with a change of the heart.

I grew up in the American South, in one of the states that tried to break from the American Union. My forebears on my father's side were soldiers in the Confederate Army. I was reading the other day a book about our first governor after the Civil War who fought for the Union Army, and who lost members of his own family. They lived the experience so many of you have lived. When this governor took office and looked out over a sea of his fellow citizens who fought on the other side, he said these words: "We have all done wrong. No one can say his heart is altogether clean and his hands altogether pure. Thus, as we wish to be forgiven, let us forgive those who have sinned against us and ours." That was the beginning of America's reconciliation, and it must be the beginning of Northern Ireland's reconciliation.

It is so much easier to believe that our differences matter more than what we have in common. It is easier, but it is wrong. We all cherish family and faith, work and community. We all strive to live lives that are free and honest and responsible. We all want our children to grow up in a world where their talents are matched by their opportunities. And I believe those values are just as strong in County Londonderry as they are in Londonderry, New Hampshire; in Belfast, Northern Ireland as in Belfast, Maine.

I am proud to be of Ulster Scots stock. I am proud to be, also, of Irish stock. I share these roots with millions and millions of Americans, now over 40 million Americans. And we rejoice at "things being various," as Louis MacNiece once wrote. It is one of those things that makes America special.

Because our greatness flows from the wealth of our diversity as well as the strength of the ideals we share in common, we feel bound to support others around the world who seek to bridge their own divides. This is an important part of our country's mission on the eve of the 21st century, because we know that the chain of peace that protects us grows stronger with every new link that is forged.

For the first time in half a century now, we can put our children to bed at night knowing that the nuclear weapons of the former Soviet Union are no longer pointed at those children. In South Africa, the long night of Apartheid has given way to new freedom for all peoples. In the Middle East, Arab and Israelis are stepping beyond war to peace in an area where many believed peace would never come. In Haiti, a brutal dictatorship has given way to a fragile new democracy. In Europe, the dream of a stable, undivided free continent seems finally within reach as the people of Bosnia have the first real hope for peace since the terrible fighting began there nearly four years ago.

The United States looks forward to working with our allies here in Europe and others to help the people in Bosnia – the Muslims, the Croats, the Serbs – to move beyond their divisions and their destructions to make the peace agreement they have made a reality in the lives of their people.

Those who work for peace have got to support one another. We know that when leaders stand up for peace, they place their fortunes on the line, and sometimes their very lives on the line, as we learned so recently in the tragic murder of the brave Prime Minister of Israel. For, just as peace has its pioneers, peace will always have its rivals. Even when children stand up and say what these children said today, there will always be people who, deep down inside, will never be able to give up the past.

Over the last three years I have had the privilege of meeting with and closely listening to both Nationalists and Unionists from Northern Ireland, and I believe that the greatest struggle you face now is not between opposing ideas or opposing interests. The greatest struggle you face is between those who, deep down inside, are inclined to be peacemakers, and those who, deep down inside, cannot yet embrace the cause of peace – between those who are in the ship of peace and those who are trying to sink it. Old habits die hard.

There will always be those who define the worth of their lives not by who they are, but by who they aren't; not by what they're for, but by what they are against. They will never escape the dead-end street of violence. But you, the vast majority, Protestant and Catholic alike, must not allow the ship of peace to sink on the rocks of old habits and hard grudges.

You must stand firm against terror. You must say to those who still would use violence for political objectives – you are the past; your day is over. Violence has no place at the table of democracy, and no role in the future of this land. By the same token, you must also be willing to say to those who renounce violence and who do take their own risks for peace that they are entitled to be full participants in the democratic process. Those who show the courage to break with the past are entitled to their stake in the future.

As leaders for peace become invested in the process, as leaders make compromises and risk the backlash, people begin more and more – I have seen this all over the world – they begin more and more to develop a common interest in each other's success; in standing together rather than standing apart. They realize that the sooner they get to true peace, with all the rewards it brings, the sooner it will be easy to discredit and destroy the forces of destruction.

We will stand with those who take risks for peace, in Northern Ireland and around the world. I pledge that we will do all we can, through the International Fund for Ireland and in many other ways, to ease your load. If you walk down this path continually, you will not walk alone. We are entering an era of possibility unparalleled in all of human history. If you enter that era determined to build a new age of peace, the United States of America will proudly stand with you.

But at the end of the day, as with all free people, your future is for you to decide. Your destiny is for you to determine. Only you can decide between division and unity, between hard lives and high hopes. Only you can create a lasting peace.

It takes courage to let go of familiar divisions. It takes faith to walk down a new road. But when we see the bright gaze of these children, we know the risk is worth the reward.

I have been so touched by the thousands of letters I have received from schoolchildren here , telling me what peace means to them. One young girl from Ballymena wrote – and I quote – "It is not easy to forgive and forget, especially for those who have lost a family member or a close friend. However if people could look to the future with hope instead of the past with fear, we can only be moving in the right direction." I couldn't have said it nearly as well.

I believe you can summon the strength to keep moving forward. After all, you have come so far already. You have braved so many dangers, you have endured so many sacrifices. Surely there can be no turning back. But peace must be waged with a warrior's resolve – bravely, proudly, and relentlessly – secure in the knowledge of the single greatest difference between war and peace: In peace, everybody can win.

I was overcome today when I landed in my plane and I drove

with Hillary up the highway to come here by the phenomenal beauty of the place and the spirit and the goodwill of the people. Northern Ireland has a chance not only to begin anew, but to be a real inspiration to the rest of the world, a model of progress through tolerance.

Let us join our efforts together as never before to make that dream a reality. Let us join our prayers in this season of peace for a future of peace in this good land.

Thank you very much.

Appendix II

President Clinton's remarks at Guildhall Square, Londonderry

M r Mayor, Mrs Kerr, Mr and Mrs Hume, Sir Patrick and Lady Mayhew, and to this remarkable crowd: Let me say, there have been many Presidents of the United States who had their roots in this soil. I can see today how lucky I am to be the first President of the United States to come back to this city to say thank you very much.

Hillary and I are proud to be here in the home of Ireland's most tireless champion for civil rights and its most eloquent voice of non-violence, John Hume. I know that at least twice already I have had the honor of hosting John and Pat in Washington. And the last time I saw him I said, you can't come back to Washington one more time until you let me come to Derry. And here I am.

I am delighted to be joined here today by a large number of Americans, including a distinguished delegation of members of our United States Congress who have supported peace and reconciliation here and who have supported economic development through the International Fund for Ireland.

I'm also joined today by members of the O'Neill family. Among the last great chieftains of Ireland were the O'Neills of Ulster. But in America we still have chieftains who are the O'Neills of Boston. They came all the way over here to inaugurate the Tip O'Neill Chair in Peace Studies here at the University of Ulster. This chair will honor the great Irish American and late speaker of the House Of Representatives by furthering his dream of peace in Northern Ireland. And I am honored to be here with his family members today.

All of you know that this city is a very different place from what a visitor like me would have seen just a year and a half ago, before the ceasefire. Crossing the border now is as easy as crossing a speed bump. The soldiers are off the streets. The city walls are open to civilians. There are no more shakedowns as you walk into a store. Daily life has become more ordinary. But this will never be an ordinary city.

I came here because you are making a home for peace to flourish and endure – a local climate responsible this week for the announcement of new business operations that offer significant new opportunities to you, as well as new hope. Let me applaud also the success of the Inner City Trust and Paddy Doherty who have put people to work rebuilding bombed-out buildings, building new ones, and building up confidence and civic pride.

America's connections to this place go back a long, long time. One of our greatest cities, Philadelphia, was mapped out three centuries ago by a man who was inspired by the layout of the streets behind these walls. His name was William Penn. He was raised a Protestant in Ireland in a military family. He became a warrior and he fought in Ulster. But he turned away from warfare, traded in his armour, converted to the Quaker faith and became a champion of peace.

Imprisoned for his religious views, William Penn wrote one of the greatest defenses of religious tolerance in history. Released from prison, he went to America in the 1680s, a divisive decade here, and founded Pennsylvania, a colony unique in the new world because it was based on the principle of religious tolerance.

Philadelphia quickly became the main port of entry for immigrants from the north of Ireland who made the Protestant and Catholic traditions valuable parts of our treasured traditions in America. Today when he travels to the States, John Hume is fond of reminding us about the phrase that Americans established in Philadelphia as the motto of our nation, "E pluribus unum" – Out of many, one – the belief that back then Quakers and Catholics, Anglicans and Presbyterians could practice their religion, celebrate their culture, honor their traditions and live as neighbours in peace.

In the United States today in just one county, Los Angeles, there are representatives of over 150 different racial, ethnic and religious groups. We are struggling to live out William Penn's vision, and we pray that you will be able to live out that vision as well.

Over the last three years since I have had the privilege to be the President of the United States I have had occasion to meet with Nationalists and to meet with Unionists, and to listen to their sides of the story. I have come to the conclusion that here, as in so many other places in the world – from the Middle East to Bosnia – the divisions that are most important here are not the divisions between opposing views or opposing interests. Those divisions can be reconciled. The deep divisions, the most important ones, are those between the peacemakers and the enemies of peace – those who, deep, deep down inside want peace more than anything, and those who, deep down inside can't bring themselves to reach out for peace. Those who are in the ship of peace and those who would sink it. Those who bravely meet on the bridge of reconciliation, and those who would blow it up.

My friends, everyone in life at some point has to decide what kind of person he or she is going to be. Are you going to be someone who defines yourself in terms of what you are against, or what you are for? Will you be someone who defines yourself in terms of who you aren't, or who you are? The time has come for the peacemakers to triumph in Northern Ireland, and the United States will support them as they do.

The world-renowned playwright from this city, Brian Friel, wrote a play called "Philadelphia Here I Come." In it, a character who is about to emigrate from Ireland thinks back on his past life and says to himself, it's all over. But his alter ego reminds him of his future and replies, and it's about to begin. It's all over and it's about to begin. If only change were that easy.

To leave one way of life behind in search of another takes a strong amount of faith and courage. But the world has seen here over the last 15 months that people from Londonderry County to County Down, from Antrim to Armagh, have made transition from a time of ever-present fear to a time of fragile peace. The United States applauds the efforts of Prime Minister Major and Prime Minister Bruton who have launched the new twin-track initiative and have opened a process that gives the parties to begin a dialogue in which all views are represented, and all can be heard.

Not far from this spot stands a statue of reconciliation – two figures, ten feet tall, each reaching out a hand toward the other, but neither quite making it across the divide. It is a beautiful and powerful symbol of where many people stand today in this great land. Let it now point people to the handshake of reconciliation. Life cannot be lived with the stillness of statues. Life must go on. The hands must come closer together of drift further apart.

Your great Nobel Prize winning poet, Seamus Heaney, wrote the following words that some of you must know already, but that for me capture this moment. He said: "History says don't hope on this side of the grave, but then, once in a lifetime the longed-for tidal wave of justice can rise up. And hope and history rhyme. So hope for a great sea change on the far side of revenge. Believe that a further shore is reachable from here. Believe in miracles and cures and healing wells"

Well, my friends, I believe. I believe we live in a time of hope and history rhyming. Standing here in front of the Guildhall, looking out over these historic walls, I see a peaceful city, a safe city, a hopeful city, full of young people that should have a peaceful and prosperous future here where their roots and families are. That is what I see today with you.

And so I ask you to build on the opportunity you have before you; to believe that the future can be better than the past; to work together because you have so much more to gain by working together than by drifting apart. Have the patience to work for a just and lasting peace. Reach for it. The United States will reach with you. The further shore of that peace is within your reach.

Thank you, and God bless you all.

Appendix III

President Clinton's remarks at City Hall, Belfast

Thank you very much. To the Lord Mayor and Lady Mayoress, let me begin by saying to all of you, Hillary and I thank you from the bottom of our hearts for making us feel so very, very welcome in Belfast and Northern Ireland. We thank you, Lord Mayor, for your cooperation and your help in making this trip so successful, and we trust that, for all of you, we haven't inconvenienced you too much. But this has been a wonderful way for us to begin the Christmas holidays.

Let me also say I understand just what an honor it was to be able to turn on this Christmas tree when I realized the competition. Now, to become the President of the United States you have to undertake some considerable competition. But I have never confronted challengers with the name recognition, the understanding of the media and the ability in the martial arts of the Mighty Morphin Power rangers.

To all of you whose support enabled me to join you tonight and turn the Christmas tree on, I give you my heartfelt thanks. I know here in Belfast you've been lighting the Christmas tree for more than 20 years. But this year must be especially joyous to you, for you are entering your second Christmas of peace.

As I look down these beautiful streets, I think how wonderful it will be for people to do their holiday shopping without worry of searches or bombs; to visit loved ones on the other side of the border without the burden of checkpoints or roadblocks; to enjoy these magnificent Christmas lights without any fear of violence. Peace has brought real change to your lives.

Across the ocean, the American people are rejoicing with you. We are joined to you by strong ties of community and commerce and culture. Over the years men and women of both traditions have flourished in our country and helped America to flourish.

And today, of course, we are forging new and special bonds. Belfast's sister city in the United States, Nashville, Tennessee, was proud to send this Christmas tree to friends across the Atlantic. I want to thank the most prominent present resident of Nashville,

Tennessee, Vice President Al Gore, the Mayor, Phil Bredesen, and the United States Air Force for getting this big tree all the way across the Atlantic to be here with you tonight.

In this 50th anniversary year of the end of World War II, many Americans still remember the warmth the people of Northern Ireland showed them when the army was stationed here under General Eisenhower. The people of Belfast named General Eisenhower an honorary burgess of the city. He viewed that honor, and I quote, "as a token of our common purpose to work together for a better world." That mission endures today. We remain Americans and as people of Northern Ireland, partners for security, partners for prosperity and, most important, partners for peace.

Two years ago, at this very spot, tens of thousands of you took part in a day for peace, as a response to some of the worst violence Northern Ireland had known in recent years. The two morning papers, representing both traditions, sponsored a telephone poll for peace that generated almost 160,000 calls. In the United States, for my fellow Americans who are here, that would be the equivalent of 25 million calls.

The response left no doubt that all across Northern Ireland the desire for peace was becoming a demand. I am honored to announce today that those same two newspapers, the News Letter and the Irish News, have established the President's Prize, an annual award to those at the grass roots level who have contributed most to peace and reconciliation. The honorees will travel to the United States to exchange experiences on the issues we share, including community relations and conflict resolution. We have a lot to learn from one another. The President's prize will underscore that Northern Ireland's two traditions have a common interest in peace.

As you know, I have received thousands of letters from school children all over your remarkable land telling me what peace means to them. They poured in from villages and cities, from Catholic and Protestant communities, from mixed schools, primary schools, from schools for children with special needs. All the letters in their own way were truly wonderful for their honesty, their simple wisdom and their passion. Many of the children showed tremendous pride in their homeland, in its beauty and its true nature. I congratulate the winners. They were wonderful and I loved hearing their letters.

But let me tell you about another couple I received. Eleven-year-old Keith from Carrickfergus wrote " Please tell everyone in America that we're not always fighting here, and that it's only a small number of people who make the trouble." Like many of the children, Keith did not identify himself as Protestant or Catholic, and did not distinguish between the sources of violence.

So many children told me of loved ones they have lost, of lives disrupted and opportunities forsaken and families forced to move. Yet, they showed remarkable courage and strength and a commitment to overcome the past. As 14-year-old Sharon of County Armagh wrote: "Both sides have been hurt. Both sides must forgive."

Despite the extraordinary hardships so many of these children have faced, their letters were full of hope and love and humour. To all of you who took the time to write me, you've brightened my holiday season with your words of faith and courage, and I thank you. To all of you who asked me to do what I could to help peace take root, I pledge you America's support. We will stand with you as you take risks for peace.

And to all of you who have not lost your sense of humour, I say thank you. I got a letter from 13-year-old Ryan from Belfast. Now, Ryan, if you're out in the crowd tonight, here's the answer to your question. No, as far as I know, an alien spacecraft did not crash in Roswell, New Mexico, in 1947. And Ryan, if the United States Air Force did recover alien bodies, they didn't tell me about it, either, and I want to know.

Ladies and Gentlemen, this day that Hillary and I have had here in Belfast and in Derry and Londonderry County will long be with us as one of the most remarkable days of our lives. I leave you with these thoughts. May the Christmas spirit of peace and goodwill flourish and grow in you. May you remember the words of the Lord Mayor: "This is Christmas. We celebrate the world in a new way because of the birth of Emmanuel; God with us." And when God was with us, he said no words more important than these: "Blessed are the peacemakers, for they shall inherit the Earth."

Merry Christmas, and God bless you all.

Bibliography

Adams, Gerry, *Before the Dawn* (Brandon Books, Dingle 1996).

Coogan, Tim Pat, *The Troubles: Ireland's Ordeal 1966-1995 and the Search for Peace* (Hutchinson, London 1995).

Flackes, W D & Elliot, S, *Northern Ireland, A Political Directory. 1968-1993* (The Blackstaff Press, Belfast 1994).

Guelke, Adrian, *The US, Irish Americans and the Northern Ireland Peace Process* (International Affairs 72, 3 1996).

Holland, Jack, *The Irish American Connection* (Poolbeg, Dublin 1989).

Hume, John, *Personal Views. Politics, Peace and Reconciliation in Ireland* (Town House, Dublin 1996).

Mallie, Eamonn & McKitterick, David, *The Fight for Peace* (Heinemann, London 1996).

Maraniss, David, *First in his Class. The Biography of Bill Clinton* (Touchstone, New York 1996).

O'Clery, Conor, *The Greening of the White House* (Gill & MacMillan, Dublin 1996).

O'Grady, Joseph, *An Irish Policy Born in the USA. Clinton's Break With The Past* (Foreign Affairs, May/June 1996).

Wilson, Andrew, *Irish America and the Ulster Conflict 1968-1995* (The Blackstaff Press, Belfast 1995).

Newspapers

The Belfast Telegraph	*The New York Times*
The Daily Express	*The Financial Times*
The Times	*The Guardian*
The Sunday Telegraph	*The Irish News*
The Sunday Times	*The Irish Times*
The Sunday Tribune	*The Independent*
The Washington Post	*The News Letter*

Index